Early Praise for
From the Potato to Star Trek and Beyond

"What can I tell you about my friend of decades, Chet Richards? He's a fine musician, a rocket scientist, a wonderful writer and an adventurer, but most of all, he married well."

> — Marilyn Scott-Waters, writer and illustrator. Her works include, *The Toymaker: Paper Toys That You Can Make Yourself, Haunted Histories, The Search For Vile Things.*

"I would highly recommend *From the Potato to Star Trek and Beyond.* The book is informative, even educational, but author Chet Richards maintains a friendly, conversational tone throughout. The stories were a definite surprise. Who knew that this mild-mannered, soft-spoken gentleman I've known for years had so many harrowing adventures, and was so accomplished in the scientific community? If there is a lesson to be learned from these pages, it's that everyone should get to know the people in their lives on a deep level, especially the mild-mannered, soft-spoken ones. Chet's book made me look back at my own life and consider what experiences I have had that might be as interesting to others. Personally, I would never visit a country whose army actively reduces its population. For better or worse, the number of harrowing moments I've had are much scarcer. (Be on the lookout early next year for my autobiographical pamphlet.) Happy Reading!"

> — Steve Pastis, Author, *Fables for the Clarinet, Elk and Penguin Stories, Ten Good Reasons to Fix that Airplane.* Writer/Editor *The Good Life* publication for seniors. Chet's Friend

"I was so moved from the first words, how the author wrote these stories as a tribute to his wife, and as a way to heal after she died. What a wonderful way to deal with the pain so many of us experience. And the Star Trek story – really interesting to see how the process in Hollywood works. And the story of The Potato, and all the other adventures that kept almost killing him, and the rocket science stories. I loved those...as a former technologist, I'm always interested in knowing how science works."

    — Mary Kenner, Associate Editor, RKEdit, retired
       Clinical Laboratory Scientist II

FROM THE POTATO TO STAR TREK AND BEYOND

MEMOIRS OF A ROCKET SCIENTIST

CHESTER L. RICHARDS

a Pawpress book

From The Potato to Star Trek and Beyond: Memoirs of a Rocket Scientist

Chester L. Richards

Published by Pawpress

Edited by Ina Hillebrandt

Cover art and interior design by Pedernales Publishing, LLC

© 2022 by Chester L. Richards

For information on reprints, bulk purchase, or available related performance and merchandising properties, and licensing questions, please contact the publisher via email: annap@InasPawprints.com.

Or mail:

Pawpress
Brentwood Village ● 200 S. Barrington Ave. # 492213
Los Angeles, CA 90049
https://InasPawprints.com

Publisher's Cataloging-In-Publication Data

Names: Richards, Chester L., author.
Title: From the Potato to Star Trek and beyond : memoirs of a rocket scientist / Chester L. Richards.
Description: Los Angeles, CA : Pawpress, [2022] | "A Pawpress book."
Identifiers: ISBN 9781880882306 (trade paperback) | ISBN 9781880882320 (hardcover) | ISBN 9781880882313 (ebook)
Subjects: LCSH: Richards, Chester L. | Authors, American--21st century--Biography. | Aerospace engineers--United States--Biography. | Adventure and adventurers--United States--Biography. | LCGFT: Autobiographies. | BISAC: BIOGRAPHY & AUTOBIOGRAPHY / Personal Memoirs. | SCIENCE / Space Science / General. | SPORTS & RECREATION / Water Sports / General.
Classification: LCC PS3618.I342 Z46 2022 (print) | LCC PS3618.I342 (ebook) | DDC 813/.6--dc23

a Pawpress book

Printed in the U.S.A.

For Sarah

ACKNOWLEDGEMENTS

My muse was my dear Sarah. It was her delight in my stories that encouraged me to write them down. This book I owe to her.

And my parents. It isn't just that they gave me life and love, and a solid foundation for the future. They encouraged my delight in reading by letting me roam the Galaxy during the Golden Age of Science Fiction. This, when I should have been doing my family chores. Their tolerance was amazing.

With frequent changes of elementary schools I skipped basic grammar. Consequently, in junior high English classes I had no idea what the teachers were talking about. At the University of California, Berkeley, during a rigorous course in bonehead English (Subject A), I eventually did find out where to put periods and commas. Thanks, Berkeley, I needed that.

A full half of my undergraduate education at Berkeley came in only one course. This was Professor Wolfson's single semester of Classical Rhetoric. It was in that class that I learned logic, rigorous analysis and techniques of exposition. Kudos, Wolfson.

My first job after receiving my Bachelor's Degree involved writing technical proposals. The group had, on staff, a retired editor from Time Magazine. She taught me how to unravel my tangled sentences, taught me rhythm in writing, and explained the mysteries of the Gunning Fog Index. Because of this lady, I learned clarity in my writing.

Then came my collaboration with Judy Burns. From that wonderful experience I discovered I liked writing stories, and learned some of the techniques involved. I came to admire Judy's mastery of rigorous internal consistency in storytelling. Everything must be integral to the progress and logic of the story. Thanks, Judy.

From watching Nancy Alvarado Stone at work I discovered the fine art of economical expression. Nancy was a master of writing advertising copy: how to communicate a complex idea in the fewest number of words.

Thanks to Jose Ramirez, Padernales Publishing LLC, for his expert design and production of the book.

Finally, there is my editor, Ina Hillebrandt. Ina and I have had long knockdown, drag-out, battles over as little as a single word. She keeps trying to rope me in when I am obscure. I might think a description is clear because I have actually lived it, but she correctly knows better because she hasn't. Eventually we find a solution and it is always an improvement. Ina has done her job well and I believe this work shows her deft hand and excellent advice. Amazingly, we remain very great friends. Thanks, Ina.

Contents

FROM THE POTATO TO
STAR TREK AND BEYOND

OVERTURE: LETTERS TO SARAH

It HAD BEEN A GOOD DAY AT WORK, a day of considerable achievement. I was looking forward to telling Sarah. The last few weeks had been hard on her. She was recovering from a fractured pelvis, and the pain had visibly weakened my Sarah. The news, I hoped, would give her some pleasure.

After the long drive from work, I finally arrived home. *Odd. No cheerful greeting.* Something was wrong. I found Sarah sitting in her wheelchair at the entrance to the bathroom. She had been there a long time, she said, waiting for me to arrive. She got up, took a few steps, collapsed and lay still.

No doubt it was only a few minutes before the paramedics arrived, but it seemed an eternity. I knew Sarah's heart had stopped and time was now against her. The paramedics did get her heart going again, but as one of them turned to look at me, his expression, and a slight shake of his head, filled me with dread.

At the hospital I waited in the Chapel while the staff worked to stabilize Sarah. Time passed. The head physician came to get me. His pessimism was apparent.

For a long while I stood beside my beautiful wife's silent form, talking to her, telling how much I loved her. She seemed to respond to my voice, but it could have been an illusion. Soon the staff told me to go home and get some rest. I turned on every light in the house. It didn't give me much comfort, but it was better than the dark.

Later in the evening the hospital called. Sarah's heart had stopped, but they'd managed, once more, to get it going. They asked for instructions. I told them if it stopped again they were to let her go. But her heart continued strong and steady.

Much earlier I'd called Paul, her son by a previous marriage. He'd immediately started south from San Francisco. I expected he would arrive sometime around midnight, or shortly thereafter, so I stayed up waiting for him. In the morning I awoke from a short sleep on the sofa. Paul had still not arrived. Another worry.

Mid-morning Sarah's son showed up. He had been so tired on the drive south he pulled off the road and slept through the night. Good. Better late than worse. We talked. He had not realized how serious the situation was.

At the hospital I left Paul alone with Sarah. He had many things to say to her. A couple of hours later he found me, and we stayed with her together.

Shortly before the end a priest arrived to give last rites. Sarah's blood pressure slowly began to fade. The attending nurse had briefed us, so we knew this was the end. The inevitable continued until only the oxygen machine was still pumping her lungs — simulating a life that was no longer there. I turned it off.

Paul could not bear to stay. This place was now a nightmare. He headed north to be with his family. Alone in agony, I wailed, and wept long into the night.

There was much to do the next day. Work had to be notified and business put on hold. A funeral had to be arranged. A gathering planned. A grave and gravestone had to be purchased. Friends had to be notified. The day passed quickly. Exhausted, I slept, but not well, that night.

The next morning it really hit me. The house was empty. It would always *be* empty. Half of me was gone. I had been sliced in two, from the top of my head on down. I was deep in shock. There are no words to describe the experience. No language is capable. If you have suffered the like no words are needed. You know. If you have not, you simply cannot comprehend. One thing was clear, I could not stay here. I fled.

My colleagues at work were shocked to see me. I couldn't explain. I needed to be someplace different but familiar. Most of all, I needed the human companionship of my collegial friends. I felt a certain relief being in my office, and tried to work on my project. The nature of my work as an engineering physicist often requires intense focus. This concentration was now out of the question. I couldn't do a thing. At least, though, I was in a place of comfort.

Sarah was universally loved. At the upcoming funeral our friends would want some reminders of her life. That was my task. I sat for a while, remembering the stories she had told me about the years before we met. I remembered the many things we had shared. Yes, there was much I could report to our friends. Much, but not all. Many things were just between the two of us. I sat in my office and began to write.

I wrote *A Great Lady*. I told about Sarah's early life and gave some hint of the troubles she had experienced. I wrote of her talents and triumphs. I wrote about things we had done together. I told of the great privilege I had had spending so many years with this wonderful woman. I wrote my love. And as I wrote, my mood lightened.

The days passed. Friends from all over came to the funeral. It was good to see everyone again. We talked, we told stories, we laughed, we cried. We said farewell to the one we all loved. All gave me comfort. All gave *me* their love.

After this brief bright moment I sank back into darkness. This depression, I knew, would be fatal. And I knew I must find some way back up towards the light. While I brooded over the question of how to move forward, the warmth I had felt when I wrote my eulogy flooded through me. I knew what to do.

Sarah liked my stories. She liked to hear of my travels to exotic places, of my challenging and rewarding experiences as an aerospace engineer. Most of all she liked to hear about the people I'd met along the way.

Many times Sarah said I should write these tales. I never did. I never wanted to, but now I needed salvation. If writing would put me on the upward path, I would write. I would write stories drawn from my experiences. I would write in memory of Sarah. Writing worked. I began to heal.

Each story is a letter of love to my dear Sarah. Each is an adventure. Each stands complete by itself. Each is meant to entertain or inform. Each is true.

Popped an oar, out of control, at Lava Falls
Photo taken from nearby boat

ADVENTURES

"WRITE YOUR PASSIONS," Bob Duncan, veteran pro writer, told me one evening long ago. At the time I was young, a graduate student in engineering, and had no intention of becoming a writer. To be sure, my friend Judy Burns and I had collaborated on a speculative Star Trek script which Bob had read and liked. And this led to an unexpected series of rewarding events for the two of us.

I knew writing was not to be my career. Nonetheless, Bob's advice did affect me, and in a most profound way. Though I was an engineer, not a writer, what he said applied to me at a much more fundamental level. Bob was advising me to pursue a richness of experience. This would apply whether I wrote or not. Sitting in an office repeating routines would not suffice. And so, I made a decision I've never regretted — to fill my life with adventure.

Well, easier said than done. After all, I needed to earn a living. Luckily, there would be vacations in my future, and these would provide me with the time and resources to dive into a series of hazardous, hair raising odysseys. On those occasions I did write, keeping a daily journal. Moreover, Bob's wisdom changed my perspective about ordinary things. It was clear: Looked at in the right way, day-to-day affairs can become extraordinary. Especially if these everyday adventures involve taking risks, professional risks as well as physical ones.

In time I did have stories to tell, a few recalled from my youth, but most inspired by following Bob's advice.

STAR TREK

Beginnings

I WAS ON THE BRIDGE OF A STARSHIP in the far future. The ship was haunted. The crew was terrified. The terrible tension spun me back down through the centuries to the safety of my darkened bedroom. I awoke. *A ghost story,* I muttered to myself, they've *never done a ghost story.* I picked up a pad by my bedside and scribbled some notes. *I must call Judy in the morning.* Satisfied, I laid back and drifted off to sleep.

Judy Burns had once been my principal political adversary, and I hers. With this in common, we soon became fast friends. At the time of my dream I was still an engineering graduate student at the young University of California, Irvine. Judy had recently graduated from UCI. A couple of years before, as charter students at the new university, we were elected to help write the new Student Constitution. I led the Liberals, and she the Conservatives.

After Judy graduated she moved, for a while, into an old World War II Quonset Hut off the end of the runway at Orange County Airport. This choice had not been her original intention. An anthropologist and stellar student, she had caught the attention of Louis Leakey (she says by dropping a note in his pocket) and he had invited her to work with him in Kenya. But, at the last minute she had to hold back — lack of money, you see. So, she decided to try her hand, for a while, as a professional writer.

For Judy, writing stories had been a hobby from the time she was a child. Now she suddenly became serious about writing, for money. As an impoverished ex-student, writing for Hollywood struck her as an excellent way to raise the needed cash for her Kenya plan. As things worked out, she never did go to Africa to dig bones.

A secondary motivation, which helped develop her specific interest in *Star Trek*, was her admiration for Leonard Nimoy as Mr. Spock. Judy wanted to meet and get to know him. Being a consummate schemer, the best way to Make It So, she decided, was to write a script for the show. This she did, collaborating with her roommate, another talented young lady.

Their story was a good one. But her script went nowhere. It was lost in the slush pile when the show was canceled after two seasons. This was not good. How could Judy become friends with Nimoy if *Star Trek* was off the air? To sell a script the show had to be on the air. So Judy made up her mind to help bring the show back to life — a seeming impossibility. No show had ever been successfully resuscitated. Fortunately, Judy was not alone. There were a lot of talented people with the same idea. A well-orchestrated effort, including a massive letter writing campaign, succeeded in reinstating the show — for one more season.

With the show back on the air, Judy needed to have a new script to submit. We talked over some of her ideas, but nothing had caught her fancy. After all, writing a script is a lot of hard work so the inspiration for a story should be a knockout.

Then came the dream. I called Judy the next morning. She loved the idea of a ghost story, and invited me to collaborate on a script. We settled down and got to work.

A ghost story — hmmmm — how are we going to sell the concept to Gene Roddenberry? He was convinced no one in the centuries to come would believe in ghosts. After all, *he* didn't.

Aha! We'll make it sound scientific. Suppose we introduce parallel universes, an old science fiction theme (these days the notion is accepted as a possible theory of physics). Maybe a character's wave function somehow oscillates back and forth between these nearby universes (an idea straight out of quantum mechanics). This should provide a suitable ghost.

So be it, parallel universes it was. The oscillation was made plausible by formulating a local distortion in the hyperspatial continuum so the parallel universes were no longer fully orthogonal.

So now we had the physics of the ghost. Next, we had to find a suitable candidate ghost. We kicked around the possibilities among various prominent cast members, trying out different story ideas around each of them. This exercise brought lots of giggles. But there was little doubt from the outset our victim would be Mr. Spock. He was perfect. Spock was easily the most popular character in *Star Trek*. Killing him off, and turning him into a ghost, would attract fantastic attention from the fans (Trekkers in those days, Trekkies later on). We speculated a whispering campaign, ahead of the airing of the episode, would suck in all the faithful, plus many newbies. Of course there was also Judy's infatuation with the character. After we got through laughing, we started to build a plot around killing off Spock.

Of course we couldn't actually kill Spock off and eliminate him from the series. That would stab a knife into the heart of *Star Trek*. So we contrived it so everyone would *think* he's been killed. We had our ghost. Said apparition would haunt the Enterprise and scare everyone half to death. In reality, he'd be alive, in the other universe. The story would become one of discovering this fact, followed by trying to retrieve the still living Spock. Lots of jeopardy here, because the Enterprise, itself, might easily get sucked into interspatial limbo if it does anything foolish.

We needed a MacGuffin to get the Enterprise in trouble and Spock killed. This is why the Federation warship, Scimitar, was introduced.

Trekkie Trivia Alert! Originally, and through several versions of the story, we called the MacGuffin ship the Scimitar, but because, as we were told there was a conflict with the Star Trek Bible (the show's continuity manual) we later had to abandon that name. Of several under consideration, I liked the name Defiant; it reminded me of the movie "Damn the Defiant," a cracking good sea story. Defiant it eventually became.

Since we were going to temporarily kill off Spock, we needed another science type character to take his place. Thus, Dr. Reilly was born. This aggressive PhD type human was a weapons expert the Enterprise was hauling out to Carn's World to beef up their defenses. Reilly not only causes lots of mischief — being a good scientist he *has* to experiment with this weird gateway to hyperspace — but he also later figures out how to save the day.

We'd finally finished the story treatment, an effort of considerable work and pride. I was back at my studies when Judy called me up one morning. She was troubled. "We have to talk. This is going to take some time. Let's go down to the beach." So we did, driving out the Balboa Peninsula to its end and walking the rest of the way to The Wedge. I was wondering what was wrong, but Judy kept mum until we had spread out a blanket on the nearly empty beach and sat ourselves comfortably down.

"Chet, I hope this isn't too disappointing," she opened with, "but the story just doesn't work." There simply was too little tension to properly propel the plot. Actually I was relieved by this. On the drive down I'd been speculating maybe I'd done something dreadful, serious enough to destroy our friendship. Changing the story was the least of my concerns. Relief washed over me. We would simply invent what we needed to make the story work. It was a pleasant, sunny and softly warm day. Properly attired for the beach, we didn't have any sleeves to roll up, so we got to work with no loss of time.

We realized we must have a backstory, some additional jeopardy to force risky decisions. So we conjured up the Tholians. Originally we'd conceived of the Tholian Assembly as a composite piratical empire of humanoid races, well known to the Federation, and treacherous. But it's good practice for writers to flesh out the background information, even if it doesn't go directly into the story. This gives internal consistency. So we figured out *why* the Tholians were particularly protective of this dangerous patch of space, which played an important role in influencing later story choices.

The name Tholian was my tribute to a friend at the time, Jack Green. The term was derived from Mycenaean Tholos tombs. Jack was a volcanologist. Not a Vulcanologist, who spend their time studying Mr. Spock and his relatives, Dr. Green was the kind who studies volcanos. Near the island of

13

Thera, Jack discovered a Tholos. It was an important find but it soon was dramatically overshadowed.

At the time Jack made his discovery, he was on an expedition with Spyridon Marinatos, the Director General of Antiquities at the Greek Ministry of Culture. Marinatos, along with other archaeologists, had a nutty idea — the ancient volcanic explosion of the Aegean island of Thera had destroyed Plato's supposedly mythical civilization of Atlantis. As the story goes, Jack was wandering close to the beach on a nearby island, Kristiana, when he noticed some rocks were completely out of place — the wrong type of rocks for the area. With a bit of digging, the crew unearthed Jack's find — the top of a collapsed Tholos, complete with its treasures. What kept that wonderful discovery from the acclaim it deserved was this: Shortly thereafter Marinatos came up with an astonishing well preserved Minoan city at Akrotiri. As he was hoping to do, Marinatos actually did discover Atlantis, or so many people now believe.

Meanwhile, while Jack and Marinatos are in a different space-time location, uncovering incredible ancient earthly history, we return to The Enterprise, which is on its own expedition in space, and earthly development.

When the ship arrives at the mysterious patch of the cosmos, its sensors pick up a shimmering visual image of the Scimitar, overdue on its passage back from Carn's World. Only the Enterprise's visual sensors see the Scimitar, vaguely; the other sensors report nothing is there. Dr. Reilly, aggressively elbowing past Mr. Spock, reports to Captain Kirk the Scimitar is, "In essence ..... nothing." (Thus, *In Essence ..... Nothing* became the original title of the story.)

Soon, however, the Scimitar solidifies and can be boarded. Naturally, Captain Kirk leads the exploration party aboard the Scimitar. Why the captain of a galactic battleship leads every risky boarding and shore party is a real mystery to those who understand naval affairs. (Perhaps this mystery could be cleared up if we could interview the ghost of Gene Roddenberry.)

In any event, true to form, Captain Kirk, accompanied by Spock, McCoy and Reilly, activates his personal force shield (no clunky space suits, please!) and transports the team aboard the newly materialized Scimitar. The Scimitar is a ghost ship. The crew is dead from some mysterious cause. When the ship starts to fade back to its alternate universe, Kirk, McCoy and Reilly beam back to the Enterprise. Spock elects to stay behind to make some critical last minute measurements. However, before Spock can be successfully transported back to the Enterprise, the Scimitar winks out, carrying Spock with it.

Spock is dead. His funeral is held. Everyone is so sad.

Suddenly the lead battleship of a Tholian fleet appears. The suave Tholian captain is mock friendly. With iron fist in velvet glove he *suggests* the Enterprise accompany him away from this dangerous region of space (and into captivity deep within Tholian territory). The Enterprise prepares to fight its way past this *Space Pirate*.

But Spock's ghost starts haunting the corridors of the Enterprise. The crew is in a panic at these deathly apparitions — surely they portend defeat and doom. Adding to the jeopardy the rest of the Tholian fleet arrives and envelops the Enterprise. There is no escape now.

Doctor, smart guy, Reilly finally proves himself useful by figuring out what is going on. He proposes a perilous journey into the alternate universe — both to recover Spock and to escape the deadly trap of the Tholians. The Enterprise escapes and recovers Spock in the nick of time. Whew! That was close.

All through this process of writing the story and the script I was learning. From the beginning it was evident a script is not merely a dialog sequence. A script is far more complex. Motivation — the characters' silent internal chatter — is often more important than what is said out loud. Camera directions, too, are a vital part of the script, standard call-outs writers use to propel the scene.

One way a screen writer might create a scene is to define the characters and the action needed, then let the characters do what seems natural. For me the process proved to be no great stretch. I would simply set up a scene in my mind and let it evolve. Once I'd gained enough familiarity with Star Trek's actors, and the characters they'd created, I could let my imaginary clones walk through the scene, say whatever seemed appropriate, and write down what occurred. Because I'd watched so many movies, and so much television, camera angles also came naturally, once I understood the relationship between the script and the images on the screen.

The Middle

As soon as we finished the script we had to get it before the right people at *Star Trek*. Judy already had an agent, Polly Connell. Polly specialized in developing young writers. Truth be told, a good Hollywood agent is essential. Without a good agent a script doesn't get through the front door — too many liability problems for the studio.

Polly delivered our newly finished script to the powers that be. Nothing happened.

All the while, Judy had been taking a University of California Extension course in script writing taught by Bob Duncan. With Bob's permission, she invited me to audit the course. Now Bob was an old pro in the business. He'd started his career writing jungle bodice rippers for *Argosy* magazine, and "I was an unwed mother" stories for *Confidential,* under the pen name of Roberta Duncan. From that lowly station he worked his way up to writing several movies, a hundred tele-plays and dozens of novels. Maybe I had learned something during the writing of the *Star Trek* script, but attendance in Bob's course told me how much I did *not* know about writing, about people, and about life itself. Bob could take the most mundane situation and turn it into a work of art. Judy had the same gift. Quite frankly, I was intimidated.

Months passed and still we heard no word about our script. Bob's course wound up with a party at his house. During the evening Bob and I sat alone and chatted. He was curious about me because he almost never had a scientist or engineer attend his course, and I was both. This was the night he said the words that shaped much of my later life: "Write your passion... Write your passion, for without passion your story will fail." Valuable advice, as I understood later, though in seeming contradiction with what another writer, T.C. Boyle, told a mutual friend: "Don't preach, just tell a story." Staying at the center of tension between these two seemingly opposite poles, I learned, is essential in producing a compelling story.

After a while Judy wandered over and joined the conver-sation. "Whatever happened to the *Star Trek* script you guys did?" Bob inquired. "That was a pretty good story."

Judy replied the production company had been com-pletely reorganized for the upcoming third season, and some fellow named Fred Freiberger was taking over as producer. "Oh, Freddy," Bob said, "I've known Freddy forever. We worked together on *Wild, Wild West* and a bunch of other things. I'll give him a call in the morning." And so he did.

Nothing happened for a few days. It was June 1968 now. Stanley Kubrick's *2001 – A Space Odyssey* was playing at Grauman's Chinese Theater in Hollywood. With the school term having finished I was free for the summer. So Judy and I drove up to the Chinese Theater. *2001* turned out to be a strange, but interesting, movie. After dining at the nearby Mongolian Barbecue, we drove the long drive back to Judy's parents' house, which she now called home. As we pulled up, Judy's sister flung open the door and ran toward us. "Judy, this guy has been calling all day for you. He said to call him back as soon as you got home — any time, day or night. I've got his home phone number. His name was Fred something, Fred Freeman, or something like that."

"Fred Freiberger?" Judy asked.

"Yes, that's it, Fred Freiberger."

We rushed into the house. Judy grabbed the phone and called the number her sister had written down. Sure enough it was *Star Trek's* producer. He wanted us to come up, first thing in the morning, for a story conference. Hooray! We were in business.

Early the next morning we drove up to Hollywood. In the lobby of Paramount Studios, the guard did not have us on the entry list. Judy did the talking and charmed the guard enough for him to phone and get clearance from *Star Trek* to pass us through. (Although we were there for a legitimate meeting, the guard was naturally suspicious because posing as a writer was a common ploy to get through the gate.) After getting directions we walked to one of the two story bungalows occupied by Desilu Productions. Once inside I asked directions to the *Star Trek* Producer's office. The lady behind the desk pointed to an unmarked door right behind us. Judy and I entered, encountered the usual protective secretary, and were soon ushered into the Inner Sanctum — the Producer's Office.

If you have visions of a Hollywood Palace, forget all that. Fred Freiberger's lair was just another office. A bit larger than some, so a few people could sit comfortably and chat, and with a window — a small window with curtains — otherwise it was fairly plain. In front of Fred's desk was a sofa. The producer sat us down there and offered refreshments. We talked for a while, Freiberger asking us about our backgrounds. He was not only getting acquainted and probing to see how well we would work with him, he was also stalling until the rest of his staff could arrive.

Bob Justman, the associate producer, came in first, together with his ever present secretary. Shortly thereafter Arthur Singer, the story editor, sashayed in from a side door and swished his way across the room to sit himself next to me on the sofa, snuggling in a bit. I recoiled and snugged myself up to Judy, leaving a gap of a few inches between Arthur and me.

After the appropriate introductions, we got down to work. Now it was Justman's habit, while thinking things through, to wander around the Paramount lot and talk out loud. His secretary would follow in his footsteps with a pad of paper and write his musings down in shorthand. Later this discourse would be typed and circulated among the senior staff for comments.

In Freiberger's office, Justman, hyper with energy, couldn't sit. He pulled out a thick stack of yellow typed pages and walked nervously around the office, reading his previous thoughts to us. His secretary took down, verbatim, any new ideas. Bobby Justman started by assuring us we had an excellent story and *Star Trek* was going to buy it. Judy and I exchanged quick, happy, glances. He continued. Only a *few minor changes* were needed. Pacing around the office he read from the yellow pages. As he read from his notes my heart sank. A few changes, indeed. *Keep Spock alive. Let Captain Kirk be lost with the 'ghost ship.'* Here he stopped, pulled out a black felt tipped pen and inked over some words. Somewhat later he repeated this ritual. *This stuff isn't relevant.*

Justman continued with his briefing. Get rid of Reilly. Jazz up the Tholians. Add more punch to the deaths on the lost ship. Add more hazard to the Enterprise. Put Kirk and his fellows in *real* space suits — none of that stupid force field stuff. Change the relationship between Scott and McCoy. The litany went on and on. I glanced again at Judy. She shook her head, slightly, telling me silently to keep my mouth shut and agree to everything. Both of us now knew the story would have to be rewritten from scratch — the original, tightly woven logic of the story had just been shredded.

When Justman was finished, he asked if we had any questions. I stole a look at Freiberger. He sat quietly at his desk, observing how we were reacting. Judy said we understood what needed to be done and we agreed. I nodded along with her.

"One thing," added Freiberger, turning the screw a bit more. "We're on a tight schedule. We'll need the revised script in a week." *Impossible,* was my silent reaction, but Judy responded that was fine.

Justman handed me his notes. The meeting was over. We had our assignment: *Charge up the hill and do or die!*

As we were leaving the conference I asked about the trailer prominently placed in the courtyard outside. I was informed to avoid it at all costs. The trailer was the domain of Lucille Ball and you definitely did not want to catch the attention of *that* monster. Thus were we clued in to the common opinion of the minions of Desilu Productions.

After being warned, Judy and I were careful not to go anywhere near the trailer. But there was a nice compensation to working in the *Star Trek* offices. In those days the show occupied the downstairs suite while *Mission Impossible* had the upper floor. This was neat because I occasionally passed by my favorite *Mission Impossible* actors — especially the absolutely gorgeous Barbara Bain (much more beautiful in real life than on the screen).

The long drive home passed quickly. We had much to discuss: How we were going to reshape the story, what additional elements (other than Justman's dictates) had to be deep sixed, what was the new logic of the story, what were the new elements we might add to make the new logic bullet proof. Most important, how were we going to accomplish writing a whole new script in less than a week.

The way Judy and I worked, we'd create the draft story treatment first, and pick alternate scenes to flesh out with motivation, dialogue and camera directions. When we completed this initial effort, we'd exchange scenes and make whatever modifications to the other person's work each felt was necessary, get together again, review the changes and negotiate any differences. The process was efficient and effective. We also learned, along the way, each of us was better at certain things.

This understanding of each other's strengths helped greatly in planning the recovery. By the time we reached Judy's house we had the basic outline of the new story in our heads and a pretty good idea of the scene structure and who was to write what.

Judy also had an idea which helped greatly. The university housed a brand new marvel: a *word processing machine!* By today's standards this IBM computer-driven Selectric typewriter would be considered medieval technology. In those days this clattering hunk of metal and glowing vacuum tubes was a godsend. The university agreed to let us use the machine at night, provided we supplied our own computer tape. The tape was extremely pricey — each of us had to lay out around $1,000 in today's money, a princely sum for two impoverished young people. But the investment proved to be more than worth it, especially on that last nocturnal session before we had to deliver the new script.

Far into the night we talked, Judy and I both taking notes. The scene on the Scimitar was tragic. The crew had been fighting some dread brain distorting malady which appeared to be the consequence of the fractured space they were trapped in. This malady snuffed out the lives of the entire crew of the Scimitar in a single instant and later threatened the Enterprise. We worked up a rationale for trapping Kirk on the Scimitar, while his three companions made it safely back to the Enterprise. The Scimitar was fading out, and distorting the electronics of the transporter in the process so only three at a time could be beamed back aboard the Enterprise.

In this, and other early versions of the story, the Tholians had had their own troubles with this unruly patch of space, having lost ships there. Maybe they came to realize this region could work to their benefit, since it behaved something like quicksand, or a tar pit, trapping ships and rendering them vulnerable to capture. All this was background; we did not intend to spend time explaining it, for the people on the Enterprise would not have known the history of this patch of space and the Tholian's hand in it. *Show, don't tell.*

Sometime during the night a miracle happened — the Tholian's web was created. The story now had a much more powerful theme. No longer were the Tholians rather raffish humanoids. Now they were totally alien crystalline creatures — completely incomprehensible in action and intent to organic life, such as ourselves.

During the initial contact with the Tholian ship, commanded by a character named LoCene, the Tholians became illogically aggressive and made the mistake of firing on the Enterprise. The Enterprise was shaken, but fired back and severely damaged the Tholian vessel. Captain Kirk, in the midst of being transported, was lost during this skirmish.

Having been crippled, the Tholian ship fell back out of effective combat range and called for help from a companion, which subsequently arrived and joined up with the damaged ship. The two ships separated and a mysterious strand of glowing force was spun between them — the beginning of the Tholian's web. This was a completely novel type of weapon — a kind of enveloping force field which would allow the Tholians to safely capture the Enterprise. The new story thus became *Spiders in Space!* Well, that was our private name. The official title remained *In Essence....Nothing.* Until sometime in July when *The Tholian Web* was born. The "Essence of Nothing" had evaporated completely.

The new story had much greater psychological potential. In particular we were able to develop a major conflict between Dr. McCoy and Mr. Spock. Spock became excessively focused — obsessed — on technical problems interfering with the ability of the Enterprise to escape. McCoy started ragging on Spock, accusing him of arrogance in his monomaniacal attempts to retrieve Captain Kirk — thereby jeopardizing the entire crew. The distortions of perception caused by the strange nature of this region of space enormously magnified inner suspicions until the mutual conflict got completely out of hand, right up to the point of hysteria, by the normally reserved and controlled McCoy. Only the intervention of a posthumous message, left by Captain Kirk and addressed to both Spock and McCoy, saved the day.

Kirk had been perceptive enough to anticipate this personality conflict. His message directly addressed the problem and provided the psychological key to its resolution. In listening to Kirk's wisdom both McCoy and Spock gained deep insight into each other's motivations. Thus the crisis passed.

And so, over the next few days we evolved and wrote a completely new script, while retaining several of the original elements. Much to our surprise the new story was much better than the old. Whatever his true motivations, Bobby Justman had shown excellent instincts. And, maybe, with both practice and great incentive, we were becoming more skilled at spinning a yarn.

A week of intense labor culminated that night before we had to deliver the new script. Judy and I worked through the long hours, trading places typing on the University's solitary word processor. More than once the cranky machine balked and we had to reboot and retype sections. Finally, as the sun

24

was starting to rise above the hills to the East we printed out the last few pages. We were on our way to Hollywood.

Another miracle: Our new script was immediately accepted and put into what software people now call "configuration control." We were free of the drudgery. Paramount took over the task of typing changes. Each page of the retyped script was dated and cataloged. Each subsequent revision was again dated but was now typed on different color paper. The finished shooting script resembled a rainbow.

Nothing much happened immediately. Several weeks passed. Pre-production hit. All hell broke loose. We found ourselves entangled in revisions. The Scimitar became the Defiant. This is when the name of the story changed to *The Tholian Web*. LoCene became LoSkene, apparently because the Network's Standards and Practices guru thought LoCene sounded vaguely obscene. These were minor changes which did not affect the story. More significantly, timing exercises showed the script was too long. Accordingly, dialog was trimmed, or cut out altogether. We found the judicious pruning to be beneficial; the same thoughts could often be expressed in many fewer words.

Word came down from on high the Big Boss liked what he was seeing. So, one day Judy and I were taken for a walk. We wandered around for a bit, climbed a narrow flight of stairs and were ushered into the Sanctum Sanctorum. There, waiting for us was Gene Roddenberry. The meeting was short — a quick look us over, and we were on our way back down the stairs.

The script was starting to converge to the finished product. But still there were revisions. Some of the revisions were coming from the *Star Trek* staff. We agreed most of these were fine.

But, sometime in July we got notes, with a new version of the script. *Good Grief!* Where did *that* come from? A mutiny on board a starship? Preposterous. At least that was *our* opinion. The mutiny was Bobby Justman's idea. Hype up the emotions was his mantra — then hype them up even more.

I took back what I'd said about Justman's good instincts. He had once again wrecked a tightly wrought, tension filled drama, turning it, with this change, into a self-parody, we thought. But Bobby was our boss, so we did as directed. The logic of the story no longer held. Judy and I had only a few days to rewrite whole sections of the script. A witty scene in the dining commons had to be scrapped and Checkov was turned into a Mad Russian. We reworked the logic and dialogue of the story as best we could.

Fortunately, Judy was able to protect and polish a scene where McCoy directs Spock and Scotty to drink a derivative of a deadly nerve gas poison, Theragen. The evolution of the scene caused us to realize how the germ of an idea can blossom into something really charming.

On August 6 the last script revisions (nice pink paper) were typed and inserted. Our work, at last, was finished. Production began shortly thereafter. We were invited to be on the set during shooting. I went up for a couple of days during the two week shoot. Judy had other things to do those particular days, so I just sat and watched what was taking place.

Days on the *Star Trek* set were, quite frankly, boring. The technicians fiddled endlessly with spot lights, creating what became the unique visual signature of the first *Star Trek* series, the flat lighting. Mostly we all sat around waiting for the shadows to be precisely filled in. On the screen, the light appeared to come from nowhere and from everywhere. And yet, the actors always stood out from the slightly dimmed background. The lighting was pure wizardry.

Unlike the other actors, Jimmy Doohan — Scotty — rehearsed constantly while he was on the set. He was always master of his lines so his rehearsal was directed towards the camera. Keenly aware of where its eye would be at all times, he carefully rehearsed his hands. Part of one hand was missing, but this never showed. He oriented and moved this hand so it appeared natural, but the missing part was always safely hidden. What fighter pilots call "situational awareness" was a central part of his craft.

One evening I heard Doohan tell the stories of his *Star Trek* audition, and of the various characters he improvised while Gene Roddenberry was trying to make up his mind about what kind of engineer he wanted. He went through a variety of accents and body languages as he spoke. Sequentially he *became* East Indian, German, French, English, and finally a Scotsman. Scottish it was. My appreciation for his acting skills rose exponentially with each change of character.

After a couple of days of sitting on the set and waiting for something to happen, I gave up and didn't return.

Judy was more diligent, went on set frequently, and became well acquainted with the film crew and actors. She was already thinking ahead to a career in Hollywood.

Months passed. Judy had made friends with Mike Minor, the episode's special effects genius, and the three of us shared a delicious evening dining and swapping stories at the Mongolian Barbecue. Mike described how he had created the images of the Tholian's Web. His technique used painstaking stop action animation. As I recall, his method was something like the following.

He would start with color film which looked completely black. With a ruler as a guide, he'd scratch away a short line. This left some of the colored dyes embedded in the black film visible. He would take a photograph of this scratched section of film, and that would become the background of the first frame of an animated film strip. For the next frame he'd start with a fresh piece of black film and scratch a somewhat longer line. Because the scratching did not exactly match, from frame to frame, the colors that were revealed did not exactly match, and the result looked like a sparkly strand of web. Upon each new frame the Tholian ships, and the Enterprise, were matted in and a final frame exposure was made. This process had to be repeated, with precise registration until the entire cross-linked web had been constructed.

The process was a tour-de-force of stop action animation. It was also expensive. Our episode's special effects budget ballooned, along with the cost of filming, until it doubled the cost of a normal episode. Part of the excess expense could be attributed to the episode's first director. He had fallen in love with the possibilities presented by crew madness. Using special lenses he created POV (Point of View) shots with extreme visual distortion. These tricks consumed so much time and budget he was fired and another director was brought in to salvage the show.

The airing was in November. Family and friends gathered at Judy's house for the viewing and celebration. As familiar as the story had become for us it was still amazing to see the final result on TV.

One thing puzzled me, however. At one point of the story the dialogue between Scott and McCoy didn't seem to fit — the logic was wrong. Judy laughed. I was right. When DeForest Kelly and Jim Doohan were rehearsing the scene they didn't like the way it played, so they simply traded dialogue. Naturally their trade busted the logic of the whole act.

Still, our endeavor was, and remains, something of a triumph. Though, at the time, Judy and I had no idea we were participating in a major cultural phenomenon. Neither did anyone else.

Endings

After *Star Trek,* Judy and I collaborated on a speculative script for *Mission Impossible.* We never got screen credit for it, but Rumor Control has it the story, highly modified, did subsequently air. Mission's problem with our story was it was built around a fake assassination. In the story this assassination was faked so cleverly it completely fooled the bad guys. The people at *Mission* thought the technique proposed was too gory for family television. The clever trick I invented to fake the assassination was to mount explosive squibs on protective plates. The plates would be molded onto the skin of the "victim" in such a way as to be invisible. When the "bullet" struck the "victim" the squibs would be triggered on both his front and back, thereby simulating a real hit from a bullet. Sound familiar? Shortly thereafter Sam Peckinpah used precisely the same technique as a special effect in his sensational movie *The Wild Bunch.* Was there a connection? I suspect so.

Not long after this script was submitted to *Mission Impossible* I got a call from its producer. He wanted to meet with me to discuss my becoming a screen writer for the show. I begged off and told him the real talent was Judy Burns and he should give her a call. He did and Judy was hired as a staff writer.

This was after the third season of *Star Trek* had wrapped. The actors on the show were back on the street, looking for jobs. With Judy at *Mission,* one *Star Trek* actor quickly found work. Judy convinced the execs at *Mission* Leonard Nimoy would fit perfectly into the IMF crew. And so, Nimoy was hired and became Agent Paris, and Judy *did* get to become friends with the target of her admiration.

Judy's career blossomed. She became a story editor and ghost writer, including performing these roles on a couple of the *Star Trek* movies, and went on to write for many TV series. Finally, she became a producer as well as a writer for various shows, including the iconic MacGyver series.

The Tholian Web episode received an Emmy Nomination for special effects. We heard it actually received the Emmy, but I have not been able to confirm this. Mike Minor, though he did the work, did not receive the credit. He was working as a subcontractor to a certain opticals house, which gleefully took all the credit. Word got around, though, and the opticals house lost considerable business. Mike, on the other hand, prospered. Hollywood sometimes does things right. In later years Mike worked on several major motion pictures, including many of the *Star Trek* films. He was the art director for *The Wrath of Khan* and continued his career in the film and television industries.

Sadly, Mike Minor died young, as they used to delicately put it, "after a long illness," another talented victim of Babylonian Hollywood.

We received reports that *The Tholian Web* received a Hugo Award Nomination for best screenplay — one of science fiction's highest honors. But we didn't have much of a chance. Stanley Kubrick's *2001* won the Hugo that year.

A few years ago a major exhibit of *Star Trek* memorabilia was mounted at the Smithsonian's American History Museum. Our rainbow script for *The Tholian Web* was prominently displayed.

What a surprise! The Smithsonian. I had no idea what I'd taken on as a lark would turn out so well.

Grand Central Airport, Glendale, CA
Cover of Grand Central News, Grand Central Aircraft
Company magazine, March, 1953

MY GUARDIAN ANGEL

NOTHING TOPS THE JOYFUL EXHILARATION of soaring high above the spring-green earth through stupendous cloud canyons, weaving effortlessly among giant cloud towers, brilliant angel white against luminous sapphire sky.

From my earliest childhood I was drawn to an irresistible dream, having grown in the empire of the air — post war Southern California, the heartland of aviation.

In those days this sun baked land was a special place for lovers of the sky. Los Angeles was still young and still mostly empty space. A multitude of airfields mingled with truck farms and orange groves surrounding widely spaced small towns.

When we moved to Southern California in 1949 the city ended at the end of the runway next to the massive war-built Lockheed aircraft factory in Burbank. Beyond, extending the full length of the San Fernando Valley, were farms.

Nearer home was Glendale's legendary Grand Central Airport, a place where I spent part of my youth. Grand Central was grandiosely named, and for a number of years, it well deserved its name. For it was at Grand Central that the aviation industry in the Southland first coalesced. Here was the early home base for such legendary figures as Charles Lindbergh, Howard Hughes, Amelia Earhart, Roscoe Turner, Glenn Martin, Jack Northrop, Donald Douglas and the Lockheed brothers. Here is where Howard Hughes filmed much of Hell's

Angels and designed and built his world record racing plane. Here was the home for some of the earliest major airlines. Here was where the movie stars and business tycoons and politicians gathered and flew. Here is where the wartime Army Air Corps trained its mechanics in the Curtiss-Wright facility, and also trained many of its pilots. (Here, also, is where Walt Disney dwelled and later designed Disneyland.) Here was a place of glamour.

Here is no longer there, for it evaporated by 1960, converted into slab-sided tilt-up industrial buildings — except for the old crumbling zig-zag Art Deco Grand Central Terminal, and the new Disney studios.

For a few years my special boyhood birthday present was to be treated to an airplane ride out of this much acclaimed airport. I flew as the sole passenger in different types of light aircraft. My favorites were the fast V-tailed Beechcraft Bonanza and the slow Piper Cub with its wonderful view of the world below and the sky above.

It was in 1953, the lone passenger in a Cessna this time, that I experienced my first White Knuckle Flight. I was twelve years old. This was indeed a flight to remember, not only for me, but for all who witnessed it — and there were many. The flight became the stuff of legend.

It happened on a warm, sparkling December day, a day of desert clarity. Santa Ana winds had cleared the air of Southern California smog. More strong Santa Anas were predicted for late in the afternoon. But light westerly breezes would prevail for many hours to come, so we had plenty of time for a safe flight. My pilot was strongly muscled, ruggedly broad-faced, sun bronzed and movie star handsome — a man in the full flower of manhood. Straight out of a Milt Caniff cartoon strip, he could have been the prototype for Steve Canyon. In the flight ready room one of the other airmen mentioned I was going aloft with someone special, an outstanding World War Two fighter ace.

Together we walked out onto the flight line. The pilot opened the door of the small, high winged airplane and ushered me inside, warning me to be careful and not step on the thin skin of the airframe. Climbing cautiously, I swung up into the seat. The pilot buckled me in and dropped into the seat beside me. The prop was spun and the engine idled for a few minutes, warming up. We started our long taxi down to the east end of the runway.

We moved past the faded hulk of an old Curtiss C-46, the homely, workaday step-sister of the sleek and glamorous Douglas C-47. We passed a multitude of war-worn trainers, fighters and bombers; past the bare bone skeletons of old biplanes, a few fluttering tatters of rag still attached to those bones. We taxied until there was no more pavement, then we turned around into the wind.

Takeoff was routine. We soon soared high above Sonora Avenue, which now bisected the long wartime runway. Banking left over Griffith Park, we successfully avoided the air traffic circling around Burbank Airport. Soon we were flying over Hollywood, beginning our sight-seeing tour. Below, lining curly hillside roads, were the toy-like mansions and parklands of the rich and famous. The air, on this desert day, was utterly transparent. From this altitude one could see most of the Channel Islands, from San Clemente in the south to Santa Cruz in the north, and San Nicolas far out to sea. Sharp-edged mountains ringed the landward horizon. The buildings down below formed a photo clear diorama, seeming so close they appeared to be almost within reach. The flight was exhilarating.

Suddenly the radio crackled. It was Grand Central calling. The wind had unexpectedly picked up and was strong and gusty, with a powerful cross wind, so the runway was now closed. We would have to find another place to land. The pilot reassured me he would get me back to Glendale, even if it meant a long taxi ride. He started radioing around to other airfields, of which there were quite a few in the area.

His voice grew progressively more quiet, and took on something of a strain, as airfield after airfield reported high winds and closed runways. The pilot had a long conversation with Grand Central. Finally he told me we were going to go back to Glendale, but the landing was going to be a bit rough. He reached over and rechecked my harness to make doubly sure I was well secured. He banked over, and headed back north.

We circled the field. The pilot looked down intently, gauging the wind from the long, turbulent streaks of tan dust ripping straight across the runway — dust picked up from the railroad tracks north of the airfield and funneled between the buildings lining the airstrip. Not good. The wind gusts were intermittently peaking with velocities about as fast as we were flying. We circled again, the pilot analyzing, timing the gusts, plotting various tactics.

We circled again. Down below, people were pouring out of the nearby buildings, lining up along both sides of the runway. A fire engine pulled out of one of the structures and sat idling beside the runway. Men were climbing into several jeeps arrayed haphazardly among the throng. All stood watching, intently following our circling.

The pilot turned to me and said, in a subdued voice I could barely hear over the roar of the engine, "Brace yourself. This landing is going to be interesting and a little rough."

We began our final turn, the sound of the engine muted as the pilot throttled back. It was a little bumpy as we approached the runway, but not too bad. The pilot crabbed the plane into the wind, oscillating direction across the runway with each new wind gust, then back down the runway as the wind let up.

The plane banked slightly to the right as we neared the ground, compensating for a funneled gust of wind. One wheel touched the pavement — hard, jolting. The plane bounced up and came down, again hard, on its left wheel. The nose rose and fell. The wings see-sawed up and down, each wing tip dipping inches from impact with the concrete as the plane made short hops upwards, each time swerving around left and right, facing now down the runway, now facing across the runway. Sharp squeals of protest rose alternately from tires being severely punished. The pilot was torturing the plane to bleed off speed as fast as possible, timing the hops to compensate for the periodic wind funnels made visible with entrained dust.

Our landing traced out a zig-zag pattern part down and part across the wide strip of concrete. The plane was decelerating rapidly now, and we finally swung fully around into the gusting wind, headed almost straight across the runway. We were down, safe at last. The pilot turned the plane left and headed slowly toward the distant south side ready room.

From all directions people came running across the airfield to meet us, jeeps heading the pack. Seeing we were safe, the firemen started backing their truck into its dark lair.

The ride to the ready room was still bumpy, the pilot fighting to maintain control as strong, sharp wind gusts tried to lift our small plane back into flight. At last we arrived at our parking place. The pilot swung the plane around and shut off the engine while volunteers emerged from the growing circle of well-wishers to tie the still quivering aircraft down. The two of us sat there for a few moments catching our breath as the crowd pressed in close.

They didn't give us much time; our doors sprang open as if by magic. Someone reached in and unbuckled my harness. The same happened to the pilot. I started to climb out of the plane, but the commotion from the other side made me look back. I was puzzled by all the fuss. The pilot was being lifted bodily from his seat by grinning, laughing, happy faces. His feet never touched the ground as he was hoisted up onto husky shoulders and hustled back towards the ready room.

I climbed shakily out of the plane, helped by a strong hand, only too glad when my feet were planted firmly on the solid ground. The hand shifted to rest on my shoulder. I looked up to see the hand belonged to one of the pilots who had been present in the ready room. "Son," he said as we walked together across the apron, "that was the greatest piece of flying any of us have ever seen. If anyone else had been flying that plane you wouldn't still be alive. Your Guardian Angel was with you today." Maybe my Guardian Angel sat on my shoulder during the landing, but more likely he had been sitting right next to me.

AIR TRAVEL

THE FAMILIAR CONTOURS OF THE LAND slid by, far below. Crossing the continent by air had become a routine without adventure. The airline scheduling had been carefully put together to permit several hours for the plane transfer at JFK in New York. I had the suspicion legendary New York frictions would take their toll. The abrasive reputation of New Yorkers was not mere rumor. Each of my previous trips through that part of the world had been an unpleasant experience. I was not looking forward to this part of the journey. But it was essential I make connections through Kennedy, in a timely fashion, for I had to make a time critical connection in London or lose a considerable pile of money.

True to form, trouble started before we were on the ground. Our plane found itself stuck in a holding pattern high over the airport. Minutes passed as we circled, and expanded into hours. It was unbelievable. For more than two hours we were in the air over New York. My carefully planned reserve of time was dwindling to a miniscule margin.

Once down, baggage retrieval took the best part of an hour. I had decided not to trust the airlines to make the baggage transfer because of the probability a switch from one terminal to the next would be fouled up. And I absolutely needed the gear I was carrying. None of it could be obtained where I was going.

At long last I found myself on the sidewalk in front of the terminal. It was necessary to commute to the British Airways pavilion a couple of miles down the road. I planted myself optimistically at the airport shuttle bus stop and waited for the tram. It wasn't long before the big special cruised up the road. I waved at it, without success. Two more airport buses with the correct markings sped by without the slightest hesitation. I was growing desperate.

By standing at the airport transfer bus stop I had also given the game away to onlookers — I was only going a short distance. Calls to the nearby fleet of taxis produced only shrugs of disdain.

It was time for action, dramatic action. Another airport special was threading its way through traffic on the approach ramp. Quickly I grabbed one of my suitcases and lugged it into the middle of the street to make a barricade. Adding a couple more items from my stack on the sidewalk I enthroned myself in the middle of the street's chaos.

The bus cruised up and stopped, its massive front only inches away from my nose. The driver leaned out of his window and inquired, with less than polite language, as to what I thought I was doing. I told him to open the door and I would explain. He did, which I suppose was his mistake.

I jammed my suitcase in the door just as he decided to close it again. I told him he was the fourth, half empty, bus which had decided to ignore its obligations to pick up travelers. I informed the infuriated driver he was going to let me aboard and was going to transport me to the British Airways terminal — or else.

He was having none of it. Picking up his microphone he radioed the cops. Excellent! I informed him his call was precisely what I was hoping for. Now I would have unimpeachable witnesses. I told him time was growing short for me to make my connection; several thousand dollars had already been spent on the assumption I would be on that plane; the money was irrecoverable and I would see him and his employers in court if he didn't do his job.

"How do you like driving buses? Would you rather be unemployed, unemployable and bankrupt?" I asked him. It was brutal, but effective — and very New York. Capitulating, he let me aboard.

I was down to my last half hour by the time the driver deposited me in front of the British terminal. A porter wrestled my gear up to the check-in counter. I had some extra heavy boxes to check, and as I usually traveled light, had overlooked the problem of excess baggage. This was going to be costly — I was way over the limit. But with a bit of explanation about my problem I was able to get the price down.

The issue of excess baggage resolved, I headed for U.S. Customs to get my camera gear registered. I saw no point in having to pay import duties on all this expensive stuff when I tried to get back into the country.

The customs clerk was courteous and efficient and expedited the several forms required. I grabbed my certification, thanked him profusely and ran for the airplane, various gear bags slapping against my back and sides. As I sprinted along the corridor I could hear the final boarding call over the P.A. In the distance the last passengers were disappearing through the tunnel to the plane. The pneumatically operated door was already starting to shut. I hurtled a barrier, (this was long before OJ's famous TV commercial), and jammed my arm through the narrowing crack. The rubber safety bumper squeezed around my arm before the dim-witted sensors of the robot door control detected my presence and reopened the passage. So much for Kennedy. Good riddance.

The flight to London was uneventful, except for a peculiar thing British Airways has about meals. Somewhere over the Atlantic, not long after we reached altitude, it was time for supper. The usual fare was provided. It was my intention to settle down immediately after dinner and get some sleep. This was not feasible as long as the tray of table scraps lay in front of me. No one appeared interested in removing this obstruction so, after a long while, I made an inquiry of the rarely seen and somewhat harassed stewardess.

"I'm sorry sir. We can't remove your tray until after tea."

"But I don't want tea. I wish to sleep."

"Regulations sir, we can't take your tray."

I tried propping myself in an awkward position so as to keep from falling into the two hour old remnants of my meal while I dozed off. No go. At long last tea was served, and eventually the trays were removed.

The cabin lights dimmed and I settled in for what remained of the night. Settling gives the wrong impression since the seats on British made airplanes are clearly scaled to Pygmies, not average sized Americans. The result was a bit like being tucked away, upright, in a straightjacket.

Sleep finally came, welcome after an exhausting day of mostly sitting around. Almost immediately the cabin lights blazed on. A cheery voice over the intercom announced morning and breakfast before landing at Heathrow. I checked my watch. About fifteen minutes had elapsed since I had last glanced at it. I figure the permitted sleep period had been all of half an hour.

At some point along the line flying lost its romance. Likely this trip was it.

Sam Street and his signature sombrero

THE CLIFF

SAM STREET WAS STANDING AT THE EDGE OF THE RIVER. Tendrils of water rushed up to shyly kiss his toes, then quickly fled back to the safety of the stream. A slight smile animated Sam's face as he gazed at his crew cavorting wildly in the shallows, kicking up sprays of sun sparkled diamonds and whooping in demented frenzy at the record high flow.

Sam was average in height and deeply bronzed. His long, well groomed, sandy hair hung down almost to his waist and his face was swathed in a similarly long sun bleached beard. He wasn't wearing much — a ragged pair of gym shorts with patches of skin showing through, and a colorful bandana tied over his head. There was little to distinguish this Trip Captain from the rest of his piratical appearing crew. Except for his crown. Snugged down over his bandana was a large, battered, broad brimmed hat of dubious origin and considerable character.

Legend has it Sam was moseying down the road one day when he came to an intersection with a sign reading Sam Street. This, he thought, was a most excellent name. So he went to the Court House and *became* Sam Street.

Sam was a minimalist. He conversed in a slow, dreamy manner, his words picked with care. His movements were equally economical. Beneath that placid surface was remarkable depth, I was to discover a few days later.

This trip we were on was all about The River — the Colorado River. We were gathered, nearly five decades ago, under Sam's leadership for a voyage through the depths of the Grand Canyon. Sam's command was a small fleet of inflated rafts powered by long oars. O.A.R.S. — Outdoor Adventure River Specialists — was the name of the renowned white water company.

It was always hard to read Sam. Experienced as he was in conducting tourists down the river, Sam had to have been something of a showman — most boatmen are. Like a practiced stage magician he often misdirected your attention a split second before pulling a rabbit out of his hat. But something more was involved. While the other boatmen had a camaraderie, they instinctively kept a bit of emotional distance from him. Sam was somehow different, and the boatmen unconsciously recognized this.

After a brief lecture from our singular Trip Captain, mostly concerned with protecting our life saving Mae Wests at all costs, we shoved out into the river and began our adventure. Quickly those remaining behind shrank to tiny dolls and disappeared altogether as the swift current glided us silently towards the rising walls of Marble Canyon. A few gravelly riffles from the outflow of the Paria River and we were into the canyon. We'd had a late start, waiting for Sam and his contingent of passengers to arrive from Page, Arizona, so we soon beached our boats for lunch not far downstream from the Paria inflow. Peanut butter is said to be the river man's fuel. Without it everything quickly grinds to a halt. Lunch was mostly peanut butter sandwiches and Kool-Aid.

After our meal, Sam gathered us around for another lecture. This time it was about the canyon and the river and the magical mood the place can inspire. He spoke in a slow drawl, taking his time to say simple things which were deeply felt. As he spoke the water started rising. The circle of listeners closed in until there was no more room around the small sand mount from which this sermon was being delivered. Gradually people climbed onto the rafts until Sam was alone on the newly created island. He looked perfectly oblivious to the rising waters of the river. But, with magnificent timing, he spoke the carefully measured last word of his speech and stepped dry-footed aboard his vessel at the precise moment a wavelet finally submerged the lost Atlantean island. The man was indeed a showman.

Sam dealt quietly with things. Long before a rapid was fully in view he studied the river intently, reading the surface ripples for information about position and currents. When he was satisfied he understood it all he would unship the oars, and waggle them a couple of times, and bring them back in. Period. We would now be set for the run. Occasionally Sam would poll the passengers before setting up to find out what kind of a run they would like — wet or dry. The choice depended on the time of day, the temperature and how tired we were from previous activities.

There was much more to Sam than his style. There was something uncanny about him — some kind of magic. Perhaps it was because he had wintered with a Navajo Shaman, and had absorbed much of the old man's lore. Knowledge which came in handy when he healed the ankle of a crew member. Or, maybe Sam derived it from the canyon. The place itself was magic.

We all felt it. The precipitous, flame painted, canyon walls, seemingly rising to infinity, propelled us to a different world — one completely outside our experience. This world filled us with tranquility, for it was *quiet*. Yes, there were rapids. And, yes, those rapids were loud. But the rapids on this river were formed by alluvial dams which back up the river for miles. Drifting down those miles, suspended like angels above glass-like emerald green water, there was no sound save what we created ourselves, and of course the pleasant sounds of occasional animals, dragonflies and birds. It was not uncommon for quiet conversations to be carried out between boats spaced dozens of yards apart. That is how deep the silence was.

Within days the impositions of civilization, with all its tensions, had dropped completely away. One typical morning we drifted with the stream and soaked up great draughts of tranquility. Civilization had become remote, as if a wrong way telescope intervened. It appeared the river and canyon had won completely. I had become as detached as a swami on a mountain top. However, such moods do not last forever. The reality of existence in what can be a harsh world brings its own intrusion into such a state of tranquility. And the intrusion is magnified by any piece of careless foolishness a misdirected sense of tranquility can engender — as I soon discovered.

We beached our flotilla in a lagoon formed by a long spit of sand projecting into the river. This was at the foot of Saddle Canyon, another tributary of the main formation. This was to be the location of a side hike which would last most of the day. I unpacked the black rubber bag that kept my gear dry. The process of searching out the hiking boots I'd carefully packed away delayed me, so I was compelled to follow a couple of minutes behind the hiking party. I missed the trail head and had quite a scramble before I finally got back on track and joined the second party ascending along the base of the red painted cliff.

The trail circled above a dry waterfall and continued up the tributary canyon. The walls of this upper canyon narrowed in and the floor became sandy. Not much further there was the trickle of a stream flowing over the sand. We headed up, back towards the source of this disappearing stream. As we followed the twists and turns of the hanging valley the vegetation began changing. Dusty dry clumps of Sonoran flora became the grassy spaced tree system of the African Veldt. Another twist in the trail and we were ambling along through light jungle. Finally the limestone walls of the Muav formation (which lies beneath the Redwall) closed in to create a passage so constricted there was only room for the now substantial flow of water. We could go no further; a sizeable waterfall blocked further passage. The warm pool below the fall was inviting, so most of us took the opportunity to rinse off the grime of the hot and dusty walk.

The existence of an impassible wall did not deter the more intrepid boatmen, however. Searching around the alcove one of the river guides discovered there were two channels to the waterfall. The one right next to the filled and flowing fall was dry and formed an easy chimney for climbing. The boatmen had to give it a try. Soon several had made the ascent. A couple of the more intrepid and skilled passengers joined them. Off this patrol went to explore still another level of the series of narrow hanging canyons.

Those of us remaining behind waited at the falls for a considerable period of time, some people taking naps, others conversing and a few reading. Finally, with the growing hunger from a postponed lunch, most of us decided to head back to the boats and rustle up some food.

After we ate, the time beside the river began to pile up and a worry started to grow. The people who had elected to stay behind at the falls had long since come down to the boats and reported no sign of the exploring party. A rescue effort was organized under the supervision of the training boatmen. Gear which appeared to be of appropriate utility was stripped off the boats, including a couple of long ropes. We were about to start making the ascent up the trail when off in the distance there came a hailing shout. The missing group had returned.

Scrambling down the loose shale talus above us, the boatmen almost tumbled in their haste to reach the security of the boats. Their behavior afterward was most strange. A couple walked out to various parts of the projecting sand spit. Others planted themselves, each alone, in a shaded clearing of the Tamarisk forest.

Curious about what had happened, I approached several of the boatmen with questions. I got no response except a vague communication of resentment for my intrusion.

Finally, I cornered one of the passengers who had made the trek. He told the following remarkable story.

Having climbed to the top of the waterfall, the party started hiking up what was obviously a pristine wilderness. No sign of any previous human presence could be discerned in either the sand or the plants growing there. There were signs aplenty of small animals, though, and these little furries, showing natural curiosity about these strangers, appeared quite tame.

The group continued up the narrow slit canyon until it was apparent no further progress could be made. There they found the giant whose spirit dominates the spot. It was an ancient cottonwood. The gnarled old tree completely spanned the canyon from wall to wall. Forming a hand to hand chain, the group estimated the circumference of this old creature to be a whopping twenty-four feet.

Having completed their exploration, the group returned to the waterfall. By now everyone waiting had returned to the boats. To their horror the explorers found the wind had shifted and the explanation for the second channel of the waterfall was all too apparent. The water was now flowing down the alternate channel, thus blocking the passage up which they had made their climb. Worse, the moss at the top of the original channel was so thoroughly soaked descent by this route was suicidal. A couple of attempts at this route nearly ended in disaster, with only the quick hands and strength of a backstopping boatman saving the would-be climber from a plunge to the stone pavement far below.

The boatmen tried a different possibility. Extending out along the cliff face, above the waterfall, was a ledge. It appeared there might be a route down from the end of the ledge to the stream below. But all the skill of these experienced mountain men provided no solution to the problem of finding the route.

The answer came in a most unexpected way. Sam Street went off by himself and coiled into a meditative trance. For a long time he sat there, no one disturbing his contemplation. Finally, he started giving directions, eyes closed, talking in a measured voice from the depths of his dream. He ordered one of the boatmen out to the end of the ledge. Where the ledge ended the wall curved around to invisibility. Sam described a hand and foot hold from his mind's eye. He told the boatman to go ahead and reach out for them and not be afraid. Trusting his remarkable leader, the boatman did as instructed. And sure enough, the holds were as described. Step by step Sam guided the first boatman, and then the others, down to the safety below. After the last of the party got safely down, Sam, unassisted, made his own blind descent.

The wonder of the experience sealed the lips of Sam's hard headed followers. They obviously were convinced they had witnessed a true miracle, something supernatural.

Was it? Perhaps.

On the other hand, without question Sam had the most acute powers of observation. He demonstrated this numerous times. If natural explanations are called for, one might suggest Sam had unconsciously taken in every detail of the wall during the ascent along the trail below. The trance permitted Sam a hypnotic recollection of the surface which, together with the responses from the descending climbers, gave a sure picture to Sam of what was happening and what had to happen next. Whatever the explanation, there was indeed a miracle at the waterfall, if only in the demonstration of the wonderful powers a human being possesses when survival is at stake.

Years later Sam had another epiphany. He trimmed his hair short, applied a razor to his luxuriant beard, donned starched khakis, a badge, a Smokey Bear sombrero, and strapped on a heavy caliber pistol. Sam Street had transmogrified into Sam West, ace Grand Canyon River Ranger! That is, when he wasn't down on the river, near naked again, and getting paid handsomely, by oarsman standards, to do what he dearly loved doing.

LAVA FALLS

KEN WAS ROWING. The issue had been settled a week before, upstream at Crystal. Now it was his time. He stood solidly on the high rock perch years of tradition had confirmed as the boatman's lookout. Sun hot dark basalt, beneath his feet and at his back, reflected an oven's touch onto his bare, tanned flesh, creating little glittering jewels of sweat in the thick hairy matting of his broad chest. His eyes peered nervously from the black bush that was his head, down towards the boiling, raging turmoil below the cliff.

The time of confrontation had come at last. This was Lava Falls in the Grand Canyon, the Emperor of Rapids, and Ken, for the first time in his life, was gazing on the great legend. There was in his manner a trace of awe, laced with fear. His skills were great, it is true, but they had been honed over the years in California, on rivers much smaller and more technical in their challenge. This was the Colorado, the giant of white water. This was the place where the sport was born. Here the rapids are titanic snarls. These rapids are engines of great power which can casually flip a multi-ton boat with the slightest flick of the edge of a wave. The challenge of the Colorado was not to dance gracefully among the rounded rocks of a boulder garden, but merely to survive.

So far we had been lucky, Ken and Mark and myself. We had had some close calls, such as the time I had nearly upset our raft at President Harding. And the bleak day at Horn Creek when two other rafts in our flotilla met disaster and a helicopter evacuated one of our crew to the hospital. But those events were mere prelude. For the man of the river, the Colorado signifies one thing: Lava Falls.

We three were the trainees. It was our job to learn the ways of the river in preparation for the prospect of rowing the Colorado commercially. We were rowing for OARS, the California based company which pioneered the use of small rowing rafts in the Grand Canyon. Mark was the senior of our trio, having run the Colorado eight times, either as a passenger or a boatman. Before the summer was through he would likely be earning his pay here. Ken was an experienced pro from the Sierra rivers. Skilled in the ways of white water, he worked summers as trip leader for OARS on the Gold Country rivers. But the Colorado, that was a challenge at a much higher level. My background was more diverse. I had run rivers around the world, mostly as a passenger. My experience in command of a white water vessel was primarily in kayaks. Somehow I had talked my way onto this trip as one of the trainees.

This was not my first time on the hot rocks above Lava. Years before, during my first trip down the Colorado, I had stood in this same place, gripped with foreboding. The river was running big — something over three times its normal flow. The boatmen stood at the lookout in the broiling sun and watched. They had never seen the river in such a rage. No one appeared willing to try his luck. For more than an hour the debate ricocheted among the boatmen about the best course of action. Finally a decision was made. Terry would try the usually forbidden left side run carrying his passengers with him. That included me.

We didn't make it. The top part of the rapid was OK, but we stalled out in a keeper hole near the rapid's foot. The other two passengers onboard were flushed out immediately by the crashing waves of a thirty knot current. I hung on, desperately, through cycles of breaking waves. In the end I was flung free. My last vision of the raft, before I was driven to the black bottom of the silty river, was of Terry, half overboard, his outside leg caught between a maverick oar and the side of the boat. The gnawing jaw of the vise had trapped his leg, and was locked tight by the pressure of the current.

Somehow Terry survived. When we met again my eyes were filled with the image of his leg — tatters of flesh where the trap had gripped him, the torn folds of his skin draped down about his ankle like an unruly sock. He had used his wrestler's strength to break the lock of the river and somehow managed to lever the boat out of the keeper and back into the main flow. But Terry was not again quite the same free spirit, after he had found his hole in Lava.

Lava sometimes does that to people. It was toying with Ken, Mark and me now, working on our fears and memories of the scrapes we had each barely survived. The sparkling day darkened as we thought of the grim possibilities. We knew of the undercut, razor sharp, drowning rocks that lined the shores and depths of the rapid. We contemplated the narrow margins of the run. There was, here, NO room for error. All forgiveness had been used up in earlier places. The river between these shores was hard and cruel.

Below us was the reality: The waterfall at the top, stretching from bank to bank, pouring the mighty river's fluid into a churning trough. The narrow, tenuous bridge, showing vaguely on the right, provided the only possible route at this water level — the massive triple series of holes, lurking along the right wall, gulping and gnashing any and all within reach; the awesome breaker at the bottom of the rapid, unavoidable, inevitable.

While there was no room for error, the correct road was obscure. The entry was extremely technical, quite invisible during the approach, but still it had to be finessed to perfection. We received our briefing from the elders. The rapid was runnable for a single reason: The Bubbles. The bubbles are the key. The marker is subtle, hard to see, irregular at best and, on many days, not there.

By some trick, not understood, the river traps air in the rocks upstream of the falls. Or perhaps there is a gaseous leak, courtesy of the remnants of volcanism. Whatever the cause, one can see, if one knows where to look, bubbles rising to the surface. Five seconds, eight seconds, three seconds apart, sometimes not at all for critical periods of time, they rise. They burst on the surface, forming nebulas of foam which are instantly swept, by the accelerating current, towards the precipice. By some kind fate, the track of the bubbles takes the traveler right towards the bridge which breaks the waterfall. Follow the bubbly road. Take the bubble route. Advice of the experienced, given freely to the novice.

The first two boats made their run. Mike, the trip leader, was positioned on the bubble run to perfection. Big Bruce, one of the most experienced boatmen around, was more daring in his run. Confident of his strength, he ran the sketchy right, plowing through the three great holes. The river toyed with him a bit, knocking his rig askew and disabling an oar. Bruce kept his poise and plunged his raft through to safety with powerful strokes of his remaining oar.

We were in the next group. We watched intently as the boat ahead of us dropped out of sight over the edge of the waterfall. A long time later the boat reappeared, shrunken to a tiny dot by the distance, apparently OK.

Ken stretched the oars to set up our entry. Mark stood up on the bench to gain a sighting of the bubbles. I joined him shortly. A few feet of altitude makes a wonderful difference. What had been nearly invisible sitting down was quite clear standing up. Too clear. We were way off course — too far to the right. Mark was trying to point the bubble marker to Ken. Ken could not pick it out in the glare of the sun. We were drifting for the edge. I was growing fatalistic. I felt no panic, no fear, only a sense of the inevitable and of being along for the ride.

Ken never did see the bubbles. Mark took over command, directing Ken to stroke to the left. Ken did so, with too much power. We slid across the bubble line immediately above the precipice, our momentum carrying us past the now visible bridge and flinging us into a split in the current. We accelerated left with the new stream of water.

Ken slewed the boat around to meet the rapid head on. Our fate became fully apparent. We sat on the lip of the waterfall. With majesty we tilted over and started our slide. The drop is twelve feet and vertical. From my eyes to the bottom of the depression in the trough below the falls was twenty. It was a long drop.

It did not seem to take forever. It took as long as it took. We simply fell. I have no doubt Ken was stroking to keep the nose into the foot wave as we went down; I could feel the corrections. His quick thinking probably saved us from extreme consequences. What happened next was inevitable. The boat smashed into the bottom of the waterfall and kept on going.

It dipped below the surface. Our downstream momentum, created by the swift current above the falls, carried us straight into the tumultuous haystack of the fall's reversal wave.

An inflated raft may weigh, fully laden, nearly a ton. But its buoyancy is many times greater. Like the leviathan our raft breached up through the foam, arrowing towards the blue sky. The bottom current neatly tripped our tail and the raft spun over on its back.

I was hanging on through all of this — with desperation. The raft came over on top of me, solid, impenetrable, the black floor now a ceiling over my head. Turbulent foam forced me up into the well of the craft. For a moment I was trapped. Instinctively I fought to get clear. Flipping my legs up and planting my feet on the bow tube, I pushed off, down into the depths of the river. And was swept free.

The turbulence buffeted me, tumbling me around until I lost all orientation. My life jacket played its role. I rose to the surface. Daylight. Air! I gasped for breath. Before I could swallow a cupful of the life giving stuff a wave crashed over from behind. The animal in me started to take over, crying in mounting panic.

Then experience gained command. Thirty seconds, I told myself, and the worst would be behind me. Relax and go with it. The panic was quenched. I reoriented myself to survey the prospect downstream. A trough, a quick breath, a plunge through the next wave and I could see the situation.

It was easy. I was at the center of the river, well away from the murderous dangers of the right side holes and rocks. Time to go into my drill, legs out front, downstream. Breathe regularly, before dunking through the waves. Wait for the tail of the rapid, backstroke to the left bank. Glancing back I could see Ken and Mark upriver with the overturned boat beyond them. The rock wall on the left was coming up fast now. I crossed an eddy line and snagged a spur of rock. My legs were instantly sucked under. The rock wall was undercut. Get out of there! I pushed back out into the current and kicked free.

Back in the stream I checked my situation. I could feel the cold now. Funny how I had not been aware of the bitter river chill during the action upstream. Was there a problem with hypothermia? With my rain clothes on, worn as protection against the anticipated splash of the rapid, I felt no water circulating against my skin, no numbness. I decided to swim down to the beach I knew lay below. The boat had passed, bottoms up, while I'd anchored at the side of the river. So had Big Bruce, racing to the rescue. I followed our disabled vessel into the eddy, swam around the jam-up near shore and walked onto dry land.

I trembled slightly, standing there, not from chill but from the slow draining of accumulated adrenalin. I remembered Ken struggling to drag himself up the rocks, and volunteered to search him out. After scrambling through a tangled jungle of razor sharp saw grass Ken appeared in a clearing, lost and upset. We walked through lacerating blades of saw grass. As Ken walked behind me, matching me step by step, his bare skin shielded by the protection of my nylon weather suit, we shoved through the green knife edges.

Mark was not so lucky. Coming onto land far upstream he had to force his way, bare legged, through hundreds of yards of the cutting blades. By the time he made the beach his legs were crisscrossed with bloody lacerations.

In time the other boats arrived to help in the task of righting our raft. With lines rigged across its bottom, and with plenty of muscle power, we performed the flip, adjusted the skewed gear and rowed back out onto the river.

There were gains and losses in the incident. Lost: one hat, weathered, given character by weeks on the river. Lost: one new, expensive rain jacket, earned over a long winter, penny after penny, by an impoverished boatman. Lost: pride and cockiness.

But on the other side of the ledger there were new riches. Most importantly, lives were saved. Experience, to be savored, was added to the treasure house of each person present. A boatman, at first upset with himself, had added the raw material to carry him through at a future time when his passengers would be innocents, not the experienced watermen of this day.

And there was the tale to be told, repeated to the amused and disbelieving on distant nights when issues of life and death are remote.

Lava Falls
View from the west side of the Toroweap area

"Land of Troubles": Awash River Falls, at the put-in

LAND OF TROUBLES

September 1976, Heathrow Airport, London: A pair of five fingered spiders skittered lightly up and down my body, quickly probing every crevice, searching for contraband. Briefly, delicately, the fingers traced the outline of the Swiss Army Knife nestled in my pocket. This guy was a pro, quite unlike the clumsy TSA searchers of today. He knew about the knife, but I didn't fit the profile. I passed inspection and proceeded through the boarding gate. I was on my way to Ethiopia and an expedition down the wild and still unexplored Omo River.

My friend had warned me. Don't do this. It's far more dangerous than you can possibly imagine. I didn't listen. He was right.

The flight from London to Addis Ababa was long delayed. At last it was time for my bags to be examined. Every single item was removed, unraveled and looked at closely, then remarkably, precisely repacked. I went through the body inspection and was allowed to board.

The passenger cabin of the airliner was near empty on the long flight. All but one of the few passengers were fellow members of our expedition. The outsider proved to be the president of Ethiopian Airlines. During a friendly conversation he mentioned the long delay resulted from a warning – a bomb had been placed aboard.

We refueled in Rome and headed out over the Mediterranean. After a long and restless night, dawn found me gazing down at Khartoum spread along the pointed tongue between the merging streams of the Blue and White Nile. We flew on.

The next day I opened my journal and began to write. What follows is based on those journal entries.

THE PLANE BEGAN ITS SAG towards the high plateau of the central Ethiopian massif. It was clear from the outset Addis Ababa was a different city from most I had seen. On flights into many cities around the U.S. and, on this trip, into London and Rome, I had observed each is certainly different in its own way. But they are all variations on a pattern – a western pattern. Addis was a completely unfamiliar world. On the approach to the metropolis, small farms, scattered about the landscape, broke up the countryside into unlikely patches. The farm buildings themselves were small and densely clustered, making compounds which were surprisingly large. Each farm center appeared to be a small village. But these villages were not laid out along streets and blocks. The pattern of the cluster was rectangular but the buildings were irregularly spaced.

There was no edge to the city proper. Farms became smaller and closer together as we approached the airport until they fused together. Fields diminished in size, gradually becoming backyards.

Occasionally a large structure would appear — almost invariably in these outskirts this would emerge as the gleaming golden dome of a church whose architecture was a legacy from the Age of Justinian.

Eventually we were on the final approach to the mile high capital city. And finally, we were down.

The long walk across the runway apron from the plane to the small terminal building gave plenty of time to soak in the atmosphere. The air of the high mountain plateau was crisp and a gentle breeze carried aromas of a subtle alien quality.

The land was verdant with the growth of the rainy season. The margins of the runway held back charging legions of golden blossomed bushes. I was reminded of California Mustard in the spring. But spring and California were two seasons and half a world away. Here it was Meskel, the holy day of the true cross, in the season of the yellow flowers, and of rain.

Things became unpleasant in the terminal. The few of us who were from the plane jammed into a line that had piled up long before. One of my companions for this expedition, Kathy, was plucked from the milling confusion by a matron and hustled into a tiny cubical to be strip searched. She was seething on her return. My problems came later.

I collected my baggage from the cart and hauled it over to the custom inspector's table. The official, in a slightly disheveled uniform, poked around in the innards of my pack and suitcase without much enthusiasm. Turning his attention to the tightly sealed carton I had carried from California, he asked me to open it for inspection in fractured English. No way! That box had factory packed tents. Once opened it would be impossible to put everything back together. The inspector got stubborn. I changed my tack. Okay, I would let the inspector open the box, but he was going to have to repack it. I assured him this was going to take several hours. The message got across, and rather glumly the bureaucrat passed me through, box undisturbed.

I discovered how narrowly I'd escaped real trouble later. The new "Socialist" government had, a few days before, ordered all the currency of the country be turned in and replaced with a new issue. Of course the new money would be worth less than the old, with higher denominations redeemed at a lower rate of exchange. Soak the rich, as usual. Since the new government had declared it, ex post facto, to be illegal to take money out of the country they were searching travelers for money being smuggled back in. This was the critical day because the deadline for turning in the old currency was on the morrow. No wonder a sealed carton of the right size attracted so much attention.

Outside the terminal the straggling survivors of the customs inquisition were gradually collected by a tall, bronzed, boatman type. He introduced himself as John Yost and said he would be one of the guides on the trip. The trip leader, Jim Slade, was on his way from the city and would pick us up in a few minutes. Sure enough, Slade cruised in, driving a battered old car and leading a squadron of colorful taxi cabs. We sorted ourselves out and I found myself seated next to Slade for the drive to the city.

We approached Addis Ababa — the Little Flower — along a broad boulevard. Scattered at random along its margins were buildings of an amazing variety of architectural styles. Italian Baroque dominated — the legacy of Italy's long, sometimes unfriendly, association with the country. Otherwise there was no obvious organizing principle. The pavilions were plunked down wherever a patron's fancy chose. Orientations of the various structures were also random. One was as likely to see a back porch as a front door. Many of the structures were large and elegant. Jim said much of the Capital's diplomatic community was housed along this highway.

Presently we passed a low cluster of solid but unkempt structures. To one side was a tall flag pole. As we drew abreast a gust of wind ruffled the limp rag at the top and it briefly snapped to attention. Its insignia was a dark gray ball on tattered gray background. The frayed edges of the cloth were like decorative ribbons, signifying ages of dutiful service. It was the embassy of Japan, literally at the end of the world for the poor, devoted folk within.

A few miles further and the scattered structures thickened into city. Traffic picked up. It was time for the game. Jim Slade has been driving streets like these for years — fortunately. On these broad streets cars and pedestrians mix indiscriminately. Traffic is not so dense as to be bogged down, so the game of dodge-em is played at high speed. A pedestrian steps off the curb straight into the tangled weaving of traffic. He strides, apparently oblivious to the hurtling machines, straight across to his destination. It is the task of the driver to make just enough allowance to prevent the pedestrian from getting trapped in a no-win situation. In turn, the stroller might supply a slight hesitation at the last moment so the car does not deposit a fresh carcass in the road.

This dance of death lasted its fascinating minutes, but in the end, the motley caravan pulled up in front of the Ethiopia Hotel. We collected and sorted our gear and worked out our room assignments. Dinner was in two hours, Yost announced. It was to be a special treat at a restaurant serving native fare. Not for me. During more than two full days of travel I had totaled only a few minutes of fitful slumber. Crushed beyond endurance, I staggered to my room and collapsed on the sagging foam rubber mattress of my bed. This time I slept.

The next day our group boarded a chartered bus for an excursion down the steep escarpment into the Afar triangle. Our intent was a short warm-up river trip on the Awash River before we headed out on our expedition down the Omo River. All day bus trips can be long and boring. This one wasn't.

Along the way we traded rumors about the current situation and what it portended. Two years before, following much rioting in the streets, young military officers, members of the Derg, had carried out a coup, and deposed Emperor Haile Selassie. It was said this had been done in what appeared to be a uniquely civilized way. The elderly Selassie was never told he had been deposed and he continued to give orders as usual. The orders were never carried out, of course. While the powerless emperor was sequestered, most of his former government officials were executed without trial. A year later Selassie himself died under suspicious circumstances, barely one year before we arrived.

A more bizarre rumor claimed before the original coup pairs of conservative and communist opponents in the Derg had been handcuffed together, day and night. This was to prevent mischief by the opposing parties. Nevertheless, somehow all got guns, and the outcome was decided by a close quarters gun battle during a meeting of the Derg. The few surviving communists were the victors. After the coup, the country descended into chaos. Whatever the truth, these and other recent events had brought things to a boil. And we were now immersed and unsafe.

We passed by an old village. Plastered houses were randomly scattered around a central open area, the whole shaded by ancient trees. Under one of the trees a crowd of men had gathered. They were standing quietly, several deep in a circle, listening intently to a man in the center who was elevated above them. The man was haranguing the swaying circle, gesticulating with both arms partly raised. Suddenly, in a fit of excitement, the circle of men raised their weapons — old muskets and spears — thrusting them to the sky and jumping and yelling wildly. The fleeting scene vanished in the dust behind us.

Military checkpoints along the highway caused us some trepidation. We were stopped at one and some of us got off the bus to relieve ourselves. Along the roadway to our right was a high embankment covered with bushes and trees. A militia man with a rifle, well polished with use, followed us back onto the bus and started walking down the aisle checking our passports. Someone in the bus called out to be careful with his gun. "Gun" was one of the few words of English he understood. So, he immediately started a search to see if we had any weapons which could be confiscated. When he came to me he saw the camera in my lap. He swung his rifle around and pointed it towards my belly, his finger nervous on the trigger. I froze. John Yost, fluent in Amharic, talked him down and we all relaxed — especially me.

Finally he convinced himself we were harmless and let us go. As we drove away we realized the cause of the incident. A military air base was behind the embankment. Such incidents, together with the multitudes of soldiers parading with live machine guns, made us all the more anxious to move out into the bush.

We started our warm-up river excursion below Awash Falls, a most remarkable place to put in. Above the falls the river drifts lazily across a flat prairie, with trees clustered along its banks. Stretched straight across the river, the waterfall is like a miniature version of Niagara Falls. Unlike most waterfalls around the world, it is not tall and narrow. Its height might be thirty or forty feet, maybe somewhat more, but the width is much larger, more than the length of a football field. Below the falls the river drops into a shallow canyon, which progressively deepens downstream until its depth becomes quite substantial. There are occasional open areas where the walls of the canyon recede and there is ready access from the terrain above. In these areas natives come down to the river for various activities.

Monkey invasion, first Awash campsite

A few miles downstream the sounds of singing and laughing drifted up the canyon to meet us. This was not at all primitive music. The words were sung in familiar three part harmonies and two and three line counterpoint. Yet the melodies and rhythms were completely new and beguiling. I did not expect such enchanting music in this primitive setting. Was the music entirely native and ancient? Or, did the Italian influence in the high country filter down to these backwater regions. Maybe both cultural streams had merged.

As we drifted out from the narrow canyon, and around a bend, the river banks widened out into a gravel bar forming a gentle rapid. We could see the songs were coming from a group of Danikil women bathing and doing laundry at the gravel bar. The scene was reminiscent of the Odyssey, where shipwrecked Odysseus chanced upon women laundering clothes at the riverside.

The women were friendly enough until I got out a camera, whereupon they became most upset. Photography of these people must be surreptitious, if at all, I learned. The Danikil are still definitely wild. Young men kill and take "testicular trophies" from neighboring unfriendly tribes as a rite of passage and signal of marriageability. Efforts by the government to change this bloodthirsty custom have not been too successful. Generally they are friendly but if you cross them they might start shooting.

Downstream a few miles we saw three men, one of whom was carrying a rifle. No one made the slightest move to get out a camera. But still, the sharp eyed rifleman saw the camera dangling from a strap around my neck. He leveled his rifle straight at me. Someone covered up my camera with a hat. I raised my right hand high. (Definitely not an unsanitary left hand — that is reserved for unspeakable things and deadly insults.) The left went high enough to show it was empty. With my right hand raised, and many Salaams, I managed to pacify him, and he lowered his rifle. It is definitely unsettling to stare down the barrel of a rifle held by a man you know has killed others for sport.

The Awash interlude was entertaining, but at its end I got a violent case of what was later dubbed Chet's Revenge. It took me a couple of days to recover. When I was finally feeling up to it I joined Kathy and Murphy for an excursion to the Mercato.

This is a vast market of small shops. It is typical of African markets, I was told, except this one was reputed to be the largest such market in Africa.

Kathy, a tall, slender young woman, comes from the exclusive schools of the East coast and is preparing, in graduate school, for a career as a wildlife biologist. Like me she is a Turner freak and could not resist the opportunity, when we were in London, to visit the Tate and see the world's treasure house of Turner paintings.

Murphy is a stocky, sandy haired, good humored young man with a soft Cajun accent. A petroleum engineer, he specializes in reconstructing African oil fields and refineries blown apart in the Continent's perpetual wars. This river excursion is a vacation between assignments. His last was down in Angola where there is still a fracas going on, engineered by a Cuban expeditionary force. Next, he was going off to Nigeria where a lively civil war was underway. "I'll probably leave my bones around here, somewhere," he grinned, "but the pay is excellent and so is the adventure."

Murphy's intention was to chase down Maria Theresa Tallers — a reliable trade currency. He wanted to gather enough silver for a belt buckle. Maria Theresas, somewhat larger than a U.S. silver dollar, were minted in the eighteenth century when the Empress Maria Theresa ruled over the Austro-Hungarian Empire. The coins were going for only a couple of U.S. dollars, which shows the true value of American money in the backwaters of the world. Quality original Maria Theresas are worth thousands of dollars among coin collectors. But Murphy insisted he only intended to cast a belt buckle. Being picky, he wanted near mint coins so we spent a long time searching. In the end he made a good haul.

The three of us were milling around at the plaza end of the Mercato when I caught sight of a flash of steel. A knife. Whipped out of a lean man's cloak and thrust expertly into the belly of another man, and quickly stuffed back into the cloak. The victim dropped to the ground like the proverbial sack of potatoes, and lay still as the assassin melted into the crowd and vanished. This happened less than ten yards away. Naturally I was urged by curiosity to move towards the gathering circle of bystanders. Murphy, with wisdom gathered through many years of experience in Africa, grabbed my sleeve and tugged me in the opposite direction. "We don't want to be here!"

We skedaddled down a long row of shops and ducked inside one of them before the commotion got out of hand. Murphy immediately started dickering with the proprietor for coins.

The next morning we began the real expedition. A bus ride would take us from Addis to the Gibe River. From there we would drift down the river, past the junction with the Omo River, and finally make our first camp.

Morning started early — before seven we were at the bus station. We were taking a regular bus this time. None of those fancy charters for this trip. Few people were on the streets at this early hour but as we approached the station we quickly merged with a rapidly expanding mob.

Our taxis parked across a dusty road from the station. In our walk to the station's entrance we passed over the local underground sewer, evident from the fetid odor rising from beneath our feet. The sewer was only a short distance under-ground. Its roof culminated in a grated slit running along the sewer's length, likely engineered to prevent the accumulation of explosive methane. It was the presence of this vent that made us aware of the existence of the facility. A few steps further and the odor had completely vanished.

There was nothing special about the bus station, although John Yost said it had been completely rebuilt since the previous year. The scene was a big rock strewn dirt lot filled with buses, baggage and milling people. Ticket counters, taking the form of adobe cubicles, lined one side. An adobe wall ran round the compound with two gates.

I was impressed with extraordinary juggling feats performed by the baggage handlers. One fellow balanced a huge, boxy, heavy load on his shoulders and proceeded to climb hand over hand up the back ladder of the bus, to deposit his burden in the rack on top.

John returned after a bit with a handful of tickets. When he approached the ticket counter he was confronted with a solid wall of people, all hoping to catch the same bus, the last one of the day. Not a chance to break through that barrier without a stratagem. Although we were traveling only a minor part of the route, John needed to get our tickets before they were all sold so he yelled out to the ticket seller, in Amharic, "Twelve people to the end of the line!" The ticket seller promptly scattered the crowd and took John's order first.

We boarded the bus together with a crowd of locals, many of them piled on top of the bus and nestled into the stacks of baggage, and proceeded out of the city. First stop was a military checkpoint which we slowly filtered through. Once again a soldier pointed his AK-47 at me while his companion puzzled over my passport, an experience becoming common, but always frightening. This unpleasantness behind me, I climbed back aboard the bus.

Along the highway out of Addis we passed neat farms. The houses and out buildings were sometimes circular with adobe walls, and thatched roofs, interspersed with an occasional roof of corrugated tin.

As we rolled along lively music started pouring from a loudspeaker above the driver. Familiar with native South African music, for it has been fashionable in American liberal circles, I also have heard much Middle Eastern music. This was quite different. The melodic lines were contrapuntal, with Western harmonies. Though the rhythms were completely novel, the music had something of a jazz flavor to it, perhaps because the instruments were saxes and trumpets. Quite appealing. Africa is a BIG continent, so it should not have been a surprise to find such a wide range of musical genres.

Second stop was Ghion, and all of a sudden we were plunged into a Rudyard Kipling story. Crowds instantly gathered around the bus, some people importuning the conductor with reasons why they in particular should be allowed to buy tickets. Peddlers clustered about the windows selling hats, knives, walking sticks, bread and a local variety of popcorn.

Many passengers got off the bus to stretch their legs, some to bargain with the vendors while they were out. This cleared the aisles and food sellers came aboard. Soon after, the beggars arrived in force. Two blind men paced slowly up and down the aisle of our bus, each chanting his long sad tale. The chants were duotone and the two beggars, working off each other, wove a subtle, rhythmic, four note counterpoint.

We were about to pull away when the town psychotic accosted the bus. Dressed in a bright pink turban, which hung loosely and flowed down his back, and little else, he sidled up to the bus and started to flirt with us *Feringes*. His method was to hold the triple prong of a long stick right in front of his eye and grin at us. As we were starting to move I got my camera out to take a photo. He went berserk, threatening to clobber my window with his stick. I was in no danger, however. He obviously was going to do nothing to harm his most precious possession, his magic stick.

An hour or two later the bus stopped and we transferred to waiting expedition vans. After a short drive we reached the river. Since the boats, four rafts this time, had already been prepared, we needed only to change into river gear, pack away our city clothes into the familiar black, waterproof bags, load our stuff onto the rafts, have lunch, and launch our boats.

While we ate, I sat with a young American physics professor from the American University at Addis. He was supporting our expedition with the necessary city arrangements and field logistics. The professor was proud of his small contingent of promising students and the rapid progress these bright youngsters were making. He expounded eloquently on the exciting socialist future Ethiopia was now entering. I had my doubts about this and cautioned him not to be too optimistic. Bad things were happening and the situation would get far worse, I felt convinced. He shrugged off my pessimism.

Before we put in we had a brief lecture on do's and don'ts. This river has hazards which are quite different from what we had already experienced. The tag line was: "Don't sleep on a hippo trail!" Our party found this most amusing. Imagine laying out a sleeping bag, or tent, on such an animal highway. Glancing around, I saw the cryptic smirks on the faces of the experienced boatmen. But Jim Slade appeared to be serious.

He assured us hippo trails don't look like what we expect, and someone, sometime, will attempt to sleep on one. I couldn't determine if Jim was pulling our legs.

We launched onto a tributary of the quite substantial Gibe River and drifted under the Mimma Bridge and through a narrow gorge. Some miles downstream the smaller Omo River joined us and the two together became the Mighty Omo.

Most of a month on the Omo provided plenty of adventures. That certainly was unexplored territory. A steep river canyon impeded travel except by river. Tse Tse flies carried cattle diseases and made it impossible for the cattle herding Nilotic natives to live there. The benefit: The river was indeed wild and so were the animals, and they were in great numbers. Crocs and hippos were always a threat, as was the painful nuisance of the ever aggressive Tse Tses. Below the canyon of the Omo were natives so primitive and unknown some were yet to be reported to the outside world.

So, dangers were everywhere – from animals to accident and more. We took great precautions since a serious accident or injury could mean a two week walk out to civilization, quite likely in agony. Despite our precautions I was the victim of what turned out to be a most dangerous creature. Right at the end of the journey a tiny scarlet tick got into one of my socks. In time both feet were a great mass of blisters. Field surgery by the light of a camp fire eased the pain. But I suffer still from the disease it gave me – a usually lethal cousin of Lyme disease.

Until the next evening after the surgery I was in no condition to walk much. At the time we were camped at the Mui game reserve.

At the present time I am sitting in the shade of a make-shift lean-to, hiding from the midday sun and waiting for the plane to Maji and points north.

Anticipating our air transport would arrive mid-after-noon, my friends packed my gear early, and, still crippled, I was driven up to the so-called Mui International Airport. The rest of the expedition will walk up from the camp when the plane arrives.

Mui International Airport is a grand name for a patch of grass land and a pile of construction material intended, some day, to become a small building. A large herd of fearsome Cape Buffalo is grazing up and down the center of what is purported to be the runway. Carl Forsmark, the creator of this game reserve, told me in order to land, the plane will first have to buzz the air strip to chase the Buffalo off. He says this is necessary every time.

The plane never came. Mid-afternoon I was picked up and driven down to Carl's camp beside the Mui River. By evening I was starting to recover, and could walk a little. We enjoyed a leisurely period drinking and chatting beneath a shaded canvas canopy before walking along the river to our old campsite.

Carl Forsmark is a legend in East Africa. He told us part of his story. At the end of the Second World War he decided to fulfill his dream of setting up a commercial hunting camp in the African wilderness. The logistical challenge was formidable as it required transporting tons of supplies and vehicles several thousand miles across war torn Europe and the Middle East. With what must have been remarkably daring and skill he established fuel caches all along the route and managed to keep these highly valued stores safe from thieves. He also had to make arrangements, in what amounted to

establishing a treaty, with the newly reinstalled Ethiopian Govern-
ment. The Government apparently created the National Park at Mui
in order to give cover for Carl's enterprise.

The next morning we broke camp early so as to be ready if the
plane should show up. Show up it did, buzzing the campsite
shortly after breakfast. We hurried our gear up to the airstrip
and loaded aboard a venerable C-47. This was the first time I
had flown in one of the famous old Gooney birds and it was
quite an experience. We strapped ourselves onto the canvas
benches lining the interior walls. Around us, precariously
lashed down, were the tons of gear and boating equipment
we had used.

Before takeoff, the plane had to make a slow speed, and
rather bumpy, passage down and back up the runway to chase
away several large herds of grazing Cape Buffalo. Then came
the takeoff. This plane is a tail sitter, which means we were
already perched on a steep slope on our benches. As the plane
accelerated down the runway the apparent force of gravity
increased and the slope became precipitous; we were soon
hanging precariously from anything handy. After the tail
lifted off and the plane leveled out, things were not bad at all.

What was particularly surprising about the takeoff was its
smoothness. After all, about the only thing done to prepare
the landing strip was to burn off a section of the savanna. The
plane has great lift in ground effect. And, it also has oversize,
low pressure tires for rough field operations. No wonder
this bird still flies after nearly half a century of continuous
operation.

We flew to Jimma, and after waiting a few hours, caught another C-47 to Addis. Ah, for a hot shower and a relaxed meal, with no bugs to bother us.

We were greeted at the airport by Conrad, our anchor in Addis, and by the young physics professor I had lunched with before the Omo put-in. The professor looked distraught about something so John Yost took him aside some distance. The two sat huddled together in intense conversation.

Meanwhile, Conrad briefed Jim Slade and the rest of us about the mix-up with the aircraft. Through government ineptitude the aircraft's travel orders had been lost. When our airplane failed to arrive on the appointed day, Conrad moved heaven and hell to get a plane to us on the next day.

Several times, while Conrad was briefing us, I glanced over at John and the professor. The two were sitting close together, John's hand on the professor's shoulder, apparently comforting him. After a while the two stood up and John came over to give us the news.

The previous night, Government goons had dragged the professor's students from their beds, hauled them out into the street and shot them all. Their bodies were left lying in pools of blood waiting for their families to come for them.

Our trip back to the hotel was somber.

For those of us flying out this morning, Conrad had arranged a chartered bus to the airport. Unexpectedly, part way there we picked up a police escort. We needed it. When we arrived at the airport it was like the fall of Saigon the previous year. As we approached the gate we found ourselves immersed in a vast sea of humanity — people desperately trying to flee the country. Our police escort knifed through this immense crowd like the prow of a ship plowing through the ocean, our motion sending waves of reaction propagating across the endless mass of people as those nearest us backed away from our vehicles.

Now I am going home from that land of growing horror. I fear the real blood bath is about to begin.

It did.

*Omo River Hippos charge into the water to stand guard
over baby as we approach on our rafts*

HE WAS DEAD SERIOUS

OCTOBER 1976. Nine days into our three-week Omo River expedition we had a most memorable day. An unpleasant one, but fortunately a day with a happy ending.

It was on this day that we came to a formidable rapid. As usual, when approaching what looked to be a big rapid we needed to stop and scout. We went ashore on river left and followed a narrow animal trail up to a vantage point above the rapid. I was walking barefoot on this trail when I almost stepped on a poisonous snake lazing at the trail's edge. Fortunately I missed it by about three inches or that would have been the end of me. The colorful creature was happy to scurry back into the bushes and save its venom for something it could swallow.

On the first Omo expedition, three years previously, there was a drought, so the river was at a low level. It ran to the right of a long, slightly up-sloping rock platform on river left. The rapid was an easy river right run.

This time, the area had been experiencing a heavy monsoon season so the river was swollen. Its flow was significantly greater than the Colorado River. This made all the difference at this rapid. Instead of modestly flowing down the river-right channel, the river switched over to the left and accelerated to high speed down a steep entry. This gave it the momentum to shoot straight up the left side inclined platform and catapult into the air over its far edge. It then arced like the torrent from a stupendous fire hose. When the deluge plunged back down into the river bed the mass of water smashed into a field of giant boulders and exploded back into the air. Amazing!

In all my years of river travels I have never, before or since, seen anything like it. My companions, experienced professional whitewater boatmen, were equally astonished. This rapid was likely the most treacherous and lethal on any navigable river anywhere in the world.

Still, there was the sneak route on river-right which skirted the main flow over the platform. Should we risk it? To attempt this route and fail to stay in its minor current meant being swept away to certain death. What to do? The expedition leaders debated this for more than an hour while the rest of us stood by, slowly broiling in the equatorial sun. Finally the decision was made to portage the rapid. It was too dangerous to take a chance. What delayed the decision: No one wanted a portage because it was going to be a misery.

The determination made, we rowed across the river to the large alluvial fan that, by constricting the river, created the rapid. We stripped the boats, and prepared to portage them and the gear to the downriver side of the fan. Each fully equipped raft weighed in excess of a thousand pounds, and we had four rafts. There was a lot of hauling to do.

The portage wouldn't have been out of the ordinary but nature had a nasty surprise waiting for us. Splitting the large alluvial fan in two was an impenetrable wall of giant boulders eight to ten feet tall. This wall extended from the river's edge right up to the mountain side of the canyon we were in. We had no choice but to go *over* the wall.

The strongest stood atop the wall and hauled up, while the rest of us pushed up from below. This took hours. Making matters worse, it was now late afternoon and the sun was mirroring off the river. So we had high humidity, an air temperature above a hundred and reflected, as well as direct, sun to make our lives miserable.

Eventually, by evening, we got it all done. The alluvial fan was far too rocky for our camp, so we decided to cross the river to what appeared to be a nice looking campsite on the other side. Far too exhausted to refit the rafts, we piled everything inside and paddled across the river.

Unfortunately, small cobbles were strewn all over this promising camp site. However, there was an inviting animal trail on the down-river end of the site. Several of us started to lay our sleeping bags out on this trail. Seeing this, the expedition leader came over and advised us this was not a good place to sleep. "You see," he explained, "that nice, narrow, smooth, animal trail is a hippo trail!" What had seemed, at the first put in, absurd, was nevertheless true.

In Disney's movie *Fantasia*, hippos are portrayed as ballerinas. Wonderfully funny, but hippos on land actually do walk in an elegant way. They carefully put one foot directly in front of the other. Thus, hippo trails are narrow, not wide. It now became obvious the trail we had earlier followed up to the rapid's scouting overlook was, in fact, a hippo trail.

I decided to move to the up-river side of the campsite where there was a small stream and some smooth ground, and pitched my tent. Soon it was dark and I was enveloped in a friendly cloud of fireflies dancing merrily.

Late into the night the hippos in the river bellowed their hunger. Finally they decided we were not going away and offered no threat. One by one they left the river and followed the narrow trail up the hillside to their feeding ground, walking, head-to-tail, in a long graceful line — a picture straight out of Disney's film.

Hippos waiting for dinnertime

Boatman with undersized Omo River catfish,
about three and a half feet long

NESSIE

I CAUGHT A FISH. This was notable because I had never caught a fish before. In truth, I haven't caught one since — for the simple reason that I don't go fishing.

I had not previously caught a fish despite many attempts to do so. Back when I was a kid, my buddies and I used to ride our bikes along the dusty, poison oak infested bridle path around the skirt of Gould Mesa and down through the cascade of parking lots ringing Caltech's Jet Propulsion Lab. In those days JPL was still a holdover from the Second World War, with mostly wood structures or concrete blockhouses, and the rumored mysterious tunnels drilled deep into Gould Mesa. Today's ultramodern facility was far into the future. Leaving JPL behind we peddled several miles up a dirt road, past the water treatment plant, past burned out, and flooded out, ruins of nineteenth century resort cabins and up into the deep Arroyo Seco Canyon with its beautiful, tree shaded, mountain stream and trout filled pools. Into our favorite pools we would drop our lines and fish.

My buddies caught plenty. I caught none. No one ever told me I was supposed to set the hook when the fish nibbles the bait. So I caught plenty of empty hooks. Setting the hook is easy, they say. All you do is jerk the pole when the fish first nibbles the bait, so the hook catches the nibbler's mouth. Thanks to me, the fish along this stream were well fed.

When these many years later I landed that first fish, it was perhaps notable my catch was four and a half feet long and quite hefty. But on this expedition my feat was no big deal. It wasn't the biggest catfish we caught. And it was simply my turn, at the start of evening camp, to bait the hook (a *big* hook) with an old chunk of catfish, and drop the line (a *heavy* line) into the water from the outermost raft. A couple of hours later the taut fish line told us there was a drowned catfish on the other end.

We had been doing this, out of necessity, on a regular basis ever since the accident at Double Trouble. Double Trouble was a rapid we had named on the Omo River in southern Ethiopia. This was on our second expedition down the Omo. No trouble had been experienced in that particular rapid on the previous expedition. No trouble was expected on this day, so in a fit of carelessness, the lids on both of the lunch boxes on our four rafts had not been locked down.

The Omo was a wild river in those days. Wild and unpredictable. And, sure enough, the two lunch box boats flipped in a rapid grown unexpectedly mean. Gone were the supplies we needed for another three weeks on the river. We had been thrown back to hunter-gatherer days. This meant fishing. Fortunately we had some cheese left, and this got us going.

We started off baiting with cheese. After catching our first fish we used chunks of catfish to attract the hungry cannibals of the river. Catfish love to eat other catfish. It rather reminds me of Washington politics. No, rather, academic politics, which can be much more brutal, in a polite, slimy, back stabbing way.

Catfish is a delicious meat. It doesn't taste like fish. It almost tastes like the proverbial chicken. Nearly everything unfamiliar is reputed to taste like chicken; this catfish actually does — almost. But for weeks thereafter, we had catfish for dinner (usually fresh), catfish for breakfast (less fresh), catfish for lunch (distinctly old), catfish for snacks (who now cared about snacks) and catfish on all other occasions (yuck). I doubt if I will ever again ingest catfish, now that I am freed from the necessities of survival.

The problem with catfish is not the catching. As I have noted, even the exceptionally unskilled, such as yours truly, can easily catch catfish. The problem with catfish is the cleaning. My catfish caused all kinds of mayhem. And therein lies a tale.

I had learned about catfish a few years previously. One day I got a phone call from Bob Rines. Robert Rines was an associate of my patent attorneys, Leonard Golove and Marv Kleinberg. They traded cases. When a case was to be argued before an eastern Federal Court, Bob Rines made the presentation. Golove and Kleinberg argued the western cases. During the Second World War, Bob, with his physics hat on, contributed some important inventions to radar development. Later, with his lawyer hat on, he founded a successful Law School. Versatile Bob also wrote the music, lyrics and playbooks for Broadway musicals. However, to the general public he was best known for his Loch Ness investigations. He was even satirized in a long Doonesbury cartoon series about Nessie. Bob had lurid tales to tell about his encounters with the monster.

Over the years Bob and I had been trading favors. On one occasion he mentioned a friend, Tim Dinsdale, was coming from England and headed for the West Coast. Tim was a retired aeronautical engineer. His connection with the

Loch Ness Monster was having shot an unusually high quality movie of the creature while it was swimming on the surface of the Loch. Bob asked if I could arrange for Tim to give some lectures at local universities.

I was immediately skeptical, but agreed to try. My impression with universities was they were likely to be pretty stuffy when it comes to harebrained folk tales. Much to my surprise, every school I phoned turned out to be delighted at the prospect of a presentation on Nessie. Unfortunately, however, I was calling too late in the season to book his talk at any of them. The one place where my call was timely was the most unexpected of all: The Scripps Institution of Oceanography in La Jolla. They most definitely wanted Tim to come and present his findings.

The day came when it was time for me to pick up Tim. I drove to LAX and from there we headed down towards San Diego. Mid-morning we descended the steep driveway to the Institute and parked. There, we were greeted by the director of Scripps. He took us on a tour of the labs before the event. It was on this tour that I became acquainted with catfish. Scripps had considerable research underway on a variety of catfish like their cousins, electric eels. These two types of electric fish cruise over muddy river bottoms and use powerful oscillating electromagnetic fields to detect their prey hiding in cavities deep in the mud below. The research proved to be fascinating. Tanks containing these electrified fish were heavily instrumented to measure the emanations of the fish as they swam back and forth. The signals changed dramatically when the fish passed over a hollow in the sandy bottom. It is no wonder Omo catfish grow quite large and fat; there must be plenty of creatures hiding below the bottom of the nutrient-rich river.

During lunch the Lab's director, a Chinese gentleman, talked about his childhood experience of being taken captive by South China Sea Pirates. This was back in the nineteen thirties. The ocean liner he was on was captured by a fleet of pirate junks and the passengers were being held for ransom. Naturally, this caused a major international uproar. All the Pacific Ocean navies sent warships to the area — British, American, Dutch, Australian, Russian and Japanese. An ad-hoc war fleet was assembled and they chased down, captured and hung the pirates without the loss of any of the passengers. This was the last time the Allied and Japanese navies cooperated before the onset of the subsequent War of Annihilation.

After lunch we drove back to the Lab, ascended the stairs to the parking lot in front of the lecture hall and found ourselves the center of attention. A large crowd filled the parking lot — far more than the small auditorium could accommodate. Televisions had been set up outside to relay Tim's lecture. As we arrived a kilted Scotsman started playing his pipes and the crowd roared a greeting. The welcome inside the auditorium was no less enthusiastic.

To be sure, the auditorium was filled with professionals. There were things these biologists and oceanographers wanted to know, as Tim was well aware. He began with a review of the Loch's geography and ecosystem. The Loch is deeper than most lakes — around a thousand feet — and it is connected with the North Sea, so there is significant migration of sea creatures into and out of the Loch. The Loch has a large population of benthic (deep dwelling) fish, much more than enough to support a large colony of monsters.

These facts were what the marine scientists wanted to hear. As the lecture proceeded the atmosphere grew progressively more relaxed and enthusiastic. Tim's film nailed the case shut. At the end of the presentation, after many questions were asked and answered, a resolution was passed by the Institute's staff formally establishing the Scripps Institute Chapter to Investigate the Loch Ness Phenomenon.

As we were exiting the auditorium, passing out into the well wishes of the crowd outside, the director told us this had been, with one exception, the largest and most successful public event in the Institute's history. The exception was when Jacques Cousteau came to town.

Despite the Scripps experience in my memory I was startled by what my fish would do. The catfish, of course, was dead, though still twitching with electricity. Its powerful array of batteries were still at full charge and could deliver a nasty, stunning jolt to the unwary. The boatmen knew this and, with long experience, were prepared to deal with the problem.

Tugging on the stout fishing line, the monster fish was hauled out onto the sand of the beach, all taking great care to keep well away from it. A long bladed hunting knife was lashed to the end of an oar. With this improvised spear the fish was to be gutted and its batteries discharged. On this occasion it was Tom Moody's turn to execute the procedure. He did everything according to tradition. Only, this time, the oar had a slick of water running its length. As he plunged the blade into the belly of the fish a powerful jolt traveled up the wet oar and into Tom's body. He convulsed and was flung backward, unconscious. Fortunately, he recovered after a while. Afterwards he had no memory of his electrocution. I imagine, though, his muscles ached for some time to come.

Yet greater care was exercised by the old pro boatmen as they finished the task of discharging the fish's remaining batteries. There was no difference in the taste of the meal to follow, but we could *imagine* an extra tang.

Rocket launch from Vandenberg Air Force Base, (now Vandenberg Space Force Base), headed for Kwajalein Atoll

STORIES FROM A ROCKET SCIENTIST

I STARTED MY CAREER AS A BLUE COLLAR WORKER — mopping floors, refining metal, assembling electronics and laying up fiberglass plastic (the worst job of the lot). From this experience I developed a keen appreciation of the unsung heroes who, with grit and wit, keep our civilization going.

After leaving the university I found myself sitting at a desk writing equations. Supposedly dull stuff, but it wasn't — not even close. Almost immediately came a succession of difficult technical challenges and great professional adventures. When you are immersed in these tasks they may not seem exciting. It was only in retrospect that I began to understand what remarkable experiences these really were. Memorable because I have spent my career working on the Aerospace frontier of modern technology. The work presents a continuing stream of seemingly impossible problems. The people attracted to the industry are in the main highly gifted, fascinating individuals, and very much worth meeting. There is high adventure in working with extraordinary people. There is high adventure in the kind of challenging projects that are commonplace on this frontier.

I have stories to tell about the best (true geniuses) and the worst (there are some monsters), but always extraordinary characters. I have stories to tell about the unusual situations that I have found myself in. I have stories to tell about the kind of work that I have found to be endlessly fascinating. I have stories to tell of these adventures in the professional world — mostly a different kind of adventure than physical peril, but there's been a bit of that, as well.

DICK BAXTER'S WONDER PLANE

IN 1970 I DECIDED TO BAIL OUT of graduate school and descend to the real world. It was fortunate that I did for I found myself working for William F. O'Neil, one of the true seminal geniuses of the aerospace industry. It was the beginning of a life-long friendship.

Bill, in order to further my *real* education, installed me in the office of Dick Baxter. Dick, several years my senior, was an unassuming, but highly intelligent man. I didn't know it in the beginning but in certain arcane circles Dick was an international celebrity. The reason was Dick's hobby. Even as an undergraduate at the Massachusetts Institute of Technology Dick was known internationally for his highly innovative flying aircraft models.

After graduation from MIT, Dick had worked for NASA's predecessor, the National Advisory Committee for Aeronautics and continued on with NASA. Eventually he became disillusioned with the NASA bureaucracy and its hidebound ways and sought relief by joining private industry.

Dick's approach to the world was an effective combination of directness and subtlety. He was a modest man, so I didn't know much about his past successes. But this story Bill told me is just one example of Dick's remarkable insight and creativity.

One of the most remarkable technology competitions of that era was the indoor model airplane championship. Its goal was to create rubber band powered airplanes that can stay aloft for as long as possible. These delicate machines are constructed of ultra-light-weight balsa structures of great sophistication — designed to take as much rubber band tension as possible with the lowest possible weight. The models are covered in a special microfilm created by carefully depositing a single drop of lacquer into a quiet pool of water. The drop spreads out across the surface of the water and its solvent evaporates, leaving behind a monomolecular layer of polymerized lacquer. This cured microfilm is carefully lifted out of the water and then simply draped across the structure of the model airplane. The tiny burrs on the surface of the balsa wood grab the microfilm and hold it in place.

During the contest a plane's rubber band is wound up until the structure shows signs of distress and then the plane is released. Up it flies, nearly to the ceiling of a sports arena. The propeller stops, the stored energy in the rubber band having been exhausted, and the little airplane slowly glides in large, lazy circles back to the floor.

Upon analyzing this traditional engineering solution, Dick realized that the energy in the rubber band was not being used efficiently. The plane needed to draw energy *slowly* out of the rubber band and couple that energy properly into the passing air. His solution was to drive a redesigned propeller through a very small and *very* light weight gear box. As he predicted, the airplane could now sustain powered flight for exceptionally long periods. No longer was the plane merely a good glider with a short boost time. Now it was a continuously powered airplane.

The trouble was that the darned thing was *too* good. Flight times of substantially more than half an hour were not unusual. How could you conduct a contest with dozens of entries when flight durations were so long? After Dick's spectacular victory the organizing committee changed the rules. No more gears, no more half hour flights. Dick Baxter will forever be the indoor rubber band model airplane champion.

To this day, half a century later, Dick Baxter is *the* Guru of that special clan of rubber band powered model airplane enthusiasts. You can easily find him on the Web.

SYSTEM ARCHITECTURE

UNCLE BOB WASN'T MY UNCLE. He was an older colleague I happened to call Uncle Bob because the name seemed to fit. He liked the name as well. Uncle Bob was a big, bluff, booming-voiced, story-telling, good old boy. Being a big man from Texas, he was well suited to conquer the world, and so he did.

Uncle Bob was *smart*, to say the least. At an age when most folks are graduating from high school, Uncle Bob received his Bachelor's Degree in Engineering from Caltech. With that kind of talent his rise in the automotive industry was swift. At a relatively young age he was named Chief Engineer of the Cadillac Engine Division of General Motors.

The upper echelons of any society tend to party together while they engage in combat with each other. Ancient Rome provides the model. Julius Caesar's enemies and assassins were also his friends and family. Thus it was that Uncle Bob made the acquaintance of Henry Ford. Now, Uncle Bob had no great incentive to take up Henry's standing offer to come to work for him. No great incentive until one day something happened to change his mind.

The story goes that on that day Uncle Bob was in the General Motors Board Room, presenting his latest engine design to the Powers That Be. In the center of a line of senior executives was the Big Kahuna — maybe he was the Chairman of the Board, or maybe the CEO of General Motors. At this late date I don't remember. Arrayed to the right and left of the Big Man were executives of descending rank and power. All sat in stolid, stone faced, silence throughout Uncle Bob's pitch — unconsciously imitating the long row of stone potentates on Easter Island.

Uncle Bob simply could not get his message across to this unreceptive audience. He varied his tactics, he changed his presentation on the fly, he tried various ways of explaining the obvious to these pillars of stone, until, at last, the Head Honcho in the middle gave a slight nod. Then, miraculously, two waves of nods, left and right, propagated from the center to the ends of the line of executives and evaporated, the executives repetrifying again into a row of stone statues. Uncle Bob had made his point, and he had learned. That night he called Henry and asked if the standing job offer still stood.

Now Henry had something special in mind for Uncle Bob. In those days the fabled Offenhauser engine was, in American racing circles, King of the Road. Henry Ford wanted to prove that Ford's engine technology was the best in the world. Build an engine to beat the Offenhauser was Uncle Bob's challenge. Uncle Bob intended to do better. He was going to win them all, everywhere in the world. And so he, and his crew, did.

In order to avoid the stifling stuffiness of Dearborn, Uncle Bob moved his people to Newport Beach, California, and lodged them in the new Aeronutronic aerospace plant that Ford had recently built high atop Jamboree Hill. (Jamboree Hill was named for the World Boy Scout Jamboree which had encamped there a few years before.)

The engineering challenge was straightforward. Much had recently been learned about what really took place inside an automobile engine — materials, resonances, fluid flow, timing, friction, combustion, wear and tear. The trick was to put all this new knowledge together, in full harmony, in the lightest possible, but still robust, engine. Uncle Bob succeeded. The Ford V8 racing engine swept the world — much to the dismay of Offenhauser, Porsche and Ferrari.

Henry was well satisfied. Time to call a halt to this public relations stunt. Time for Uncle Bob to return to Dearborn and do something really useful — like make money for Henry. But Uncle Bob liked it just fine in sunny Southern California. He could design engines here better than there, with its talentless, pinch nosed, penny pinching, bureaucrats second guessing every design decision. He decided to stay where he was.

"Very well," was Henry's response. "You're fired!"

Uncle Bob shrugged his shoulders, picked up his termination paycheck, walked out the Aeronutronic Main Gate and across the street to the Aeronutronic Administration Building and applied for a job as an aerospace engineer. Now, everyone of consequence knew and respected Uncle Bob so he had no trouble getting what he asked for. Thus Uncle Bob was there waiting for me when I later went to work on Jamboree Hill.

Meeting Uncle Bob was not hard. One day my boss, Bill O'Neil, told me to go to Bob Pon's office and make his acquaintance, which I did. The rapport was instant and we spent the afternoon cackling away at one piece of silliness or another. After that my visits were frequent and I would spend hours by his desk watching the transactions, asking questions about what was transpiring, and learning. What I learned from this Grand Master was what is now called "System Architecture."

Nowadays System Architecture has become a *Big Deal*. It is wrapped around with curious names, such as DoDAF and Zackman Framework. It has even become enshrined in engineering courses taught in third rate colleges — the ultimate symbol of its establishment. In reality, System Architecture is as old as the earliest villages of antiquity, and just as obvious.

Whatever the scale of endeavor, the system architect puts lots of different pieces together so that they work harmoniously. On a somewhat large scale, a village needs a water supply, a food supply, it needs to get rid of sewage, it needs means of communication and transportation, it needs to provide shelter for families, and it needs some kind of defense against both marauders and Mother Nature. All very straightforward. As we all know, there are many different good solutions, depending on the circumstances. There are vastly more really bad solutions, as well. The guy who figures out how to make the village a practical affair is a good village system architect.

While system architecture is now fashionable, and professors purport to teach it in the classroom, the reality is that system architecture, at all scales, from the microscopic to continent-wide, is an art form; formal instruction doesn't really help much. More important, by far, than formal instruction is shear, raw, creative talent. And, if a young, and talented, engineer is really fortunate, he will have the opportunity to serve as an apprentice to a true Master. He will learn his lessons sitting at the feet of the Master, watching what the Master does, trying his hand at it, and receiving practical correction of missteps.

While I knew him, Uncle Bob had a couple or three projects underway. Henry had partially forgiven him and given him a contract to look at automotive applications of the Stirling engine. In Thermodynamics the Carnot cycle predicts the best possible efficiency of an ideal heat engine. The century old Stirling engine, except for some friction losses, met the efficiency limit predicted by the Carnot cycle. In other words, you cannot get better gas mileage than what a Stirling engine delivers.

Europe had the leadership in Stirling engine development. As I recall, a Combine of the Swedes, the Dutch and the Germans was pushing automotive applications of this machine. So Uncle Bob pulled up his britches and took a tour of Europe. He wasn't impressed. Apparently the engine was too sluggish to be practical for modern cars. Most people rightly demand an instant response from their cars when they press on the accelerator. This responsiveness isn't just a matter of feeling in charge, it is also a critical safety issue. Quick acceleration is often the best way to avoid an accident. Uncle Bob predicted, correctly, that the Stirling engine had no future on the highways. Thus, the First Lesson in System Architecture: *It's the unexpected simple things that kill a promising idea.*

About the only interesting automotive finding that his excursion produced was the odd observation that almost all the executives at Volvo and Mercedes Benz drove American cars: typically Cadillacs and Lincolns. "American cars are the best," they reported. "Why should we drive less than the best?" I guess the grass is always greener.

Uncle Bob was pragmatic. If Stirling engines were not suited for automotive use, maybe they would be ideal for a different application that did not require instant responsiveness. Solar energy conversion looked like a good bet. The recent applied optics literature contained several discussions of what came to be known as a "Solar Power Tower." This idea was derived directly from Archimedes' destruction of the Roman fleet by reflecting sunlight from myriad mirrors. (Recently an experimental archaeologist easily duplicated this feat, which many had come to believe was merely a myth.) The solar power tower is a simple idea: Put a boiler on top of a tall tower, surround the tower with steerable mirrors, steer the sun's reflections onto the boiler and use the resulting incandescently heated steam to drive an engine and generator.

Uncle Bob got a contract to look into this proposition in more detail. The Stirling engine was just about right for an intermediate sized solar power tower. Whether or not it was Uncle Bob's design which ultimately was constructed near Barstow, California, I don't know. But, as you drive by it, the giant glowing light bulb, high atop a tower amidst a field of mirrors, is a very impressive sight.

Unfortunately, Barstow, as is the case with most other desert locations, is windy. And wind means blowing dust. And dust means grit in the gears, sand blasted mirrors and coats of dirt obscuring their reflective power. It turns out that the extensive and expensive maintenance required simply to keep a solar power tower in operation means that it has marginal economic utility. Thus, the Second Lesson in System Architecture: *It's the unexpected simple things that kill a promising idea.*

At that time, the mid 1970's, an interesting idea was floating around in the electrical engineering literature. I mean to say it was *literally* floating around — floating on an intangible cushion of magnetic fields. This fantastic idea was the notion of a super high speed, magnetically levitated railroad train. Such a revolutionary system would be a major technical challenge — and achievement. Uncle Bob decided that he was going to master mind this development — and Uncle Bob did indeed become the project's Master Mind.

Master Mind conjures visions of a plush, mahogany appointed, suite of offices with hordes of flunkies catering to every whim. The reality was not that — not even close. Uncle Bob still had his old, cramped cave with its usual hand-me-down industrial furniture. Since this was a working engineer's office, papers, plans, books, reports and miscellaneous items and instruments were haphazardly stacked and strewn all around his quite ordinary office. It was what was taking place within this small world that was so very exciting. Here, being born, was a wonderful and fascinating vision of the future.

Most of us have played around with magnets at one time or another. North Pole to South Pole and the magnets attract each other. North Pole to North Pole and the magnets repel. Long ago magnets gave people the idea that vehicles could be suspended in midair — either by magnetic attraction or by magnetic repulsion. Easy enough to say, *very* hard to do. It turns out that magnetic suspension is *inherently* unstable. Unstable, that is, unless *something* is moving.

In the Good Old Days, Michael Faraday had a bit to say about all this. (Every generation seems to believe that the old days were the Good Old Days — but, trust me, you wouldn't want to have lived then.) Faraday, being a careful observer, noticed that when he moved a wire near a magnet he created an electric current in the wire. He also knew that an electric current in a wire would move the needle of a magnetic compass. Being a clever fellow, as well as a careful observer, he figured out that there was a simple quantitative relationship between the electric current and the changing magnetic field.

Legend has it that when Queen Victoria inquired as to the utility of Faraday's great discovery, Faraday replied, "Your Majesty, of what use is a newborn child?" Of course the legend is not true, although Faraday keenly appreciated Ben Franklin's famous witticism about electricity.

Thanks to Faraday we now have the wonderful modern electric world, with electric lights, and telephones, and radios, and television, and radar and ...and ... *toaster ovens.*

We also have a special magic which might someday give us magnetically suspended trains — *maglev* trains, in the jargon of the trade. Trains that could speed along at more than three hundred miles per hour! Or so it was thought back in the 1970's.

The Germans adopted attractive magnets to suspend their maglev trains. Maybe they chose this approach because this technique required extremely high precision engineering to work. (It is rumored that German's just *love* extremely high precision machines.) Unfortunately, the required precision is also extremely expensive, and the close suspension tolerances leave almost no margin of safety should things go wrong.

Fortunately, there is another way to float a vehicle on magnetic fields. One can simply *move* the magnet over a sheet of electrically conducting material, such as aluminum. The motion of even a permanent magnet over a conductor creates a repulsive force. It does this because, as Faraday first observed, a moving magnet creates an electric current in the conductor and this current, in turn, creates a magnetic field which pushes back. If the force is strong enough, a fast moving vehicle can float on a magnetic cushion.

This is neat. This electrodynamic suspension, it turns out, can also be made inherently stable through the motion of the vehicle. Moreover, this induced suspension floats the vehicle well above the electrically conducting track — so that the vehicle is very much safer, and the roadway is much less costly to build. All you would need for the road was a sheet of aluminum.

Uncle Bob definitely liked the idea of floating the vehicle on a dynamic magnetic cushion. So did I. There was so very much that you could do with this technique when you let your imagination run free. While Uncle Bob focused on the engineering needed to make the magnetic cushion practical, I looked at its possibilities. This was fun for me: dreaming up all kinds of wonderful applications. Fun also for Uncle Bob and his team, for they were doing what they loved: the hard part, the real engineering.

Real engineering meant figuring out how to get suitably strong magnets. A superconducting magnet, at a temperature near the coldest possible, was the only plausible answer — permanent magnets, in those days, were just too weak.

By Mother Nature's standards, we live in a relatively hot world. The temperature of frozen water — ice — is very, very hot compared to the temperature of outer space between the stars and galaxies. In that bleakly cold realm, near absolute zero, certain materials behave much differently than they commonly do in our familiar warm environment. Superconductivity is one such different behavior. You can set up an electric current in a superconductor and the electrons will literally flow forever. There are no losses. The magnetic field that can be produced this way can be extremely strong. Those of us that have been scanned with Magnetic Resonance Imaging — MRI — have been subjected to these ultra-strong superconducting magnetic fields.

Another useful property of superconductors is that electric currents can be created in them which expel any magnetic field completely outside the material. The superconductor thereby becomes a perfect magnetic shield. This provides a way to protect passengers with heart pacemakers, or with metal implants, that might not otherwise be able to ride flying magnetic trains.

Propulsion seemed, at first, like it was going to be a problem. The literature was filled with proposals for linear induction motors which were to be embedded in the roadway. However, such motors would be very expensive. A different solution was simpler and much cheaper. The traction needed for propulsion was to be created by a caterpillar-like wiggling of the cushioning magnetic field.

The fundamental engineering problem with superconductors was how to keep them so very cold without spending an arm and a leg doing it. Superinsulation techniques had to be devised, or adapted, to make this possible. Compact ultra-refrigerators, that used minimal power, also had to be designed. And, too, the whole thing had to be packaged to fit, unobtrusively, within a railroad car. All this was accomplished.

Then there was the problem of wrinkles. I mean wrinkles in the roadway. It is very hard to make a roadway perfectly smooth — at least not a road which is miles, or hundreds, or thousands of miles long. Any practical product of civil engineering is going to have some bumps along the way. At more than three hundred miles an hour even a small bump is going to create a very large, sudden, shock in something that is magnetically coupled to the roadway. That nice soft magnetic cushion is going to feel harder than a rock when it zips over even a small wrinkle in the roadway.

The solution turned out to be simple and time honored (at least to automotive engineers): Install the magnetic suspensions in separate undercarriages beneath the railroad cars. These undercarriages do experience the road shock, but then standard shock absorbers, much like what you have in your automobile, prevent the shock from being transmitted to the cabin of the railroad car. The ride becomes smooth and comfortable.

One by one the various engineering challenges were met and mastered. I was becoming increasingly enthusiastic as each problem was solved and put to bed. One day I visited Uncle Bob to tell him of some new system level concepts that I had for applying this technology. But Uncle Bob had other things on his mind that day. While I was sitting by his desk, waiting for the usual engineering discussions to taper off so I could chat about my wonderful new ideas, one of Uncle Bob's engineers came into the office with some new data. It was what Uncle Bob had been waiting for. The engineer reported some numbers. Uncle Bob didn't show much reaction, just a grunt. He did a quick calculation and then said, "I was afraid of that."

He was looking at the cost for the aluminum road sheets. It seems that the new numbers were the cheapest quote they could get for mass produced aluminum sheeting of the needed thickness. Even at minimum price the roadways were going to be far too expensive for the maglev system to be economically viable — everything else was doable. "Maybe someday, but not now," was his response. Uncle Bob anticipated a program shut down. Thus, the Third Lesson in system architecture: *It's the unexpected simple things that kill a promising idea.*

A few days later I again visited Uncle Bob. He was surprisingly cheerful. I asked what was up. He said the program had been canceled. I was astonished that he was so upbeat. He responded that the White House had directed that all the designs and engineering data be turned over to the Japanese — gratis.

This shocked me. After all that outstanding work we were just *giving* it all away — and to our primary economic rivals, to boot. But Uncle Bob just grinned. "Listen," he said, "the Japanese are going to spend billions of dollars, many billions, on this thing and all they are going to get out of it is a ride for their new Disneyland. Better them than us! Those White House guys are pretty clever, don't you think?"

ROCKET SCIENCE

"THREE...TWO...ONE...FIRE!" *Hissss. Pop.* "Uh, oh!" said the technician as the meters all swung to zero and red lights lit up down the length of the long control panel. My signals also had disappeared.

"What's up?" I asked.

"We just blew up the test stand."

"That little pop?"

"Yeah, that little pop."

I moved toward the door to see what had happened. I visualized some minor damage. The little pop made it seem like the technician must be exaggerating. "Hold on, don't go out," he said. "Safety requires an hour wait." He was right. Hydrogen and Fluorine were the propellants for our rocket engine — nasty stuff those, and they had to be fully dissipated before we could pay a visit outside.

The test stand consisted — I should say *had* consisted, before our recent, most rapid remodeling — of a concrete blockhouse, a neat tangle of piping and tanks above a concrete pad, and the rocket mounting fixtures. These fixtures projected the blast from the engine horizontally over the lip of a steep canyon near the fabled California town of San Juan Capistrano. The blockhouse was long and narrow — perhaps twice the size of a large living room. It was situated about thirty yards from the canyon's edge and oriented parallel to the edge. The control panel stretched along the entire length of the blockhouse wall facing the canyon. Doors at each end of the blockhouse opened onto narrow, concrete walled, and labyrinth shielded, walkways which led to the canyon lip. Between the blockhouse and the canyon was the tangle of silvery pipes and tanks — all of which were suspended over our heads by massive steel girders. These girders also supported the cradle which mounted the rocket engine.

With nothing to do, time passed slowly until the all clear was given. Eagerly, I walked out the door and passed the labyrinth shield to find that the entire far end of the test stand had simply . . . *vanished.* Ten yards from the edge of the canyon the piping and girders, the rocket engine and its cradle, all had been sheared off, as neatly as if with a surgeon's scalpel, and vaporized. Only the concrete pad remained, just slightly scorched.

"We won't be doing any more testing soon," said the technician. "I've seen this before. It'll be a year before we get this place up and running again." All I had, after nearly a year's hard work, was about a second's worth of now priceless data. I realized we would have to proceed to the flight tests without the confidence building experiments that we had intended. That's often the way it is with National Priority programs.

What we were doing was, after all, of the greatest national significance. The United States was vulnerable and it was our job to fix that vulnerability — very quickly, very quietly. The time was the 1970's. We had about a thousand nuclear tipped rockets sitting in holes in the ground, and many more in submarines, when it was suddenly realized that those missiles would almost certainly *not* reach their targets in the event of war. If news of this were to get out before the problem was fixed, our main nuclear deterrent force would cease to deter.

The discovery of our vulnerability was made when the Air Force routinely rotated a colonel into a new billet. The colonel taking over the reentry vehicle program had previously worked at Holloman Air Force base where he conducted high speed sled tests to measure rain erosion of aircraft radar domes and cockpit canopies. At a sufficiently high speed even tiny rain drops act like solid bullets and crater any substance that they impact.

It was only natural that one of the first questions the colonel asked at his new assignment was: Had our warheads been flown into rain clouds? Embarrassing silence followed — a silence that was compounded when the colonel followed up with an inquiry about clouds over the Soviet Union.

"Sir, we always fly our tests in clear weather. That way we get good pictures of the reentry, and good radar data."

"Sir, our weather experts say that Russia is cloudy as much as 90% of the time."

"So, most of the time, our warheads will simply vanish before they reach low altitude. Isn't that right?" The colonel asked. He was none too pleased.

"We don't know that, sir. I guess we had better test and find out."

"Yes, I guess we'd better," replied the colonel.

And so our program was launched. A veil of silence descended over the whole affair. Junior officers and the colonel's immediate superiors were no longer in the know — just the colonel and "very senior government officials." Funding was invisible. It worked like this: Two contracts were let for forty-nine thousand dollars, one to us, the Aeronutronic Division of Ford Aerospace Company, and one to our competitor, General Electric. This amount of money was petty cash for the colonel and could be reimbursed outside the regular system. So the contracts remained invisible to the Air Force's accountants. But this small amount of money could not possibly pay for the intense activity. Thus, every couple of days our program manager, Bob Lyons, would drive up to Los Angeles and pay the colonel a visit. Bob would bring home an increment of funds sufficient to keep the effort alive for another couple of days. Always the increment was just less than fifty thousand so as to keep the add-on in the petty cash column. By the time the program was successfully finished, tens of millions of dollars had been spent — on a forty-nine thousand dollar contract. Our program had perhaps the world's record cost overrun. Fortunately for the security of the U.S., unscrupulous demagogue politicians in Congress never found out.

In those days Ford Aerospace was at the forefront of high speed reentry technology. The company had a crackerjack aerothermodynamics design staff combined with first rate test facilities. Foremost among these test facilities was the rocket test stand. The rocket test stand did not test rocket engines. It *used* a rocket engine to simulate the extreme conditions of high speed reentry. The idea was to shove the front end of a reentry vehicle (i.e. ballistic missile warhead) up the nozzle of a specially designed rocket motor and then turn the beast on. Good reentry designs survived, bad designs failed.

The greatest stress on a reentry vehicle is at the nosetip. Here the high speed stream of impinging atmosphere piles up into a stagnated pocket of hellfire. Only very special materials and constructions need apply for the job of nosetip. The impact of hot gasses was bad enough, but the colonel's intuition about clouds proved correct. Once the rocket engine was modified so that simulated cloud droplets could be injected into its flow, it was discovered that conventional nosetips were almost instantly sandblasted into nothingness. A new solution was required, and quickly.

My job in the game was to be Responsible Engineer for the flight instrumentation. The technical challenge was considerable. Insert a pencil into a pencil sharpener and carefully prepare the point. Slice off the cone end of the pencil. You now have a miniature model of a reentry vehicle (or RV as it is commonly called). The slender cone shape is needed to precisely place the warhead on target. There are two significant difficulties with this shape. The first is that the RV retains its very high velocity down almost to the ground. This means that the heat load will remain extremely high throughout the reentry. To counter the heat load an exotic, temperature resistant material must fill the very confined space of the nosetip. Second, the cone shape tends to be aerodynamically unstable — it wants to flip end-for-end so that the blunt side leads. To counter this instability a substantial mass of dense ballast material must be shoved as far forward as possible. The demands of heat protection directly compete with the demand for aerodynamic stability.

The problem is greatly compounded when provision must also be made for protection against cloud droplet erosion. In order to provide this protection the length of the nosetip material must be substantially extended back towards the tail so that erosion does not completely wear the tip away when the vehicle descends through thick clouds. Extending the region filled with the nosetip material means shoving the ballast further back. At some point, in this contest between erosion protection and ballast positioning, the RV becomes aerodynamically unstable.

For our flight experiment the problem was compounded because we needed to measure the recession of the nosetip during the passage through clouds. That meant filling some of critical ballast space of the newly designed test vehicle with instruments. To make life interesting the test reentry vehicles were half size, so the space available was very cramped, indeed. Figuring out how to make these measurements was now my job.

To get started in designing the instrumentation I needed to find out, in some detail, just what the internal layout of a warheaded RV was. This meant a trip to Sandia National Laboratory to view some of our atomic secrets. The necessary clearances were arranged and I boarded a plane to Albuquerque.

What I discovered at Sandia was that RVs in that era had no room for instrumentation. The job appeared to be impossible. Fortunately, our RV designers helped out with a radically unorthodox design for the nosetip. Most of the experts in the industry (including our competition) thought our design was nutty — surely the nosetip would shatter, or break off. But we were confident that we were on the right track and therefore proceeded. From my perspective this new design was a godsend, for I now had at least some room — though not much — in which to place instrumentation.

The solution we arrived at involved a dangerous amount of radioactivity. The nosetip material was slightly porous. Suppose selected regions of this porous nosetip material were to be seeded with a highly radioactive substance. The gamma rays from these radioactive regions could be collected with special crystals and measured. As the nosetip eroded away so also would the radioactive material. We could measure the residual radioactivity of the nosetip, telemeter this information to the ground, and thereby determine how well the nosetip was holding up to erosion by the rain cloud. We could even measure the changing shape of the nosetip.

The ballast used by the RV was a very high density material which was a good absorber of gamma rays. By drilling long, narrow holes, called collimators, through this ballast, and placing the gamma ray detectors at the bottom of these holes we could see selected parts of the nosetip. Viewing the nosetip through these collimator holes in the ballast was much like looking through a few translucent soda straws.

But how were we to selectively seed the nosetip? A clever scheme was proposed by one vendor. He suggested a way whereby we could seed only those areas of the nosetip which were in line with the collimator holes. His idea was to bathe the nosetip in a hot brew of a particular element. The element would diffuse through and uniformly saturate the nosetip. Later on the nosetip would be placed in the beam of a powerful cyclotron. Then we would become alchemists. Only where the cyclotron's protons struck the nosetip would the perfused element be transmuted into a gamma ray emitter. By aligning the cyclotron's beam with the collimator holes we would, in effect, be creating gamma ray light bulbs in only those places where we wished to look. Unfortunately, the intense, and dangerous, radioactivity so created would be ephemeral — lasting only a few hours. On this detail will hang the finale of our tale.

Radioactivity measurement appeared to be the right answer, so we got started. I volunteered to do the radioactive physics part of the project. Since I knew little of the subject I needed expert tutoring. I found my expert at Aerospace

Corporation and moved into his lab for a few days. There I learned the mysteries of gamma ray spectroscopy and pulse height analyzers and how different detector crystals behaved.

The facilities for further experimentation we found at our sister division in Palo Alto. I traveled up there for a couple of intense work weeks. The experiments had to be done at night because the facilities were very busy during the day. Each night I built collimators by stacking lead bricks and predrilled ballast in various ways. I donned my lead apron and hood. Then, very carefully, I would unscrew the lid from the isotope container and lift out, with long tongs, the dangerous radioactive substance, placing it in the waiting holder. Several configuration tests, and long hours of data reduction, told me that the concept was going to work. Now to select the proper detector.

We tested several candidate detectors. The winner was Cadmium Telluride crystals of ultra-purity and molecular uniformity. There were only three sources of such crystals. The French source was immediately ruled out because of security. That left crystals from the famous Hughes Research Laboratory in Malibu (the place where the first laser was developed) and those from Tyco Labs near Boston. Our tests showed the very considerable superiority of the Tyco material, so I paid them a visit to obtain an expanded supply. There I met Gerry Entine, the scientist responsible for these marvelous crystals. He agreed to provide us with his entire stock. Unfortunately, we soon discovered that the stock was not enough and that there would be no more. Mobil Oil had just purchased Tyco and shut down Gerry's operation.

What to do? On the prospect that our program needs might provide initial funding, Gerry proposed to license his crystal growing process from Mobil Tyco and set himself up in business. This was satisfactory to us and the Colonel asked me to return to Boston to certify, for the Air Force, Gerry's new manufacturing facility.

The meeting with Gerry was interesting but it presented me with a challenge in that I had to report my findings to the Colonel when I got back to California. I must admit to a certain trepidation when I approached him with the certification document, for the Colonel had a well-deserved reputation for being difficult. The interview went something like this.

The Colonel's office was typical. A standard upscale wooden desk faced the door. It was surrounded by the usual souvenir airplane models and autographed pictures of the Colonel shaking hands with dignitaries, uniformed and otherwise. The Colonel was sitting behind his desk, back to a window overlooking a utilitarian sidewalk, a dour expression on his face.

"What do you have for me?" the Colonel asked.

"Well, sir, I need to have you certify Dr. Entine's facility for manufacturing CadTel crystals. I have the document here for your signature."

"OK, but you'd better tell me about it first."

"Um, well, Dr. Entine seemed a bit reluctant to show me his facility. So we went out to dinner before the evaluation."

"Yeah."

"Well, then he invited me over to his mom's house."

He leaned forward.

"His mother's house? You can't be serious?"

".... Well, yes sir, I am, but it was appropriate for what he had to show me."

The Colonel frowned.

"Explain!"

"Well first we sat at the kitchen table while Dr. Entine went over some of the production details and the performance specs, as well as his plans for expanding production. Then he took me into his bedroom..."

I turned slightly pink. Was that a snicker? I hurried on.

"You see, he had this dresser. A highboy, only a couple of feet wide. Gerry, er, Dr. Entine, had cleared off the top of the dresser and installed his laboratory on top."

Definitely a snicker. I continued.

"It wasn't very big, sir, but even in that small space there was room for everything. Actually, I must say that it looked something like an old A.C. Gilbert boy's chemistry set."

The corner of my mouth turned up in a grin.

"Um, he had another problem because the crystal melt was a couple thousand degrees, so he had to be *very* careful he didn't burn the house down."

I was feeling more comfortable telling this.

"His mother would probably have been very put out with him if that had happened!"

The Colonel was laughing now — so hard he nearly fell out of his chair.

"But Gerry is a very careful guy, sir, and he had *lots* of asbestos around the retort."

"That's very interesting," choked the Colonel, "but how good is his product?"

Here I wasn't the least bit tentative.

"The best in the world, sir! He beats the pants off of Hughes Research. And he *delivers*, too."

"That's good enough for me."

The Colonel snatched the document from my hand, and continued with a grin.

"Where do I sign?"

And so, Dr. Gerry Entine was officially in business as a Certified U.S. Air Force Supplier of high technology materials, with probably the smallest, and most informal, manufacturing facility in the world. His greatly expanded business thrives to this day, mostly supplying customers outside the aerospace industry.

Then there was the matter of boxes. We had to have special containers for Gerry's crystals and the circuitry which energized them.

Helen Polhovsky and I worked on this one together. She is typical of the polyglot cadre which permeates the American aerospace industry. For nearly a century, the industry has acted as a powerful magnet, drawing in many of the most talented people from around the world.

Helen's story is not atypical. Her grandfather, Count Polhovsky, had been Master of the Czar's Stables until the Communist Revolution. He smuggled his family out by camel train through Persia and then went back to collect the family's hidden jewels and treasures, only to fade into the mists of history. Her remaining family settled in Yugoslavia, and Helen fled after the Communist takeover, becoming a refugee. Given her background, Helen was highly sensitive to the plight of refugees. When Saigon fell in 1975, Helen literally camped out at the Marine Base at Camp Pendleton, so as to be a sponsor of a Vietnamese refugee family. It was her theory that the best people would be snapped up right at the beginning, so she had better be there early. The father of the family she chose, who moved in with her, had been a merchant sea captain. He was, of course, fluent in French, but only knew smatterings of English; the rest of the family, the same. But, they were smart and energetic. Within months the two young children were babbling away in English and teaching their parents our language and idioms. Within about a year the family had saved enough money for a down payment on a house of their own and had achieved full independence.

Helen was the director of the hybrid integrated circuit laboratory. This facility mated silicon integrated circuits onto ceramic substrates which had been pre-patterned with connective conductors and other components. The results were tiny jewelry-like devices — abstract gold patterns on sparkling white substrates — which performed complete electronic functions. In our case her devices converted the electrical charges within the CadTel crystals into special signals which could be transmitted to the ground. After mounting the CadTel crystals onto the hybrids the combination is inserted into small, gold plated, hermetically sealed, space qualified boxes.

It happened that a few miles away was the principal manufacturer of these custom boxes. One day Helen and I took our design layout up to the box company and sat down with its president and chief engineer. We explained our need. We couldn't tell them what we needed the boxes for, but we definitely needed them quickly. When? Three weeks; four at the very outside. "Not a chance," was the response. "Maybe we can get them to you in six to nine months, *if* you are willing to pay a premium." The problem was all the other work that the company had already committed to, most of it Defense related. Besides, the production line would have to be reconfigured, which was not of great interest for such a small order as we were seeking.

We reiterated that our project was very important, but we could not say exactly why. Round and round we went, until the discussion took on the overtones of old time melodrama: "I can't pay the rent"...."You must pay the rent!".... ultimately ending in what was almost a sneer.

"We might consider advancing your order if we were asked, very politely, by a call from the Secretary of Defense."

"Okay," I replied. The president looked at me strangely. So did Helen.

Back at the plant I reported the proceedings to our manager Bob Lyons. "Don't worry," he told me. "You'll get the boxes. Count on it." The next day the phone rang. It was the box company president. He was subdued. "We will have your boxes ready in three weeks."

Well, that settled that, but more problems avalanched on top of us. Did I mention that during reentry things get hot? The peripheral nosetip sensors were buried in the ballast only about a quarter of an inch below the inner surface of the phenolic heat shield. The outer surface of the phenolic becomes an incandescent plasma, nearly as hot as the surface of the sun. The phenolic chars, which sheds most of the heat, but the inner surface still gets very hot. Somehow we had to keep the sensor electronics at room temperature. We solved the problem by wrapping a blanket of porous silicone rubber around the boxes to ward off the heat flow during the short time of reentry. We were lucky that these heat and sound absorbing blankets also helped with another problem: the noise of reentry.

Originally we had planned to bond the CadTel crystals directly to the hybrid substrate. Then someone mentioned that CadTel is piezoelectric. Sound waves would produce a detectable electric charge on its surface. In other words, this substance is a microphone. But not just any microphone. CadTel is about four times more sensitive than quartz crystal, which is the standard crystal microphone material. Thus, we had on our hands a *really* good microphone. The problem was that the reentry environment was not only hellishly hot, it was also hellishly noisy.

Of course we would have to design acoustic isolation for the crystal. But more than that, we needed a noise source that was loud enough to test our design. We started looking for suitably noisy facilities. One possibility was the rocket test stand at Huntsville, Alabama. They were still testing the giant F1 rocket engines which powered the Saturn moon rocket. Not good enough. Those stupendous engines were too quiet. Unexpectedly, the jet engines on airliners were reported to be even more noisy. I made a trip up to the United Airlines maintenance facility in San Francisco to get some acoustic measurements. The senior engineer there proudly showed off his engine test cell. The engine noise was loud enough to crack the cell's reinforced concrete walls and skate ten ton tie down blocks freely around the floor of the cell. Unfortunately, our measurements showed that the cell's noise was still not loud enough.

Then, rather to my surprise, it turned out that our group already owned the world's loudest noise source — the Capistrano reentry test facility. So we could test noise performance as a regular part of the RV design validation. That was very convenient. In the meantime we could duplicate part of the acoustic environment with shake table and shock tests. More lore to learn.

Our analysis indicated that bonding the CadTel to the hybrid circuit substrate just wouldn't work. An alternate design floated the crystal between two thin layers of electrically conducting foam. No problem, except that no one knew how to cut the foam with the necessary precision. Thinking myself ingenious, I suggested to the model shop machinist that the foam could be precisely cut if it were first frozen with liquid nitrogen. The machinist tried this and got very clean cut surfaces. Unfortunately, the surfaces were never parallel. One morning the machinist presented a pair of precisely cut and precisely parallel foam sheets. "How did you do that?" I asked. "With a razor blade," he replied, with a straight face. A good lesson for me: Never tell a master how to do his job; just tell him what needs to be done.

At last the prototype flight boxes were assembled and had passed the electrical and radiation detection tests. We were ready for vibration and shock "shake, rattle and roll." The news was not good. The design worked up to a point, but high intensity vibrations caused powerful microphone signals. The problem was beyond my expertise, but Bob Lyons figured out a simple solution. As he recalls: "I remember you and I 'coining' the first couple of boxes by carefully rolling the edge of the head of a handy wood screw across the top of the gold box, corner to diagonal corner to mitigate the 'eardrum' effect." Inscribing an X in the top of the box raised its resonance frequencies enough to allow the device to settle down nicely — it behaved itself from then on.

The first nosetip, complete with embedded flight instrumentation, was finished and made ready for the unfortunate rocket test described above. Analysis of the brief burst of data from the test suggested that the design was going to work. We had to rely on that and press on.

With completion of the flight test instrumentation my role in the program was winding down. I was soon called on to work on Laser Death Rays. From that point on, the story is hearsay from colleagues who finished the program.

One key problem was assembly of the nosetip onto the RV. The radioactive light bulbs in the nosetip had to be very precisely aligned with the collimator holes that had been drilled through the ballast. Various mechanical coupler designs were evaluated and discarded. Only one design showed sufficient promise of quick assembly and precise alignment. The nosetip and the body of the reentry vehicle would have to be joined by a type of bayonet socket. The activated nosetip would simply be pressed down onto the vehicle and then given a slight turn to lock the nose into place. Experiments showed that no automatic assembly fixture had the right "feel" to do the job without the risk of crushing the nosetip material. The job needed to be done by hand. The catch was the deadly intense nuclear radiation that would be flowing from the operational nosetip. Anyone who mounted the nosetip would receive a lifetime allowed dose of radiation in just a few seconds. Tests with dummy nosetips indicated that the job could be done very quickly. But what if something were to go wrong? All that could be done, then, would be to replace one technician with another until the problem was corrected and the nosetips on the two RV's were properly seated.

The call went out for volunteers. Rather to everyone's surprise, there were a multitude of volunteers for this very dangerous job. The final decision was made to proceed to completion of the program.

For the launch timing was everything. The weather had to be just right, just the right thickness of clouds in just the right place. All the support facilities and aircraft had to be properly scheduled, with highest priority. All the people had to be in place and fully trained. The rocket had to be prepped for instant, reliable flight. The entire operation was meticulously rehearsed until the highly professional team was perfectly drilled. Then came the wait.

And the wait. And the wait. The weather at target site near Kwajalein Atoll was unseasonably mild. Finally, at last, a strong storm front started moving towards the target. The program's well-oiled machine swung into action. The nosetips were helicoptered to Berkeley for irradiation at its famous cyclotron. Irradiation completed, the very hot nosetips were then airlifted to Vandenberg for final assembly onto the rocket. No time to waste here. High radiation also means rapidly decaying radiation. A few hours extra delay and the light bulbs would be too weak to do their job. Fortunately the mounting of nosetips was perfectly completed in just a few seconds and the hordes of extra volunteers were not needed. All was now ready for the launch. Everything had gone according to the most optimistic schedule.

Unfortunately, somehow the Russians had gotten wind of the proceedings and had placed a "fishing trawler" right smack at ground zero. So much for security. And, some fishing boat — the vessel was hairy with electronics antennas. The

Colonel in charge of the flight test sent out a warning to the trawler.

"You're in a hazardous area, please move on."

"We can't. We've got our nets out and it will take several hours to haul them back in. Besides, these are international waters. We have a perfect right to be here."

"We insist."

"We won't."

"You're in great danger."

"We are just fishing."

The nosetip radiation was rapidly decaying. Time was growing short and so was the Colonel's patience. Finally: "Screw 'em. Launch the bird!"

A column of fire grew out of the California landscape as the powerful rocket hurled upward and arced out over the Pacific towards its distant destination at Kwaj (Kwajalein Atoll). Minutes of silence followed as the four RVs fell through the vacuum. Telemetry was working perfectly. Then the screaming incandescence of reentry. Four fire streaks disappeared into the thick tropical rain clouds. Our telemetry still looked good. We were going to have a successful experiment. Our competitors did not do so well. Their RVs vanished almost immediately.

Below the clouds a camera plane captured what happened next. One frame of film pictured just the trawler, sitting quietly in the water. The next frame showed two brilliant streaks of light, lightning bolts from cloud to sea — the first hitting a hundred yards to starboard, the other a hundred yards to port. The trawler had been neatly bracketed. In the next frames two giant columns of water shot up, vertically, to meet and penetrate the cloud base, a thousand feet above. Within seconds the Russian trawler was aboil with crewmen, scurrying like agitated ants, every which way. Axes out, the nets were quickly chopped away and the trawler took off. And did it accelerate! It must have had very powerful engines to push such a large vessel at racing boat speeds.

The reaction of the Russians was quite understandable, under the circumstances. A few hundred kilos of RV, hurtling at several kilometers per second, packs an energy substantially greater than the explosive shells from the giant guns of a WWII battleship. The shockwave from a single hit would break the back of the largest warship and sink it instantly.

After that, the Russians very scrupulously, and politely, obeyed our every request to evacuate our test areas.

THE PARTY

IT WAS DURING THE REAGAN ERA, when I was making my living as a freelance consultant. One of my contracts was with TRW. Those folks sent me to Alexandria, Virginia to help with the start of a very big project. TRW had split off a group to work on behalf of the Government. Its job was to develop the requirements for a major new Government laboratory similar to Los Alamos. The new laboratory, then called the "National Test Bed," was to be devoted to developing Reagan's Star Wars dream.

To give you a sense of the scale of this multibillion dollar effort, the smallest budget item that we were concerned with was, in 1980s dollars, $100 million. And there were several dozen of these items — too many to really wrap one's understanding around. In the end I wrote the project's defining specification document, the Statement of Work for the detailed design.

Some years later I found myself wandering down a hall at the Rockwell Seal Beach facility. I passed an open door to a large conference room. Backing up I looked in, for something odd had caught my eye. The furniture had been removed from the room. The walls were entirely covered in the strangest looking wall paper. I had to see this close up.

I could not make out any details until my nose was only a few inches from the wall. At this distance the pattern resolved itself into countless tiny boxes and tinier functional labels inside them — thousands, or even tens of thousands, of these boxes. Connecting the boxes, and running all around the room was a lattice of lines which showed the relationships between the boxes. The lines were the wiring diagram for the project. What project? I traced some of the lines to their starting point. It was the National Test Bed, the very project for which I had written the Statement of Work. The walls and detail were overwhelming. Astonishing! For the first time I had a sense of what a multibillion dollar project was really all about. Our project eventually became Schriever Space Force Base, a key location for the new U.S. Space Force.

We worked hard on the laboratory definition, with meetings of the California contingent at dawn over breakfast at the hotel, meetings of the full group at TRW during the day, and meetings after dinner back in the hotel, until nearly midnight. Weekends we had to ourselves and this led to an interesting adventure.

I had a friend who had been a senior executive in the aerospace industry. For a while he had roamed the Middle East, peddling Instruments of Death and Destruction. Along the way he developed some very interesting acquaintances. One of these was a foreign correspondent of unusual experience who was now the chief editor of an important newspaper. Since I was about to spend substantial time in the Washington D.C. area my friend arranged for me to meet with this distinguished individual.

The editor invited me to dine at very good restaurant in Arlington. It wasn't just a matter of friendship. He was very interested in my work on Star Wars type programs. These programs had been underway years before Reagan was elected. Reagan's initiative brought many of them out from the Black

World and into the sunlight. I told the editor what I could without revealing classified information. At the time, the Star Wars effort — technological foundations and the program overall — was under heavy attack. I provided the editor with the real physics behind the program.

In turn, after a couple glasses of wine, the editor opened up about the Washington Press Corps. He knew well all the players and where the bodies were buried. I sat mesmerized by stories about these distinguished individuals and their frailties. The editor's comments about his colleagues were decidedly sardonic. The dinner, and its long and stimulating conversation, ended pleasantly and we parted. I did not expect more. But there was to be more.

A few days later, I got a call from the editor. He said that he had previously committed himself and his wife to attend an embassy party. Unfortunately, something very important had suddenly intervened. He asked if I would take his place at the party that evening. His wife *must* have an escort. It took some convincing but, in the end, I reluctantly agreed.

The problem was that such an event is a very formal affair. Not only did I not know the protocols, I had nothing appropriate to wear. Over the course of decades the dress code for engineers in the aerospace industry had devolved from suit and tie (the norm when I first started) into casual wear. The best I could do was to borrow a sports jacket and tie. Even this was way less than party protocol demanded. Oh well!

At the appointed time I picked up the editor's wife — let's call her milady — at their home. This charming and beautiful lady was Persian and highly cultured. Her father had been a key figure in the Shah's inner circle. The wounds of the revolution were still raw. I did not ask questions.

The party was at the Egyptian Embassy. It was an important affair. They were celebrating the tenth anniversary of their great victory over Israel in the Yom Kippur War. Silly me, I thought they had lost that war. Go figure. Actually, they did quite well the first few days, until Israel regained its balance and ascendency. Maybe the celebration had some justification, after all. At least the Egyptians believed so.

On the short drive to the Embassy milady prepared me with do's and don'ts. The Embassy proved to be an old Georgetown mansion, one of several along the street that had been similarly converted. My name was at the door. We were ushered inside and directed up a short flight of stairs.

I thought I knew what I would find, but the reality took me aback. In the brightly lit room the crowd was modest in size, but did they dazzle! You probably have encountered scenes in Hollywood movies where the nobility have gathered. Gentlemen in tuxes, women in evening gowns, lots of jewels. Let me tell you that the reality made the movies pale in comparison. The men did wear tuxedoes, or various uniforms. Most of these were festooned with colorful, and embroidered, silk sashes. Jeweled star bursts were penned to their jackets and sashes. The women wore a rainbow of gowns. Sparkling diamonds, rubies, emeralds and sapphires bedecked their bodices and hair. I was definitely the ugly duckling in the room and everyone noticed. No matter. Pretend to be a young swan.

Milady introduced me around. All were polite. Then she led me to the buffet. The buffet was a large round table with tiers stacked up like a wedding cake. I reached out for something that looked enticing. I didn't make it. A sharp slap on my wrist stopped me. She knew about my plebian tastes and that morsel was the spiciest thing there. She directed me to this, and then that. Wonderful stuff. Different from anything I had ever had, but truly delicious!

Mostly what I did after that was listen. The talk was familiar pedestrian chit-chat. No great state secrets, no intrigues, just: "How are the kids?" "Tell me about your trip." And so on.

There was one other person who stood out from the glittering crowd. He was a senior U.S. military officer. The only one there. A multitude of stars on the shoulders of his Army Dress Blues told of his high rank. A single row of ribboned medals spoke only of his most important honors. The rest of his jacket bore several medallions of various kinds. Not having been in the service I did not know how to read the story that others would have understood at a glance.

This gentleman had a quiet authority about him that was separate from his obvious rank. I had seen that calm demeanor before — in the friends who had experienced the most ferocious combat. This man had most definitely "seen the elephant." My career was of a military nature, as well, though quite different. If he had been at the tooth, I had been at the far away tip of the tail. My engineering years had been spent conjuring up "toys for the boys" as they are sometimes called.

Like myself, he had mostly stood around listening, somewhat separated from the various little clusters of people. It seemed natural that we would drift together. I suspect he had the same curiosity about me that I had about him. We soon fell into a quiet conversation. A comfortable conversation.

He naturally asked who I was and why I was there. Satisfied, he became quite interested in the project that I was working on, and asked more questions with great skill. When I mentioned my many years working on High Energy Lasers

— Death Rays — he perked up and probed much deeper. Clearly this was a subject of considerable interest to him.

After a while the conversation lagged a bit. It was my turn. "Well, Sir," I asked, "And what do you do for a living?"

"Oh," he replied, with just a bit of a grin, "I'm Chairman of the Joint Chiefs of Staff."

ICBM

Hey kid, you want to buy an ICBM? A real Soviet ICBM. Best quality. Ready to fly. I know where you can get one cheap – <u>real cheap!</u>

IN THE EARLY YEARS OF THE 1990s I was earning my living free-lance consulting. One of my important clients was Martin Marietta Corporation. Martin, based near Littleton Colorado, was the prime contractor for space based high energy laser weapons development.

Space Based Lasers are potentially devastating predators of long range ballistic missiles. The touch of their multi-mega-watt beams of light could almost instantly pop thrusting missiles like a balloon. These developmental High Energy Lasers are true science fiction ray gun wonder weapons.

Over the years I had become expert about SBL architectures. And, I had developed the very fast computer simulation tools to back up my expertise. It was as an SBL system architect that I was advising Martin.

It happened, during a visit to Littleton, that I needed some information about Russian ICBMs. I was directed to the basement. There, in a windowless office, was the man I was looking for. The office was occupied by a quiet, unprepossessing gentleman. He didn't have to go to his files to answer my questions. The answers came off the top of his head. As we talked I realized the extraordinary depth of his knowledge, not only about Soviet weapons but also about the players on the side of our former adversary. I began to guess that his real background might have involved some daring-do, James Bond style.

After we talked technical for a while the conversation drifted on to other topics and there were the beginnings of a friendship. Then he caught me by surprise. "Do you want to buy an ICBM? I know where there is a brand new Soviet SS-19 for sale. It's cheap, only a million dollars."

The missile was the last one off the Ukrainian production line. It was still in its original crate, ready to be shipped and flown. All one had to do was erect it, fuel it, spin up the gyros, and fly it.

The offer was so unexpected that for a few minutes I was disoriented. But the offer was real. The remnants of the disintegrated Soviet Empire were impoverished and the US dollar was almost beyond value. The Ukrainians were desperate for dollars.

Slowly I began to get ideas. I told my contact that I wanted to explore something that had come to mind. When I arrived home I called my friend Dick Freeman. Retired now, he had been the boss of so many of the current principals of the aerospace industry that he was exceptionally well connected. More than this, he was active, and very well respected, in charitable circles — people with money and a desire to give. Dick was interested.

Together we mapped out a way of acquiring the missile.

I must admit that receiving such an unusual offer was more than a bit unexpected since I was not part of the Intelligence Community. If I had been this would have been routine business. Intelligence, after all, has its *sources and methods* for such things.

For example, one day right at the end of the Cold War I was driving in the Mojave Desert north of Edwards Air Force Base, heading home from an assignment. At a highway intersection I was rather startled to see the latest model Soviet tank. It was sitting on the flatbed of a tank transporter truck. Given where this intersection was, it might have been coming from the Navy's China Lake facility north of where I saw it. The Navy's interest would have been to gather optical signatures as well as information about the tank's vulnerabilities. Alternatively, it might have been traveling from, or to, Fort Irwin, the Army's battle training camp in the Mojave. The Army could certainly have used a late model Soviet tank in these training exercises.

Then, too, on another day I was wandering through one of the hangers at the Navy's Point Mugu test station. There I encountered a Chinese Silkworm missile. This was a very dangerous anti-ship missile. The Navy technician who was working on the missile explained that the Navy had been trying, with American target drones, to emulate the optical signature of the Silkworm. Then some creative individual suggested that the Navy should simply acquire some Silkworms to test. That way the optical signatures would be perfect because they would be taken from the real thing. Even though this was our adversary's missile no one thought the suggestion strange.

Of course the Navy would need a bunch of Silkworms because it is expendable — each good for just one test. Amazingly, I was told that the Navy now had more than they needed. Someone in the Intelligence Community must have had very good connections to be able to deliver a large number of Silkworms. The same is true of the Soviet tank. It seems that there are *always* people who would sell *anything* to turn a big profit, even if doing so was illicit, and dangerous.

In the case of the offer to sell the SS-19 ICBM, this was after the fall of the Soviet Empire. Ukraine was on its own and desperate for dollars. So was the factory where the missile had been made. Thus the legitimate availability and the ridiculously low price.

I had in mind that the ICBM would make a fine display for an aviation museum. Make that two museums. An intact missile is not very interesting — just a long pipe with a pointy end. At the National Air and Space museum people walk by the displayed ICBMs with hardly a glance. I thought the way to make the exhibit really interesting would be to show what is *inside* the missile, so that people could get a good idea as to how the thing worked. Besides, complex machinery is attractive in its own right. Just consider how fascinating a mechanical Swiss watch is.

So, why not slice the missile in two down the middle to show its guts. The SS-19 is ideal for such a display because it is a liquid fuel missile and has substantial internal complexity.

Of course this opened up the opportunity to interest two different aviation museums. The obvious choice for one of the museums was the Planes of Fame Air Museum in Chino, California. Another possibility was the Pima Air and Space Museum in Tucson, Arizona. Both museums had very large collections of classic warbirds on display, many of them flyable.

Dick Freeman was very well known in aviation circles and had excellent connections with the Planes of Fame museum. They were definitely interested, provided sufficient funds were available.

Dick got to work on finding money for the project — and he succeeded. One of his friends would provide the funds, provided that Planes of Fame was the right place. So Dick arranged a meeting. It was to be at a restaurant near the museum.

The day came and the financier arrived at the appointed time and place. He and Dick waited for the museum contact to arrive — and waited, and waited. The museum representative never showed up. The deal was off. What is much worse, there never was an explanation for the missed meeting — never an explanation and no apology.

You must understand that Dick Freeman was a man of honor. To him a verbal agreement or a handshake deal was sacred. These were more binding than a written contract. All Dick's many years of friendship with the Planes of Fame museum were now over. That organization was dead as far as he was concerned.

So what happened to the SS-19? Who knows. Perhaps some intelligence agency bought it. Perhaps it was used to launch a satellite into orbit. It certainly had the capability. Maybe its crate was shoved off to some dim-lit corner of the factory and long since forgotten. Maybe a new generation worker would occasionally wander by and wonder what was in that large dusty box. Or, maybe not.

DILBERT

THE WHOLE AFFAIR was straight out of a Dilbert cartoon. I had planned to retire at the end of the year on my seventieth birthday. Everybody knew that. Others noticed that clearly there was something wrong with me. I was suffering from a deadly illness (later cured) and had lost interest in the work. So I joined the layoff list. Thus my actual retirement came a few months earlier than planned. That was good. Old and sick as I was I was ready to leave.

My retirement lunch was sweet — full of good friends and well wishes.

My last day was an adventure. Our company had adopted a 9/80 work week. The work day was nine hours. Five days one week then four days the next week. Every other Friday was a 9/80 day when half the work force was home. Naturally the layoff day was a Friday and half the work force was gone. Unfortunately, certain key people were on 9/80 and nowhere to be found.

These key people were needed to sign off on the checkout sheets of those who were leaving the company that day. There were over a hundred lost souls, wandering the halls, trying to find someone to sign their exit sheets. These lost souls gathered in a crowd, shuffling together up the halls, then down the halls. For hours they wandered like ghosts. This place was really big — the size of the Pentagon — so there were endless halls to wander. I exaggerate, to be sure, but not by much.

I am an old pro. Once I realized the situation I solved it. I walked to the building that had the executive offices. I walked down the long corridor to the Chief Engineer's office and said "Hi!" to the administrative ladies working there. They all knew me and thought I had come to say goodbye. Which, of course, was part of my intention. Thanks for the good wishes, I responded, but I need to solve a problem. I explained it.

Now anyone who knows anything about large organizations will know who the real bosses are. They are not the ones that sit in the corner offices. The real bosses sit right outside the corner offices. Within five minutes the problem was solved and I was instructed to round everyone up and send them to a particular location. I did that, turned in my badge, and went home. Free at last!

LAMP (Large Advanced Mirror Program)
Beam director telescope developed for
space based high energy laser program

PSYCHOPATHS

IS THERE EVIL IN THE WORLD? You bet. I don't need headlines to show me the face of evil. I have seen it. I have witnessed murder close up — the knife thrust and twist of an expert assassin, his victim falling heavily to the ground, already dead. I have known mortal fear when a live machine gun, the wielder's finger on the trigger, was thrust into my belly. I have seen the tears of a teacher telling of his students being dragged from their homes in the middle of the night and slaughtered in the street by government goons. Escorted by police, I have pushed through vast mobs of people who were attempting to flee the looming terror of a government newly turned Communist. Millions died in the subsequent bloodshed.

America is a civilized nation. But evil *is* here. It can hide behind convention, behind politeness, behind political correctness, behind the law. Nonetheless, it leaves behind its own kind of carnage. I have witnessed such evil. I have experienced such evil, suffered from it. It has left its mark on me.

Some consider the destructive manifestations of Nature to be great evil: Fire, Flood, Earthquakes, Tornadoes, Hurricanes, Disease. I have lived through all but tornadoes, and I know from personal experience the hurt and anguish these phenomena cause. But we must accept these hazards as the price for the privilege of being alive and aware. They are the cost of doing business, so to speak.

The greatest evil is what people do to other people. Some are oblivious of the harm they cause. They are so inwardly focused they don't recognize the damage following in their wake. Others know, but don't care. These sociopaths are conscious predators. Then there are the psychopaths.

Professor James Fallon at the University of California, Irvine, has discovered there is a physiological reason psychopaths have reduced capacity for empathy and guilt. Their brains are mis-wired. Because of a mutation, certain key nerve connections are attenuated. Are they evil? It depends on the individual. It depends on what they do. Often they do good. Dr. Fallon mentioned many surgeons are, in fact, psychopaths. If so, many of us have benefited from their unemotional skills while they perform surgery.

On the other hand, there are psychopaths who are what we expect them to be: *evil.* In the course of my travels I have encountered a number of them.

One was a charming individual who swindled a member of Europe's nobility out of his fortune. That victim committed suicide when he discovered he was penniless. The charming, unrepentant villain later ended up in prison for a different crime.

Similarly glib individuals — licensed attorneys — created a real estate investment company which attracted mostly retired professionals: doctors, lawyers, and the like. The company turned out to be a disguised Ponzi scheme. Suicides followed among the newly destitute. It was later discovered that the proprietors of this company had repeatedly fled ahead of the law from a succession of states where they had also worked this kind of racket. California licensed them anyway. Ultimately they ended up in prison so California finally did something right.

I remember encountering a prominent, but unpleasant, doctor. He was head of the local hospital. One day he badly injured one of his patients. The doctor's insurance company bought off the corrupt lawyer representing the victim. The equally corrupt judge recognized the felonies but let it slide. This bad doctor later ended up in Federal prison, having been charged with trading drugs for guns. The local medical community breathed a sigh of relief.

Then there are bosses: the good, the bad and the ugly.

A good boss is competent and humane, and can range, from the merely humane and competent, to the talented, to the true genius. For a creative person having a genius good boss is pure heaven — it is always a bit chaotic but it's so much fun!

A bad boss is neither competent nor humane. These characters descend from the mediocre to the "Boss from Hell," and lower — to the true sadistic psychopath. A bad boss puts you in one of the circles of hell.

The ugly boss may be competent, he may get the job done, but he is also a vampire. When he gets the job done it's at the cost of wrecking his crew. After suffering under an ugly boss one is a depleted husk. An ugly boss drags you through purgatory.

Consider this ugly boss: Relatively early in my career I was technical leader of a teamed contract. There were three co-contractors. My company was Ford Aerospace. Another contractor was Hughes Aircraft. The third was Lockheed, the lead organization. Periodically I would travel to Palo Alto for coordination meetings.

Lockheed's project manager was highly competent. The photos on the wall of his office showed he had been in charge of a large and successful program of national significance. At first I was impressed. But this good opinion soon faded away when I discovered how he actually managed his top staff.

The work day for the leaders of the Lockheed team began at seven in the morning with briefings to the project manager, followed by the usual daily routine. The team leaders spent their days in splinter meetings. At five in the evening the project manager called his team leaders together for the evening conference. This continued until seven, or sometimes eight at night, at which time the project manager gave his Lockheed staff their overnight written assignments — sometimes belittling as he handed them out — to be delivered at the next morning's seven o'clock meeting. Burnout was clearly on the horizon. This boss operated as if we were in a wartime emergency. Only, we were not. There was no excuse for his behavior. Fortunately, I did not work for Lockheed so I had none of the psychological pain of the "homework" or rebukes, though I did put in the long days mandated by attending the morning and evening conferences.

That was an ugly boss. A bad boss can be infinitely worse, as I was to discover. My encounter with such a vile creature came during the 1980s.

At the time I was consulting on a proposal with Rockwell International. We intended to become the prime contractor for the Zenith Star project. The project's goal was to orbit a high energy laser to see if it could defeat long range ballistic missiles. This was part of President Reagan's "Star Wars" missile defense program. To carry out Reagan's directive, the Defense

Department created the Strategic Defense Initiative Organization — SDIO. Zenith Star was one of SDIO's initiatives.

It was at Rockwell that I briefed some government visitors. Apparently I made such a good impression I was invited to move over to the government's side of things. The invitation was irresistible.

I was recruited into a SETA consulting company — System Engineering and Technical Assistance. SETA specialists provide the government with technical oversight of many of the Defense Department's programs. These companies are often sardonically called "Beltway Bandits" because they have major offices in the beltway ring around Washington D.C.

This particular SETA company managed a major portion of Reagan's Star Wars program. Joining the company was especially attractive because the company was heavily engaged in rocket technology — a subject of great interest to me.

The company had offices in various locations around the country. Each office was a division. Our division was located near Los Angeles.

I soon found myself settled in a corner view office of a prestige building. All of my new colleagues, a couple dozen of them, were warm in their welcome. This was going to be good. And, for a while, it was.

The quality of the people at this small division explains why this place was so attractive. For example, several of the key engineers who created the giant F-1 rocket engines that took us to the moon were in our office. These good men also created the Space Shuttle Main Engine (SSME). We had the royalty of America's rocket engine technology.

There was one person all these senior rocket people looked up to — Tom Coultas. I don't know what contribution

Tom made to the success of the F-1 engine, but apparently it was crucial. On the other hand, I do know Tom balanced the design of the SSME. This basically meant Tom was the mastermind for the Space Shuttle's engines.

Tom's title was *Principal Advisor* to the Air Force for rocket propulsion. To get a sense of this genial man, consider his Irish setter. It lay quietly at the foot of Tom's desk throughout the day. Tom always had time for my questions. His answers usually were colored with sly humor. After I was gone from the division Tom mentored me through the analysis of one of my inventions. This required my learning the mathematics of jet and rocket engines; Tom's tutoring was of great help.

When I first arrived the division manager was a congenial fellow named Spence. I liked him and we worked well together.

Spence had a deputy whom I will call Jason. Jason was a bit strange. Following my entrance interview with him I mentioned to my wife Sarah that Jason was . . . odd. After she met him later, she agreed.

My concern about Jason increased substantially after he, Spence and myself visited another company. Jason lied about a couple of things. He implied that Spence was the source of a problem Jason himself had created. Spence said nothing — at least in my presence. Several years later I discovered Jason had regularly been slandering Spence behind his back. As a consequence, in some quarters of the industry Spence had an undeserved bad reputation. Perhaps that is why Spence retired when he did.

And so, Jason achieved his goal. He became the division manager. Things carried on normally for a while. Then began a long decline.

It is often good to trust your first instincts about a person. My odd feeling about Jason was on the money. Not long after Jason took over he hired a recently retired Air Force colonel. This former officer had been in charge of nuclear weapons development for the Air Force, so he was a significant talent. He was an affable person, as well.

The colonel's office was next to mine. The partition was thin — I could sometimes hear a bit of what was transpiring next door, particularly when the words were loud. And, increasingly often the words were loud, and then louder, and became violent. It got so bad every morning Jason would barge into the colonel's office and start with a rant. The colonel had great integrity so he refused to knuckle under to the abuse. This resistance infuriated Jason so much that, day by day, the nasty attacks grew in magnitude. Jason's strange behavior became the main topic of clandestine conversation among the entire staff, particularly because the colonel was well liked and greatly respected.

Within weeks the colonel left the company. It was good he left. Subsequently he became Dean of Engineering at a technology oriented university. This was appropriate because earlier in his career he had been senior faculty at the Air Force Academy. The colonel ultimately retired full of honors and greatly loved by the students and his colleagues.

I was soon to discover what had transpired between Jason and the colonel. Jason gave me the colonel's assignment to finish after he left. This was a straightforward task. It involved abstracting a substantial number of badly written government documents into a single readable digest. This was a good introduction to the work we were doing.

Part of the package included the colonel's handwritten digest. Beautiful handwriting — elegant calligraphy. At first it was. Day by day, the handwriting progressively deteriorated until it became an illegible scrawl. I could make out a few words, here and there, but it was impossible to reconstruct the colonel's sentences. Obviously, towards the last the colonel suffered a nervous breakdown. I kept his secret.

The best I could figure, Jason had wanted to bias the colonel's work so it would become little more than company propaganda. It was apparent the colonel would have none of that. Fortunately, Jason didn't try to pressure me. I finished the work in the way the colonel had intended.

The colonel was not the only victim of Jason's desire to dominate. Another distinguished engineer was equally abused and discarded. This gentle good man was a patriarch of Southern California's black community. He had also contributed an important invention to the world of rocketry. Sarah was quite fond of him.

Jason's misbehavior was the norm during the first months I worked under him. Eventually, though, he quieted down and we got on with the work. Unfortunately for Jason he had now lost the respect of his staff.

It was inevitable that I became one of Jason's targets. What happened could have been a minor matter. But the result created a permanent barrier between the two of us, and determined what was to transpire years later.

Earlier in my career the Office of Naval Research had financed some of my research into digital holography. This results of this research attracted substantial attention. My new employer was so well connected I had no trouble getting a contract to extend some of the earlier work. Jason was excited about what I discovered and wanted my results to be presented back east.

The normal protocol in the aerospace industry is for the creator of an idea to present that idea. The practice makes sense because the creator knows best what he has created. He also gets to be known to a wider circle. I expected, therefore, I was to make the presentation. Jason said no. He would present it himself. I told him I had better brief him in detail before he left — the subject was pretty arcane. He refused to listen and said he could learn what I had done from what I had written. Big mistake!

Jason was clobbered. There is no other way to put it. Naturally, when he returned, he blamed me in a decidedly unpleasant way. After what Jason had done to the colonel, and now me, I cared little for Jason's opinion or authority.

After this incident I might have been tempted to leave, however the job remained interesting and my new colleagues were outstanding. I resolved to stay and tough it out. Good thing I did because there were lots of good times mixed in with the occasional confrontations with Jason.

The division was at the exotic edge of President Reagan's Star Wars program. Its major contracts involved applications of high energy lasers. As I mentioned, the division was also the master of rocket propulsion. Its secondary contracts mostly supported the Air Force's rocket programs.

Lasers and rocket engines may seem an odd mix of technologies, but in reality it wasn't. It was quite natural — chemical high energy lasers are actually an assemblage of tiny rocket motors. The explanation is simple. When hot gas is accelerated through a rocket nozzle the internal temperature of the gas instantly drops to near zero. The right kind of gas suddenly undergoes an electron population inversion. In other words, the gas wants to lase, or emit coherent light. Coherent light behaves as a single wave. This coherence makes a laser the ideal light source. It makes it possible to send energy over long distances without loss, and focus the beam at its destination. Pass this fast flowing gas between two special mirrors and you have a high power laser. The advantage of this kind of chemical gas dynamic laser is its power. Such an instrument can deliver several megawatts of continuous power. Nothing, and I do mean *nothing*, can withstand the touch of a light beam this powerful. It is a true science fiction ray gun. As a space system architect, my job was to discover how to properly use this stupendous machine.

I soon plunged deeply into the job of understanding and updating the proposed Space Based Laser (SBL) architecture. Any such architecture would be made up of a number of large "battle stations" orbiting the Earth. Each battle station would be capable destroying a multitude of ballistic missiles while they are accelerating in the boost phase of their trajectories. It was while working on this that I was presented with a tough new challenge.

Several months after I joined the company Jason was sufficiently annoyed with me to concoct a scheme to get rid of me. He would give me an impossible task: to figure out exactly how a laser kills a thrusting ballistic missile.

This problem had exercised the community for several years. What puzzled everybody was the laser didn't simply burn a hole in the missile, it actually *popped* the missile like a balloon — fragments flew everywhere! There were lots of subscale experiments, and at least one at full scale, to prove this was the case. Nobody could figure out why this was so.

The reason Jason considered it impossible for me to solve this enigma: So many good people — PhD physicists and the like — had tried, and failed, to solve it. Jason's twist was to give me only a month to solve the problem or leave the company. The ploy didn't work. I solved the problem. It took two extra weeks — and required a flash of inspiration.

I don't know why he hadn't fired me at the one month mark, but now the problem for Jason was my solution made me known to senior management and to our customer. I was untouchable and pretty much free to do things my own way. "Curses, foiled again!"

So, back to SBL architectures. A space based laser battle station would be a large orbiting satellite capable of destroying a boosting ballistic missile out to a range of thousands kilometers, or miles. Based on experimental data, kill times would typically be a second or two. Retarget times are likewise a couple of seconds, or less in many scenarios. These things are *fast*, and *deadly!*

A battle station would consist of the laser with its large fuel tank and a large, directable, reverse telescope called a beam director. The reason for the reverse telescope is to concentrate the laser beam into a small spot on the target. When I was young, we kids occasionally would start a fire by focusing the sun's rays with a magnifying glass. Same principle. The reverse telescope is a giant focusing mirror.

A battle station also would need sensors for acquiring and tracking the target. The rest involves fairly complex coordination optics which would be an optometrist's delight (or nightmare). This all sounds easy. It ain't!

The fundamental architectural problem was to find the minimum resource capable of doing the job. There were two distinctly different critical missions. Already existing were the massive batteries of Soviet and Chinese nuclear tipped ballistic missiles. (This analysis was taking place in the 1980's, when the Soviet Union still existed.) Soviet and Chinese missiles constituted the near term threat. A system capable of defeating these threats logically should be called a near term system but it wasn't. There was also a future threat from third world nations, such as Iran and North Korea. This was not expected to develop until thirty or forty years in the future. This was called the far term threat. A system to defeat far term threats should have been called a far term system. Again, it wasn't.

As it happens, the technology to defeat the far term threat was already maturing in the near term since its technology had started development several years before Reagan became president. On the other hand, it was expected to take about fifty years of technology development to meet the near term threat. Thus, the far term threat could be defeated in the near term and so was called a near term system. The existing near term threat was left for the far term and was designated the far term system! Well, that's government-speak. Confused? So was I. I never got used to it.

The Soviet threat was the most interesting. Finding a near term architecture to defeat this Soviet threat was my intent. Why had my predecessors thought it would take fifty years? The system they originally proposed was the legacy of an antique style of analysis. These static methods had the flavor of 1942. The techniques were wrong for the problem at hand.

A few years before taking this job I had briefly been a member of SDIO's Mission Analysis Working Group (MAWG). This was a highly classified, top level, strategic planning task force. To give you a flavor of the meetings, the room was of modest size with chairs for about a dozen people. Behind the working scientists and engineers a few representatives of the Joint Chiefs of Staff sat on a low platform. The job of the MAWG was to define exactly what a modern ballistic missile defense was supposed to do and how it was to do it. In effect the MAWG defined the missions, and the technology, needed to achieve President Reagan's Star Wars missile defense dream.

What surprised me the most about our meetings was the primitive nature of the analysis. The major contractors — Lockheed, Boeing, Rockwell, and so on — were using transparent overlays on maps to figure out how various systems would behave. Such an ancient technique seemed totally inappropriate to me in this age of dynamic computer simulation.

As I mentioned, my participation in the MAWG was brief. One day I greatly offended an Assistant Secretary of Defense with a question he did not like and did not want to answer. "Off with his head!" so to speak.

Still, the lessons of the MAWG remained with me. It was obvious such primitive static techniques had led to a near term SBL architecture which made no sense.

The problem with static analysis: Orbiting systems are *not* static. A *constellation* of satellites constantly changes its members' relationship to a rotating Earth and various launch sites. The constellation is tasked with engaging targets randomly popping up at random distances and directions. The combination of the constellation and the array of targets is actually a complex dynamic machine. It is a machine with many moving parts. Moreover, it is a machine which is asynchronous — no interaction with targets ever repeats. My predecessors did not recognize a dynamic system of this sort cannot be analyzed as a static system. They were trapped by their mathematical methodology and got the wrong answer.

What they arrived at was a small number of giant battle stations orbiting at high altitude. These stations had an important advantage: Each could see a relatively large area of the Earth. Unfortunately, this also meant they had a crippling disadvantage: Their engagements were at very long distances. Distance was the key. In order to get a sufficiently small focus spot on a target the telescope mirror for these types of battle stations had to be enormous — on the order of thirty meters in diameter. This concept was dead on arrival. Such a large telescope lacked the needed agility, even if it could be made.

Today, more than three decades later, there are still no ground based telescopes of this size. Today's biggest telescope mirrors are ten meters in diameter — a size that became operational when the Keck telescope went into use in 1992 and was therefore of interest for orbiting battle stations.

Because creating a telescope mirror of such large size was impossible, an optical phased array telescope was proposed. This was to be composed of a cluster of laser modules. Each module would have a laser, with its fuel tank, and a gimbled ten meter mirror. These modules would be coherently linked together with a complex assembly of optical trombones to provide phase control.

This concept was so implausible, and implausibly expensive, it threw a monkey wrench into President Reagan's Star Wars missile defense program. Lasers were put on the back burner in favor of interceptor rockets stationed in orbit.

That is where things stood when I started on the project. To discover a practical answer to the Soviet threat I needed to build a dynamic system simulator. The office had only one computer, an early generation personal computer. I needed my own full time computer. I had one at home. It had the added advantages of a more advanced operating system as well as a Fortran compiler. I brought it in to work and got started.

I constructed a time dependent simulation of a generic constellation of battle stations interacting with targets. What the software did was to set the constellation "machine" in motion, then sample and compile what was going on. It recorded all the key interactions — positions, distances, incident flux, angles, kill times, etc. — and presented the results as graphical plots.

Most important, each simulation run had to be fast. I designed the software with judicious shortcuts, permitting months of real-time constellation operation to be analyzed in a few seconds. With this software, a new constellation design could be quickly created and analyzed by simply typing in a few parameter changes. The graphical output consisted of time dependent plots and cumulative probability curves. These graphs showed at a glance the performance of any given system. It was now easy to study a wide variety of constellation configurations and target types. The consequences were dramatic.

A solution to the battle station enigma soon emerged. The solution came in stages. The first stage was to disassemble the phased array battle station. The new approach uncoupled each module of the original phased array battle station and transformed the modules into smaller autonomous battle stations. This had the advantage of eliminating most of the complexity of the original giant battle stations. So there would be major cost savings. Breaking up the massive battle stations into smaller platforms also added flexibility in choosing the orbits. A key result was that the altitude could be lowered and we could get closer to the target.

I proceeded to discover that adding just one of these new battle stations to the previously proposed architecture allowed a significantly lower orbit altitude while still retaining coverage of the Earth. This reduction of altitude meant a great reduction in the engagement range. It became evident the performance of the constellation was extremely sensitive to the number and altitude of the battle stations. The surprising result was that, with just one more of these smaller stations, the performance of the system actually more than doubled! It was now clear the previous architecture was far from optimum. And adding only a couple more platforms established an optimum altitude. The system performance was now more than a factor of four more effective than the original. The dynamic simulation was a vast improvement over static analysis.

At this point we had a system with only a few more "modules" than the giant phased array system required, yet the system performance was substantially greater — and much cheaper. This was now a robust system for dealing with third world threats. By adding still more of these smaller, cheaper, standard battle stations to the constellation the point soon reached a level which completely countered the Soviet threat. Start the production line, let it run, and the ballistic missile threat would soon be nothing but a memory. I had discovered a true paradigm shift.

Jason suppressed my findings. Our customer was kept in the dark. Most likely Jason had supervised the creation of the previous architecture. This new architecture far overshadowed the earlier efforts. I was frustrated but in the long run it didn't matter. My colleagues bought into my findings and their influence was what counted, as you shall see.

While I was working on the laser architecture various tasks took me back east. This gave me the opportunity to meet the company's president. This worked out well for me, partly because we liked each other, but also because the president shared my enthusiasm for Single Stage to Orbit (SSTO) rockets. The president introduced me to Max Hunter, America's great rocket pioneer. Early in a distinguished career Max developed the Thor missile. Today's workhorse Delta rocket is the upgraded descendent of Max's Thor.

Max was the leading exponent of SSTO rockets. His work had a major influence on the Star Wars effort. One result was SDIO funded the successful DC-X rocket test vehicle and the early stages of the X-33 rocket program. Unfortunately, NASA grabbed control of the X-33 program and deliberately killed it. My guess is they believed the X-33's offspring would make their darling Space Shuttle obsolete — which it would have. Well, that is history, bitter history for many of us.

I never met Max face to face, although we were in the same room together when SDIO kicked off the SSTO effort. However, we often talked on the phone and became friends. Max had a great influence on my later work.

Sometime during my employment Gary came on board as Jason's deputy. Gary became my supervisor. Gary was a mild and religious man — easy to converse with, easy to work with. He became a buffer between me and Jason. Jason was still pulling the strings, though. Though Gary was technically my boss now, Jason was still making my assignments.

You may ask why, after I had worked for him for years, Jason still behaved the way he did towards me. Who knows

what's in the mind of such an individual? Perhaps it was because he knew he couldn't tame me.

I was frustrated. On many occasions, after I had achieved
a significant result, I went to show Jason what I had discovered.
On every single occasion I can remember Jason, after a minute or two, dismissed me and rejected what I was presenting.
He never looked at my numbers or the hard work supporting
those numbers. Perhaps it was because he had been clobbered
on my account at the beginning. Still, in my half century in the
engineering profession I never ran into anyone who was quite
as close-minded as Jason.

At this point, Jason wanted me out of his hair more than
ever. He contrived to have our Rome, New York office invite
me to work with them on a task. This was to be in December
through January, with me stuck there over the Christmas
holidays. Jason suggested Rome would be a better place for
me and I should move there. I might have thought Jason was
being sarcastic but he had absolutely no sense of irony.

Few people who have been to Rome in the dead of winter
regard it as a garden spot — particularly if California is your
standard. I went, I survived, and I ignored Jason's invitation
to get lost. By this time I had too much leverage at corporate.

Jason tried another tactic. He gave me a task he was sure
would demoralize me: estimate the costs of a constellation of
laser battle stations. True enough, if there is one thing I have
never liked to do, it is estimating cost and schedule. But once
I got into it I discovered I actually liked the project! It had
fascinating aspects. Besides, my growing enthusiasm visibly
annoyed Jason.

It actually was natural I was given this task because I knew
more about laser battle stations than almost anyone in the

company. Before joining the division I had actually worked on the conceptual design of more than one of them.

In this new endeavor there was much to learn. This was completely new stuff. I started by believing this was going to be some kind of bookkeeping task. It wasn't. I was now dealing more with how to model the costs of the physical elements of a complex system. The methodology was used by the aircraft industry.

A complex system, like an aircraft, is composed of many different elements or subsystems. For example, an airplane has a fuselage, wings, tail, landing gear, engines, an electrical system, mechanical actuators, an autopilot, a cockpit, maybe a passenger or cargo compartment, radios, radar, landing gear and many other elements, which are its major components.

Each of these elements is a complex subsystem which can be further broken down into constituent components. Cost modeling creates an algebraic equation for each of these elements, first at the top level, then at each of the significant subsystem levels. Each equation, or cost estimating relationship is a plausible model of the manufacturing cost of its corresponding component.

To be useful it is necessary to calibrate the numerical parameters in a cost equation. The calibration is done by looking at a company's past manufacturing of similar items. If the new product is similar to existing products the corporation has a history to support the cost estimates. A fuel tank designer says how much fuel is needed, and what shape the tank must take. He plugs those numbers into the equation, together with how many are to be made, and out pops the estimated manufacturing cost. In many cases all an engineer has to do is hand the design specifications over to a cost specialist and walk away.

What everyone especially dreads is cost estimation when the company is venturing into a new technology area. For example, suppose an aircraft manufacturing company wants to bid on a Mach six hypersonic aircraft. The one and only Mach six aircraft anyone has ever built was the X-15, and that was sixty years ago. Some of the existing cost relationships can be carried forward, but most must be discarded and thought through from scratch.

Jason tasked me to do something even more challenging. I needed to establish the cost models for something that didn't exist except as an idea. An orbiting laser battle station is a vehicle which not only had no manufacturing heritage it didn't yet have fully developed technology. The whole project was full of unknowns. It could keep me busy for years.

Fortunately, I didn't have to start from scratch. I had the *blue books*. I had in fact everyone's blue book for space based laser systems. Naturally I had the Air Force Master Blue Book because, after all, I was the Government. I also had the blue books of all the major contractors interested in space based lasers. This was a surprise because the government typically would not have a contractor's blue book until deep into contract negotiations.

Because I had the blue books from everyone it was essential for me to not leak the proprietary information from one contractor to another. Firewalls were necessary. It turned out that was easy. All the blue books were identical — or nearly so. The cost estimating relationships were identical in all the blue books. There were some minor differences in the calibration numbers, but not enough to distinguish between the contractors. This was definitely odd.

Obviously the blue books were all derived from a common source. Perhaps the Air Force had generously given away its blue book. Unlikely. The government's blue book is used to judge the proposals coming from the contractors. Why give the contractors the answers before the quiz? More likely, the government had sponsored an industry study which generated the source blue book.

So, what is a blue book? It is the collection of cost estimating relationships, in the form of algebraic equations, for a given vehicle or system. Each participant's blue book is usually unique to that organization because it is design sensitive as well as proprietary.

All well and good — and useful to get me started. Unfortunately, all the blue books were wrong. It is likely Jason gave me this task because he thought I would get fed up and quit.

A couple of examples are illustrative: The blue book's radio equation said the cost of the radio was proportional to the mass of the battle station. The predicted cost of the radio came out to be more than a billion, in 1991 dollars. That absurd answer was because laser fuel made up most of the mass. Fuel had nothing to do with communications. A better model for the radio depended on the "link budget" and the bandwidth. The true cost would be a couple of million dollars at most. A second example said the cost of the ground based facilities is proportional to the number of battle stations. Again, a silly proposition. Only a single ground station could manage the entire constellation, no matter how many battle stations were involved.

As I got into these equations the project started to attract the attention of my colleagues. Soon I had a small group going over the equations. Jason was visibly annoyed at this but there was nothing he could do. My people were lunchtime volunteers. What was worse, there was a lot of laughter emanating from my cadre.

Several equations were the source of some of the merriment. Apparently the authors of the blue books did not quite understand economies of scale. Many of the equations had cost curves that fell below zero. So, buy enough battle stations and you could pay off the national debt!

After a while I had completed the functional decomposition of a typical battle station down a couple of levels. The next task was to start developing cost equations for each of these subsystems. I got no further. I was pulled off to work on something else. The cost exercise was turned over to one of my colleagues.

The new task was to do a trade study between the two leading chemical lasers. The office had real experts in these technologies. Gary was one of them. I was selected specifically because I was a novice and therefore unbiased. I enlisted Gary as my tutor and got to work. There was little to choose between these two laser types. They both had about the same energy efficiency. In the end I decided on one of them because it was a slightly simpler and more robust device. Gary agreed with my choice. Jason did not. He had a favorite and my choice was not his favorite. I submitted my report and forgot about it.

It was now late summer. All summer long a young man of about college age had been haunting the halls in the vicinity of Jason's office. He didn't appear to have any reason to be there since he wasn't part of the staff. Encounters with him were less than pleasant because of his arrogant sarcasm.

Our office suite had two halls which met at a right angle outside Jason's corner office. Across from Jason's office, at the apex of the two halls, was a commons room with a kitchen. This room had a doorway to each of the halls.

One day I was walking near one of the doors and heard a commotion inside the commons. I looked in. The young man was verbally assaulting one of our admin ladies. Very nasty he was. She was nearly in tears. I looked over to the other door. There was Jason, sporting a malicious grin, obviously enjoying the show. Jason caught sight of me as I turned away from this scene of horror.

The next day the lady was gone — quit or fired. The rest of the admin staff knew what happened and were upset but the technical staff never learned about it. I kept my mouth shut.

A week or so later Gary disappeared. After a few days he reappeared. He called me into his office. He looked haggard and upset. He told me I was fired.

Gary said it was Jason's decision because I had cheated on the laser trade study. Gary knew this was a lie because he had been intimately involved in the exercise and agreed with my decision. Obviously he had no choice but to deliver the message. In order to justify firing me Jason needed the excuse I had cheated the government.

Word got around quickly. As I was packing up my belongings many of the staff came to share their sorrow about this. It helped. But I was still in shock. This really hurt.

I was moving boxes out of my office when Jason came walking down the hallway towards me. He was animated with joy. I had seen that expression and dancing walk before.

Flashback to when I encountered my first truly sadistic bully. I was walking by the neighborhood pond one afternoon, on my way home from school, when this kid called me over. He asked if I wanted to see something neat. Of course I was curious to discover what he would show me.

On the ground in front of him was a good sized frog. The kid lit a firecracker and flung it toward the frog. The frog's tongue flicked out and the firecracker slid into its belly. A muffled pop and the frog turned inside out, its guts stringing along the ground as the frog dragged himself, twitching with exquisite pain, back toward the pond. I was utterly horrified. The kid, as he hopped and danced around, had an expression of satanic glee on his sweat sheening face. I fled.

Now I was confronting the same evil expression, facial sheen, and dance of pleasure when my boss, a mature sadist, thought he had traumatized me. His narcotic was power.

Jason believed he had finally crushed me. Sign these papers saying I would not sue the company and I would be given a few thousand dollars in exchange. I refused. I took his power away from him. Jason retreated back to his office, visibly deflated.

Life goes on. Sarah helped immensely though she, too, had been injured by this event.

I went back to free-lance consulting — working sixty hours a week to build a new clientele. One good thing: I was now free to talk directly to the government. I briefed the Air Force on my space based laser architecture. The Air Force commissioned a Summer Study, most likely conducted at my old office. Now my old colleagues could bypass Jason's veto. My architecture was adopted as the SDIO standard architecture.

Eventually my consulting work during this period paid dividends and I was hired as an Engineering Fellow at Raytheon. There I stayed many years until I retired. All the while I was meeting new colleagues and making new friends. And, making interesting new discoveries.

Some months after I was fired I encountered Gary. He looked better but had lost a lot of weight. He told me he was no longer working for Jason. He had taken a job in another state and was getting ready to move his family.

He told me what had happened. Those few days Gary had been out of the office he had been in the hospital recovering from surgery. A lung was cancerous and had to be removed. Jason pulled him out of the hospital (literally!) and informed him either he fired me or he would be fired. Gary did what he had to do and went back to his sick bed.

A few weeks later Gary returned to the office. Jason called him in and fired him!

The rest of this story recapitulates ancient Athenian theater: Hubris summons Nemesis. A couple of years after I was fired, Sarah and I were enjoying a celebratory dinner at a fine restaurant. There I ran into one of my old colleagues. I wondered how things were at the office. "Who knows?" was the reply. "We were so disgusted with the place almost all of us quit and formed our own company. Our contracts went with us, leaving Jason high and dry."

Sather Gate, UC Berkeley. Architect: John Galen Howard
Added to National Register of Historic Places Locations: March 25, 1982

STUFFING THE BRAIN

WE SPEND A LIFETIME LEARNING. Even the most mundane daily tasks can teach us something if we are receptive. But it is our early years that inundate us with an avalanche of new experiences and ideas. Somehow we survive the bombardment to grow and thrive until, upon reaching adulthood, the overwhelming flow of novelty abates somewhat.

There is adventure in those early years, adventure mixed with the inevitable pain of growing up. School can be fun. School can be a misery. School can be fascinating. School can be good or it can be bad. It all depends on who is teaching us and what subjects we are absorbing. Learning can be hard or easy, fascinating or intimidating, or deadly dull. What we respond to, and how we respond, depends on our individual talents for each of us is different and unique.

During what feels like the longest time of our life we are in the hands of teachers, for good or ill. Both the good and the bad have much to teach us, though not necessarily what these teachers intend. With the experience of adulthood we can look back on those formative years and find much to entertain us. We can be amused now because we no longer are immersed in those difficult times.

There are stories I can tell about my formative years. Stories of the good and the bad, the dark and the light.

I will tell of both. In the end for me it all worked out remarkably well. My education was a series of memorable, and
often entertaining, adventures.

STRAIGHT OFF THE BOAT

'BOUT A CENTURY AGO SOMEONE NOTICED the wide eyed expressions of people who were pouring off the boats into The City (you know which one) and labeled those innocents *Straight Off The Boat.*

Now, not all who fit into the broad category of immigrant were truly innocent, but all these newcomers had to make major adaptations to the New World and a new way of life, so the expression seemed to fit. At any rate, the appellation stuck and we still call the young and innocent *Straight Off The Boat.*

Of all the newly arrived, the most innocent of the innocent apparently were the Irish. Actually, I must limit myself to Irish men, for I have never met an Irish woman who was *wet behind the ears.*

Part of my education was spent in Catholic schools. Catholic Elementary School, starting midway through fifth grade, and Catholic High School. The teachers in these schools were Irish, so I became well acquainted with the type at an early age. Elementary school was staffed by nuns of varying ages. The best word to describe this formidable collection of women is shrewd. It was impossible to get anything by those hawk-eyed ladies.

High school was staffed by priests. These fellows were from Ireland as well. At least one of them was brilliant, but he was the exception. The rest could best be described as *devious.* (The brilliant priest could be devious, too, but mostly he didn't have to be.) This faculty needed to be devious, for true Americans, besides being *upright, honest* and *open* in most things, are also, when occasion demands (as it frequently did in *that* high school) both shrewd *and* devious. Somehow we students survived.

Then, one day, we students were faced with a true marvel: A priest who was neither shrewd nor devious, but was as open, upright and honest as the *best American.* This good priest was really *straight off the boat.* He had arrived in America by sea only a few days before the beginning of my senior year.

This Good Father was young and recently ordained. Indeed, he was only a handful of years older than ourselves, which gave us the advantage. Our school was his first assignment in The World as well as in The New World. So he had much to learn, and we had much to teach him. Because, at the Seminary, he had done very well in Theology he was given the impossible assignment of making us holy by teaching us religion. Our job was to make him an American. Which is to say, we intended to *straighten him out* (which could also be interpreted to mean *make him devious*). As you might expect, a collision was about to happen. The surprising thing is how it all worked out.

The contest turned on a handful of mud. A dutiful son, and a good Irish country lad, the Good Father had imbibed the Church's teachings without moderation and passed on to us, without moderation, his understanding of the Infallible Teachings. He was, in short, a biblical literalist. God created the world in six days and rested on the seventh. There was no room in his vision of reality for other possibilities.

During the course of our instruction we arrived at Noah and the Great Flood. The whole world was covered with water and all drowned except Noah, his family and the creatures he saved. So sayeth the Bible, so sayeth the Catholic Church, so sayeth the Good Father.

How silly, was the response from an unruly student who had had enough of this ignorant nonsense. The Universe was ancient beyond dreaming. Earth was billions of years old. There was not enough water on, and in, the planet to drown the world. There was continuity of life, absent occasional *partial* extinctions, such as the Cretaceous and the Permian. Besides, the story of Noah was simply a variation on flood stories that were popular throughout the ancient Middle East. It seemed to be an adaptation of parts of the much older Epic of Gilgamesh. That there had been a catastrophic flood was likely, especially since digs in Sumerian cities showed a thick layer of mud which clearly separated the more primitive Neolithic and Chalcolithic cultures from the later and rapidly flowering Mesopotamian civilization. But, however great this flood, it was purely local and had no effect on the rest of the planet.

This was all explained to the Good Father in the superior tone of voice of a know-it-all adolescent. The class murmured its collective agreement. Most of us were well read in the latest scientific discoveries.

The Good Father could not believe what he was hearing from the desks before him. This was *heresy*, and from the senior class of a Catholic High School, to boot. Had not three previous years of theological instruction, and many years of Catholic teaching before that, had its effect?

We assured the Good Father that we were in the right. He should do his homework, and stop bothering us with such simplicity. The class ended with mutual glares.

The next day the Good Father was visibly haggard when he showed up in class. He had been up all night responding to our challenge that he do his homework. He told us that he had been researching in the Catholic Encyclopedia, and elsewhere. Now, the Catholic Encyclopedia is a work of great erudition, compiled by eminent and highly intelligent scholars (eminent and highly intelligent do not necessarily go together). Among the knowledgeable, the Catholic Encyclopedia has a reputation for fairness, completeness and literary excellence which rivals that scholarly pinnacle of Victorian optimism, the Eleventh Edition of the Encyclopedia Britannica.

The Good Father opened the class with a confession that he had intended to show us just how wrong we were. But his researches surprised him. The Encyclopedia, and the other sources that he perused, confirmed *our* position. We were right! He then proceeded to fill the class in on details that were novel to us. He concluded with recent theological interpretations which showed how this section of the Bible illuminated certain questions of morality.

I was amazed and impressed. This Good Father was truly *honest, open* and *forthright.* He was a gem. The rest of the class responded likewise. From that day the class became a working session with give and take and many lessons learned both ways.

As we relaxed into a better relationship, the Good Father began telling us something of the experiences of the Irish country lad that he had been. The day came when someone asked how he had decided to enter the Seminary. The Good Father responded with his story.

It started at a dance, he said. The clear indication, from his words and tone, was that he had been highly bothered by the piercing glances from a lovely young colleen. Tall and handsome himself, I could see why he might have attracted such attention.

The hormones must have been flooding through him for he apparently suffered from highly tempting and sinful thoughts. These devilish notions bothered him considerably during and after the dance and he felt that he must have radiated some aura of his excess stimulation. For, on the long walk home a Banshee sensed his disturbance and began stalking him from high overhead. As the Banshee's wail grew louder the yet-to-be Good Father became frightened. He began running. Faster and faster he ran. Miles and miles fled beneath his flying feet. The Banshee grew ever closer until he could sense its dark shape and its burning eyes, just over his head. The chilling wail grew louder and still louder until he knew he was doomed.

He started praying as he ran and these prayers became his salvation. His prayers were a ward which kept the Banshee from closing the final distance and devouring him. At last, stumbling from exhaustion, he paced off the final yards to his front door and safety. That night he resolved to enter the Seminary and become a priest. Never again would he fall into the clutches of the Devil.

What a tale! None of us knew how to respond. We just shook our heads in wonder at what we had just heard.

The next day someone asked the Good Father if he really believed in Banshees. He assured us that not only did he believe, but that they were known to be quite common in his part of Ireland. Many people had not survived their encounters with

Banshees. These young men and women would leave their cottages one day, and would never be seen again. This had particularly been the case during the Great Potato Famine in the previous century. Some said that the youngsters had fled across the sea, but that was unlikely for it was a time of great sinfulness and Banshees abounded.

Were there other such spirits and creatures in the Irish countryside, he was asked. He assured us that there were, and not all of them were evil. Indeed, the little Fairies were highly protective if they were treated with respect and kindness.

He admitted that he had not personally seen the wee fairies, but trustworthy older women said that *they* had. Besides, he had proof.

What proof? We asked. In response he told us that every evening a bowl of milk was placed out on the step to provide sustenance for the *little folk*. In the morning the milk would be gone. That was certainly proof.

One of my classmates was skeptical. Were there *cats* in the neighborhood?

"Oh, no," he said, "cats eat mice, they don't drink milk."

True. *My* cats won't drink milk either....

THE ART OF NEGOTIATION

THIS WASN'T THE FIRST TIME I had been to Tijuana. Many years before I met Sarah I had visited TJ a few times, mostly to buy inexpensive gifts I could afford with my slim student's budget. It was on one of those earlier trips I learned the fine Art of Negotiation.

My primary purpose on that occasion was to find my way to the Candelas guitar shop, and dream of someday owning one of those renowned instruments. But that excursion would come later in the day — sometime after I had wandered down to the Glass Factory. There I worked up a good sweat, and drank a frosty Coke while watching the artisans draw lumps of glowing glass from the blazing furnaces, and blow, twist and squeeze the heavy gelatinous material into fanciful shapes full of color.

Later, as I wandered up the street toward the guitar shop, my eye was caught by a most peculiar object. Suspended high on the back wall of a shop was the tackiest black velvet painting I had ever seen. It stood out, even on a street where such garish items were commonplace. Sacrilegiously hung between two simpering Madonnas was a curvaceous but awkward nude — glowing with florescent colors against the infinite black background.

A buxom lady, she was. Her back was turned to the viewer, but she had swiveled a bit so as to show enough of her charms to beguile the fantasies of passing youths, of whom there were plenty wandering up and down the long street. I was amazed, I was amused. It occurred to me this masterpiece of kitsch might someday grace some broken down border bordello.

I could not help myself. I was drawn into the shop and found myself lingering awhile over the variety of heavy leather goods, crude ceramics and knick knacks fabricated of wrought iron. All the while I could not help but occasionally glance at the monstrosity perched on high. The shrewd proprietor of the shop must have noticed my interest, but he pretended not to.

Finally, I had to know. I moseyed up to the counter and casually inquired about the price of the magnificent work of art on the wall. I had no intention of buying it, I declared, I just wanted to know how much he was asking. The proprietor quickly suppressed a bit of a smirk and quoted a figure. A hundred dollars, I believe it was, a considerable sum in those distant days before galloping inflation. Nonsense, I responded. We both know it isn't worth a tenth of that, I said. Besides which, I added, I wasn't interested in buying it, I was simply curious. The proprietor didn't blink. A crafty look crept over his face. This was going to be fun. He quoted a somewhat lower price. It was still an insult. No thanks, I said. I started drifting towards the door. The proprietor followed me. Since I was such a nice, courteous young man he was willing to give me a special price, he cut his previous quote in half. I wasn't interested. I *really* wasn't interested, I told him. I was through the door now, and onto the sidewalk.

The proprietor followed me out. He trailed a couple of paces to one side, as we walked, and lowered his price still more. I couldn't hold my dignity any longer. A slight grin crept across my face. I suppressed it, but he caught it. He was grinning, now, as well.

I reached the crowded street corner. The light turned green and I joined the multitude crossing to the other side. As I stepped off the curb he tested me once more. Following me, and with a bit of a whine in his voice, he begged me to please take it off his hands, it was driving good customers away. No dice, I responded.

He followed me half way across the street and shouted his final offer: "Senor, I'll give you ten dollars to take it off my hands." We were both laughing, almost uncontrollably, by then.

The proprietor retreated to his shop, sure to tell a good story to his compadres. I later returned home with the warm satisfaction of having driven the ultimate in bargains. And, I escaped from the black velvet monster.

After a recital at Charles Music
I'm the guy in the front row on the left

LEARNING MUSIC

How does one get to be a pretty good musician? Undoubtedly for each the road is different. In my case it started with a tambourine. I hated the thing! Well, I did not so much hate the tambourine as hate the fact that I always ended up with the useless contraption. Invariably the teacher would give me one without even a drum head, just a hoop with jangling little round jinglies.

On these occasions the entire fourth grade would gather around the flag pole on the lawn in front of R.D. White Elementary School for "music" lessons. I put *music* in quotes because there was nothing musical about what transpired. Various percussion instruments were handed out — real drums to the favored boys. A few bells, triangles and a couple of glockenspiels went to the favored girls (in those distant days girls and boys were still thought of as different). Since there were not enough regular instruments to go around, the "orchestra" was filled out with pots and pans and big spoons. Most of these things made a satisfying noise. But a tambourine? In all that racket you couldn't hear the darned thing if it were more than an inch away from your ear, and the teacher insisted I keep the pathetic object out in front of me where she could see it.

Needless to say, not all the kids were little Mozarts, though the teacher expected all of us to become so. This was the latest educational fad, you see.

I'll leave it to your imagination what it was like, before you flee to some equally imaginary sanctuary of peace and quiet.

When I relayed these proceedings to Mom she determined I should have proper musical training. Now, we had always had all kinds of music around us. We sang together all the time and the radio supplied pop, jazz and classical music. The NBC Symphony Orchestra, led by the incomparable Arturo Toscanini, was a particular favorite. So it was natural the emphasis in my training should be towards classical music.

Sometimes when you are immersed in something you simply don't see it. Los Angeles, in the fifties, was a mecca for many of the world's finest musicians and composers. Hitler's takeover of Central Europe had driven some of Europe's greatest talents to the United States, and a good number of them had migrated to Los Angeles — partly because of the climate, partly because other gifted refugees had settled here to create a substantial colony, but mostly because the movie studios meant the money was here, big money.

Where else could you find Jascha Heifetz, Gregor Piatigorsky and William Primrose every week happily serenading Sunday picnickers at outdoor concerts?

One day we drove up to a small, old, Craftsman Bungalow. The house was freshly painted white with green trim. The yard was tidy, with pillows of colorful flowers and large trees shading an immaculately manicured lawn. Mom and I walked along a cobble brick path to the house. A little old lady answered the door and we were invited in to her front parlor. Most of the airy space was occupied by a grand piano. I was introduced to the lady and, after some negotiation, it was arranged that I would take weekly lessons there. The lady was charming, with a mild foreign accent which did not get in the way of understanding. It was clear from the discussion this was a lady of outstanding reputation as a piano teacher. I could hardly wait to begin my lessons.

The first lesson took place then and there. The teacher wanted Mom to see her method of instruction. The lesson went well, with the lady showing me the keyboard and how harmonious sounds could be drawn out with different combinations of keys. Mom and I left with both of us happy, and I particularly eager for the next lesson — a whole too distant week away.

When Mom picked me up after the next week's lesson she knew immediately something was terribly wrong. I was silent and sullen. My hands were red and swollen and I was fighting back my tears, signs my mother, good nurse that she was, saw immediately. Days passed before I began to talk about it. When she finally teased the story out of me, Mom immediately went and confronted the teacher.

I expect the teacher, given her exalted reputation, probably felt she could intimidate anyone. I doubt, though, she had ever before run into someone like my mother. Mom, young, petite and pretty as she was, had, after all, been trained as a nurse in the hell of Bellevue, had nursed the sick and dying in the backwoods and swamps of disease ridden Georgia, and had daily braved the dangers of Hunters Point's rough ghetto. When she needed to be, Mom was as hard and tough as well tempered stainless steel — all four feet, eleven inches of her. I might, in retrospect, have pity for the teacher when Mom stormed up, but what happened during my lesson moderates any such feeling.

I remember trying as hard as I could to please the woman. I remember her patience growing short and her accent thickening into incomprehensibility when I did not instantly and perfectly perform each new exercise. Ultimately I understood nothing she said, but still I tried to please. I remember my small fingers on my small hands being pulled apart — stretched, she said — until the pain was unbearable. I remember the long wooden ruler being hard slapped — *Thwack!* — across my hand with each fumbled note. The pain!

The woman may have escaped from Nazi tyranny, but she brought the worst of her Teutonic heritage with her.

I do not know what my mother said to the woman, but she had clearly crossed the line in her abuse of a child. Some months later we heard the piano teacher had sold her house and departed to a place unknown.

Sometimes light comes from the darkness. For me light soon materialized on my daily walk home from school.

The year was 1951. I was nine years old. Every day I passed a small shop. The place was a hole in the wall, but to me it was magical. It was a hobby shop, full of wonderful model airplanes, trains and ships. There was no greater attraction imaginable to a small boy. To grown men, as well. Even in mid-afternoon, when school had just let out, there always were young men, and old, hanging out in this small wonderland. The men talked about more than models and the techniques needed to build and operate them. They talked about the war, the one then underway in Korea and the big one that had ended not long before. These were veterans, no doubt, as were the owners, and the hobby shop was a place where such men could hang out and swap tales and experience. With its growing clientele the hobby shop prospered. When a new row of shops was constructed, a block up the street, the hobby shop moved there into much larger quarters and continued prospering. And I continued visiting it.

The tiny old former hobby shop was boarded up and left alone to gather dust from the heavy automobile traffic passing nearby. I pretty much forgot about the old place until, one day, I found its door was once again open. The doorway was filled with a short, roly-poly, jolly young man. He was busy painting the door jamb while smiling to himself and humming a catchy tune. I was not a shy child, so I stopped and asked who he was and what he was up to. Never one for formality, he responded his name was Dick. Dick Charles, he said. He had acquired the store and he and his wife were musicians. They were going to give music lessons.

In time this tiny little store grew into what many believe to be the largest music emporium west of the Mississippi — but this development was still many years off.

We talked while he painted. Mr. Charles told me he played wind instruments, all kinds, but he particularly liked the clarinet and saxophone. His wife and college sweetheart, Ruth, played the piano. After my brief experience with the dreadful teacher I was not at all interested in the piano. But learning to play wind instruments sounded intriguing. Dick Charles was a true pied piper and I became hooked by his enthusiasm for woodwinds. I couldn't wait until Mom got home from work so I could tell her of my discovery.

Mom, of course, was cautious after my experience with the Wicked Witch of the West. The two of us met briefly with Mr. Charles, after which Mom and Mr. Charles stepped into his office for a private conference. I waited impatiently outside for its outcome. Satisfied with Dick Charles' assurances, Mom let me proceed with lessons.

In the beginning my hands were still a bit too small for the nickel-silver clarinet I was to start with. A few months of growth would remedy this situation. Instead of playing various notes on the instrument we concentrated on developing my embouchure and learning the basics of rhythm and music notation. Embouchure is a fancy French word for how you hold and maintain the muscles of your mouth while playing the instrument. At first the musculature is weak and the instrument squeaks with almost every note. In time, and with lots of practice, the muscles strengthen and the sound becomes sweet. Creating a particularly sweet sound ultimately was one of my greatest musical accomplishments.

As I grew into the instrument, I also learned to play it. Later I was introduced to the saxophone, and still later, trumpet and flute. Musical theory acquainted me with the cycle of fifths, ornamentation and the principles of jazz performance. While attending Michigan State, Dick Charles had formed a popular swing band. Jazz was in his soul, as was the precision playing of complex rhythms swing demanded.

Dick also loved classical music, particularly Baroque. The Baroque revival was just getting started, and the Renaissance revival was still a decade away. I am, to this day, struck by this man's understanding of this early music and his comments that much of Baroque music, unlike the later Classical and Romantic periods, was improvisational in its nature, built upon a framework of chord progressions with ornamented melody, and loosely flowing, swinging rhythms. The instrumental voices, singing in counterpoint, held lively conversations

— tossing melodic ideas back and forth, much like Dixieland. As he often said, it was early jazz.

This knowledge had not, as yet, filtered completely through the classical music community. Sunday afternoon concerts on the radio usually featured chamber music groups. These groups were exploring some of the little known byways of Baroque music, with its complex counterpoint and unfamiliar harmonies. Invariably this music, in strong reaction to the laxness of late Romantic practice, was played with rigid tempo, no ornamentation and a mechanical style. In my family we jokingly dubbed the performances "sewing machine music." As ongoing scholarship soon showed, our musical instincts were right on.

I must admit for all Dick Charles' coaching on the subject, I did not do well with counterpoint. I simply could not maintain an independent line while Dick was playing his. The problem was solved when Mr. Charles started to staff up. One of his earliest staff teachers also taught woodwinds, but at an advanced level. Dick passed me on, for a while, to Studio Guy. This new teacher was a super pro, working in the movie studios. I was dazzled. Studio Guy could play anything, the first time, with perfection. He demonstrated this during one lesson by sight reading his way through a transcript of a Benny Goodman solo. I looked at the chart and could not make heads or tails of the complex notation of insanely tricky rhythms and ornamentation. I never was able to master the piece.

Studio Guy's job was to diagnose my problem and fix it. It turned out I was following the notes of the other voice instead of maintaining my own independent line. The solution was simple. We went back to basics, with a greatly slowed tempo and with Studio Guy insisting I once again tap my toe — hard, this time, in sync with a mechanical metronome — instead of relying on an internal beat. At first I felt a bit humiliated I had to regress to a much earlier stage in my learning, but after a couple of lessons Studio Guy's wisdom became apparent. Now we could play counterpoint duets together with perfectly interwoven conversation. I was exhilarated!

I learned quickly. In a few weeks we advanced through progressively more complex rhythms and technically more difficult pieces. Soon I was holding my own with almost anything Studio Guy threw at me, all sight reading, of course.

One Sunday afternoon, during the Studio Guy period, on our way back from the beach I turned on the car's radio. A chamber group was working its way through some intricate Baroque masterpiece. Bach, it must have been. Suddenly, with a flash of insight, I fully understood the composer's intentions. It was a revelation! I would never look at music the same again.

With Studio Guy's task complete he passed me back to Dick Charles to prepare me for my final, a solo recital. Recital, a word to throw terror into the heart of most any music student. We all had to suffer this rite of passage every year. A more primitive society usually was kinder — its rite of passage occurred only once in the life of a youngster.

For my final recital Dick Charles decided I was ready to perform Mozart's miraculous and challenging Clarinet Concerto. I did well at the recital. But, I must say, after playing the thing hundreds of times I simply could not listen to another performance of it. Several decades had to pass before I could hear any part of the intensely familiar piece and not reflexively switch off the radio.

This last recital completed my regular music lessons, but not my training. Soon after my final solo recital Studio Guy formed a small orchestra at Charles Music, now housed in a much larger store. I started playing with the ensemble — quite a novelty for me because formerly I had only played duets with my teachers. I found orchestral playing to be a thoroughly enjoyable experience. A few weeks after I joined the orchestra, Dick Charles committed his studio to supplying a saxophone quintet for a special upcoming concert. I was asked to be a member. Studio Guy was given the charter of preparing the group for its performance.

With the reputation of Charles Music on the line, this performance had to be something special. Studio Guy selected for us a most exceptionally difficult piece, Stan Kenton's *Opus in Pastels.* After a couple of sessions I was named the lead sax, a position I held in all the bands and orchestras I subsequently joined.

Rehearsals were brutal. We met every couple of nights for hours of struggle. In between we practiced our parts at home. Initial efforts were, to put it mildly, ragged. Studio Guy turned into a fire breathing top sergeant, unsatisfied with the slightest imperfection. He kept barking: "Listen . . . listen to each other. Listen to what each of the others is doing. Listen to how the parts fit together. Listen. Know exactly what the others must do and will do."

Slowly, very slowly, the parts began merging into a harmonious whole, as if a single instrument were playing. We started working on dynamics and varying the tempo, smoothly accelerating and growing louder when the piece was firing up, slowing and quieting as the mood shifted to reflective. All this on top of the most difficult fingerings, rhythms and shifting key signatures. Suddenly, almost as if by magic, it all came together. We literally danced with joy and exclamations that first time we achieved perfection. The true miracle followed: Slowly, very slowly, dour Studio Guy broke into a great, broad, sunny smile.

We now were a true ensemble, a single, wonderful instrument, each member having almost telepathic empathy with the others. We were finally ready. For the first time I fully understood what real musicianship is all about.

The concert performance went perfectly. It was followed by a standing ovation.

I was now ready to turn pro.

IN THE MOOD

DOUG HAD MADE ALL THE ARRANGEMENTS. We were ready. Months of intense rehearsal had polished the ensemble to form a single harmonious instrument. We knew the music by heart, but Doug had insisted we have it on the stands in front of us. Nothing must go wrong. No one should misplay a single note.

This was the Big Night. This was the Battle of the Bands. Bands from all over Southern California were here, this night, to show their stuff. But we knew we were the best. We would be the winners.

The stage at John Muir High School in Pasadena was a bit smaller than we expected. That was all right. We simply scrunched the cardboard music stands, and our chairs, closer together to form a tighter, interlocking, phalanx across the stage.

The curtains were still closed. Doug gave the downbeat and we began. We did not need a director. Long rehearsals, together with our already well developed musical skills, had blended the band into a perfect ensemble — a true Chamber Orchestra.

We began with the familiar syncopated polyrhythm:

dah-di-DAH-di-dah-DAH-di-di-DAH-di-dah-dah . . .

The opening was soft, very soft. For the audience it was as if some wonderful sound was wafting in from far, far away.

The long refrain repeated, a bit louder this time — the band was coming closer. It repeated a third time, rising jubilantly to proclaim we had, at last, arrived.

dah-di-DAH-di-dah-DAH-di-di-DAH-di-dah-dah . . .

The curtains swept opened. The lights turned bright blue, as planned. Blue for the feel of the piece: Glenn Miller's *In The Mood.*

The lights turned bluer and dimmed, and dimmed and dimmed some more, until the stage had darkened into near night. As one we bent down close to the music stands, barely able to see the notes.

Someone bent too far. His stand kicked over. Like tumbling dominoes all the stands in the front row fell over, one after the other, slowly, majestically, unstoppable. The sheet music went flying across the stage, each sheet floating frictionless on a thin cushion of air until the pages finally fetched up on the wooden reef which guarded the edge of the stage.

The audience sat stunned for a moment. Slowly, starting with occasional titters, the laughter began. The laughter swelled and swelled until its roar drowned out the tattered remnants of music — even in our ears.

But then, something amazing happened. The ragged music knitted back together, as if by magic. Before the lights again brightened to full intensity our two rows of wind instruments stood up, as one, kicked aside the remaining music stands, spread out across the stage, dancing a bit as we moved, and, stronger still, repeated the catchy refrain:

dah-di-DAH-di-dah-DAH-di-di-DAH-di-dah-dah . . .

The laughter died away, to be replaced by a swelling, happy roar of cheers as the audience caught on to what we were up to. Our entrance had been a joke — a great comic satire. Here was the real band — strutting its stuff. Soon we had couples jitterbugging in the aisles. We ended the set in triumph and swept the competition.

A nice fantasy, that. But it didn't happen. The reality saw musicians scrambling to re-erect the music stands, pick up the charts, painfully sort through the shuffled sheets and restore them to their proper places. The brass and rhythm sections struggled to maintain some semblance of music —vamp till ready, as they used say — while the admittedly comic chaos swirled around the too small stage. At the end of our allotted three pieces, the audience gave us a good round of applause for sportsmanship, but there was no banana.

Afterward we held our post-concert celebration anyway. Well, I guess a wake is a kind of celebration. We had prepared for every conceivable contingency — except for losing our light. A contingency, after all, has to be conceivable. The gloom at the party was nearly as dark as it had been on the stage. But we resolved to soldier on. After all, we still had lucrative dances to play. And, as it turned out, we became quite popular.

Doug Koch's large swing band, *The Moonlighters* (a 50s doo-wop kind of name), was already well established before I found out about it. By then I must have had a reputation as an accomplished musician for I joined the band by invitation.

I played clarinet and saxophone, my first love being the alto sax. My first teacher had helped me develop a particularly sweet and liquid tone. My second teacher gave me the ability to sight read scores of great rhythmic complexity, at speed and with musical interpretation. He also perfected my ability to blend in an ensemble. This good man, whose name is lost in the mists of time, was a Hollywood studio musician. In my opinion studio musicians are the best of the best and I felt fortunate to be trained by a man with such a high level of expertise. As a result, upon completion of my basic training I was ready for much more.

Doug's band was a good one. Each member had been hand-picked for outstanding tone, ability to sight read anything — no matter how tricky — perfect rhythm, and an ear for blending with an ensemble. On the first evening of rehearsal I felt completely at home. These guys were fully professional, though all, like me, were still high school students. The first rehearsal proved to be a lot of fun.

Before the contest we had practiced in the guest house of a wooded palatial estate nestled in the hills of Flintridge. This estate was the family home of one of our members, but he was soon to graduate and enter college. For a while thereafter, we were reduced to playing in someone's emptied out garage. Nothing wrong with being a garage band. Many famous groups got their start that way. (Eventually the parents of one of our members took pity on us and from that time on, we had the comfort of playing in a living room. Thank goodness! Southern California winters can get bone chillingly cold.)

Playing in a garage, with its terrible acoustics and horrible heat and cold, was not our only travail. We had no piano there and we soon lost our drummer — his family was moving. Prospects could not have been worse, especially since Doug was busy picking up contracts for dances we somehow had to fulfill.

IN THE MOOD

We solved the problem of the piano by bringing in an electric guitar. This instrument could support the group with bass chords, much as a piano. And, like a piano, the guitar could double any of the wind instruments and fill out the sound. Later, the living room had a piano so we rehired our pianist, and kept the guitar. This gave us the flexibility to play almost any venue, with or without a piano.

Drums were a different matter entirely. Without drums the band would die. The night our old drummer was playing his last with us he mentioned this kid he had heard about. The kid was much younger than we were, but he was supposed to be pretty good. Maybe he could help out for the interim until we got ourselves a *real* drummer.

Doug made the phone call and, at the next rehearsal, we discovered Drummer Kid was far superior to our old drummer. We were back in business, better than ever. Well, almost.

It turned out when Drummer Kid's mom eventually heard we were a bunch of high school students she vetoed our band. The kid's mom knew her son had talent and she was determined to shape his career. Drummer Kid would play only with the best — a high school age band was off limits. We didn't know this, at first. Drummer Kid would go to bed early, open his bedroom window, and sneak out to play with us. When we found this out we realized we had a crisis on our hands.

Doug and I went to see Drummer Kid's mom. She was courteous, offering us refreshments, and a place to sit and chat. But she was also a frosty stone wall. Drummer Kid *could not* join us.

We talked. Doug was a charmer and he turned it full on. Doug apologized for our role in Drummer Kid's behavior. We hadn't known. Rather surprisingly, she accepted our apology.

She started asking questions about our backgrounds and our goals, and about the other members of the band, as well. Slowly the ice started to melt and crack away. Reluctantly, and only because Drummer Kid liked our band so much, she agreed he could play with us, but only under the most strictly controlled conditions. This strictness was especially important because of his recent disobedience and also his young age.

The crisis past, we were back in business.

How good was Drummer Kid? He used to tell us stories about sitting in for Shelly Manne down at Howard Rumsey's famous Lighthouse jazz club. He was too young to be legally allowed near the bar so he had to sneak onto the stage from a grungy entrance off the alley behind the night club.

I only half believed his tales until one day Drummer Kid asked me to play with some of his friends at a New Year's Eve gig. That evening I found myself surrounded by notable jazz musicians. As I said, I could sight read most anything, and my sound production and sense of ensemble was as good as any, so my alto sax blended nicely with those guys. Don't get me wrong, they were far better musicians than I would ever be, but I felt almost at home with their relaxed good humor and style of playing. The pay for the evening was, for a high school student, outstanding as well.

The Moonlighters had a special relationship with Stan Kenton's music. When the band migrated from the garage to the living room we found ourselves in the possession of a carton box of treasures, unpublished and unknown manuscripts in Kenton's hand.

The parents who loaned us the living room were, themselves, musicians of considerable accomplishment. The father had been a member of Stan Kenton's orchestra. It happened

Kenton had, some years before, been experimenting with compositions which were half classical and half jazz. Kenton was ahead of his time. Years later this fusion of classical and jazz was to blossom into a full blown movement led by Gunther Schuler. For whatever reason Kenton never published these experiments. They were boxed up and found themselves tucked away in a closet near the living room's front door, there to gather the dust of years, forgotten by almost all.

The night these treasures were rediscovered we rushed through our regular rehearsal and dove into the box. The results thrilled us. From the first we knew we had come across something special. We decided, on the spot, to incorporate these Kenton experiments into our repertoire. How to do this? Our solution was to use the middle set of a dance as a fusion jazz concert. For the first set we played mostly upbeat pieces. After the first break we held the Kenton concert. The third set returned to dancing with the emphasis gradually shifting to slow and dreamy pieces as the evening drew to a close. This arrangement became our signature and was invariably popular.

Looming over the dance season was the question of what to do about next spring's Battle of the Bands. That we were going to enter was clear. The real question was *how* we were going to win, and win big. From our previous hard experience we knew the stage was too small for our full band. After much discussion we decided to do something completely different. We would become a chamber sextet. This meant cutting the band down to minimal size. Now, we would have to work extra hard to emulate the depth of sound of a fine string quartet, so well blended as to sound like a single instrument. But, this meant several members would not participate. There were no objections. We would all stand (except for Drummer Kid) and we would be spread out in a line across the stage. No music stands this time, just play from memory.

Instrumental arrangements figured out, we had to make the hard decisions about what music to play, and how to balance the band so the sound was full with fewer musicians. The first and last pieces of the three allowed were obvious, but we had a real challenge with what to do about the middle piece. All of us were torn between repeating *In The Mood* or premiering one of the Kenton manuscripts. We initially favored *In The Mood* because, after all, we were a dance band and this piece was perfectly suited to our purposes (besides giving us the opportunity to obliterate the memory of last year). On the other hand, the previously unknown Kenton pieces were fresh and lively, and sure to be crowd pleasers. We put off the decision until we'd worked our way through the box of Kenton treasures. The problem was solved when we found a Kenton manuscript with a swinging rhythm and sweet harmonies perfect for dancing. Kenton it would be.

That didn't completely solve our problem, however. The Kenton chart was meant for a full orchestra and we would be a small group. For counterpoint we needed to balance brass against reeds, so we settled on two saxes and two brass. This meant Doug on tenor sax and me on alto, together with a trumpet and a trombone. And guitar and drums for rhythm. It took some clever arranging — with the guitar filling out the harmonies and doubling several of the instruments — to make it seem like we were a big band.

The night of the Battle we were ready. Those of us going on the stage had, for most of the year, worked through many extra rehearsals in addition to our regular dance rehearsals, so early on the pieces were rock solid. And the last few months we had concentrated on perfecting those subtleties making us into a true chamber ensemble.

Now it was our turn. We walked onto the stage behind closed curtains. Our guitarist checked to make sure his instrument and amplifier were perfect. We had warmed up back stage so we were ready to go. The announcer, in front of the curtain, made the introduction. There was a slight titter from the audience, as many there had witnessed the previous year's debacle.

The curtain swept open. We quietly stood there for a few moments, spread out across the stage. The audience began to feel, from the way we stood, something special was about to happen. The auditorium became silent. I began to play — quite alone. From my instrument poured liquid notes, a sweet sound, but with tears amidst its sweetness. As the melody swelled I stepped forward a bit, the other band members closing ranks behind me. I carried the people with me across the continent to distant Harlem, Harlem on a hot, steamy summer night. *Harlem Nocturne* grew more powerful, every note an agony. Behind me my friends occasionally commented, their instruments softly blending with mine: *Yes brother, yes, we feel your pain, we feel your agony. Let it out, friend, let it all out. Drain away the sorrow.*

The audience was deathly still, now, hanging on every note. Gradually, as the music reached its climax a feeling of happiness started to infuse the mood. By the last chorus the music had changed from a tone of pure pain to the prospect of joy. The whole band joined in, in appreciation of this happier feeling. The piece, now upbeat, drew to a rousing close. The audience sat there stunned. For long moments there was not a sound from the black space in front of us. Then, swelling from a few scattered claps, came full applause, capped by a mighty, thunderous, ovation.

Before the applause had fully died away we launched into the Kenton — the whole band, this time, showing off our stuff: a good swinging beat, happy sounds, joyous sounds. By the second chorus couples were dancing in the aisles. The dancing grew into full-on jitterbug. The rest of the audience was standing, now, swaying and clapping with the rhythm. On stage we felt the magic, we were one with the audience. The whole place was jumping. Then, with a cheer, it was over.

Surprisingly, the audience did not return to their seats. Instead, a crowd grew deep in front of the stage. What more wonders were we to spring on them. Well, we did indeed have a surprise ready.

It started with a tom-tom. An eccentric beat flavored with the mysterious Orient. The band joined in, playing in unison. Softly, at first, we played, as if we were coming over a distant horizon. With each repeat we grew louder and closer. Then our *Caravan* had arrived. Our camels kneeled down and we climbed off, but the tom-tom carried on. The band members stepped aside and the spotlight fell full on Drummer Kid. He launched into his solo. Here was this tiny little guy, propped up behind the big drum set, wailing away in all his glory. The audience caught the fever. As the measures rolled by the audience fell full into it, clapping merrily with the rhythm. Couples started, once again, to dance — to the drums alone they danced.

This time Drummer Kid really showed his stuff. After a year of playing with him we had never heard anything like what he was doing that night. We were all, band and audience alike, overwhelmed with his talent. After the Drummer Kid's wild, exuberant solo he reverted back to tom-tom. It was time for the caravan to get back underway. The band joined in with a couple of strong unison choruses and faded back into the distance as the caravan crossed over the horizon and out of sight.

Needless to say the audience showed its appreciation — with deafening applause and cheers. That night we were Top Banana.

The Moonlighters played together one more season, disbanding as we scattered off to different colleges. All, that is, except for Drummer Kid.

And what became of Drummer Kid? Well, this extraordinarily talented youngster, in time, matured into the distinguished Dr. Craig Woodson — eminent musicologist, popular lecturer, television and motion picture featured artist, and, not least, for five years Elvis Presley's drummer.

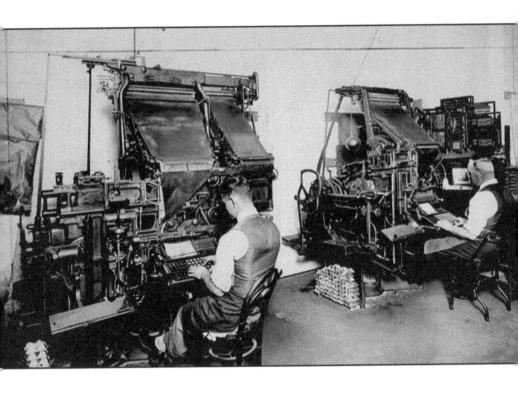

Mergenthaler Linotype Machines and Operators
Anthony Hodern & Sons Department Store
Sydney Australia, circa 1935.
The Mergenthalers were used worldwide. Note ingots stacked near
the machines, ready for operators to keep their melting pots filled.

THE POTATO

Double, Double Toil and Trouble
Fire Burn, and Caldron Bubble.

AN ACCURATE DESCRIPTION. Something the Young Devil definitely did not like. Especially the bubble part, for at this point
the task got deadly dangerous. Printer's Devil was one of those
unsung pivotal occupations upon which our entire civilization
once turned. Like Macbeth's witches this kind of devil is rapidly receding into the mists of history.

In my youth I was a Printer's Devil, like my father before
me. And, likely his father as well, for my grandfather, too, was
a printer and printers learned their trade in the time honored
way — fathers teaching their sons how to do things.

Before I was a teenager Dad partnered with a couple of his
friends and opened a small trade shop. This was a lithographic
specialty house. It prepared the four color separations needed for large scale color printing. Ultimately, Dad's business
folded after one of his partners died and the shares had to be
liquidated.

By the time I was well along in high school, Dad had
become Plant Manager of a major printing establishment in
another part of Los Angeles. And I was about to become a
real, old-time, Printer's Devil.

It was in the summer before I started college that I went to work at Dad's printing plant. While I was getting oriented I worked for a time alongside the plant's janitor. An old man, he was content with his job. He was especially proud of his contribution in keeping the prep area, where the lithographers worked, immaculate. There was no dust there, he assured me. He was proud of his contribution to work he did not understand.

A week or two later I was introduced to *The Potato*. Not any potato, The Potato had to be just right. The Potato was soft and shrunken with age and had little tendrils growing from its flanks. The Potato clearly had pretentions of becoming a Big Green Potato Plant and spawning a multitude of little potatoes. Alas, this was not to be its Destiny. We had a greater and more glorious end in mind for The Potato. It was to be the star of a Great Sacrifice. To be sure, our Great Sacrifice would not have the color and ceremony and significance of an Aztec Sacrifice. The Great Sacrifice of The Potato would not make the sun rise each morning. But The Potato's Great Sacrifice, nevertheless, was of significance. It was entirely possible American lives would depend on the Great Sacrifice of The Potato.

As each member of the tribe of The Potato was immolated in the Great Sacrifice a new Potato must take its place. Each morning I would walk up the street to the local market. The proprietor there had carefully set aside his finest sample of The Potato, for that day's Great Sacrifice.

This time honored ritual will be familiar to anyone who has worked in a letterpress shop. I was initiated into the cult of The Potato when I was assigned to assist the Linotype crew.

This propelled me back in time to an era much closer to the age of Gutenberg.

Linotype operators were once the Kings of the printing industry, and they would never let you forget it. Not all linotype operators were so supremely arrogant, though. My dear Aunt Laura, the opposite of arrogant, was Queen of the Kings for she could set a full newspaper column in record time without error or correction. Other linotype operators were dazzled by her talent.

Linotype machines. Great clattering, clacking, clicking incomprehensible Rube Goldberg piles of intricate sliding, pivoting, weaving, whirling components. Greedy machines which fed voraciously on heavy ingots of lead alloy type metal.

The refined metal ingots were placed in a pot, attached to the linotype machine, and melted down to form a silvery pool of liquid metal. The linotype operator would type, from a fantastic giant keyboard, a line of characters. With each keystroke the great machine would locate a character mold in its library of molds, and transfer the mold to a holding tray. Once the line of character molds had been formed the molds would be snugged up next to each other and the machine would deliver to the line of molds a carefully calibrated quantity of molten metal. The cast metal was quickly cooled with a squirt of water to form a line of type — a slug which would be placed below previously cast lines to make up a section of the page to be printed. Whereupon, the character molds would automatically be sorted and transferred back to their respective library racks.

Dad's printing plant had a whole line of linotype machines, eight or ten of them, served by their traditional arrogant priesthood. My job, as printer's devil, was to allow the operators to keep the ever hungry machines well fed. Dad showed me what to do. I had to learn how to sacrifice The Potato.

The Great Sacrifice took place in a tiny room, a large closet really, in another part of the printing plant. Inside the room was a large gas flame heated melting pot where old type metal was melted down, refined and recast into the ingots to feed the voracious linotypes. The melting pot was about the size of Macbeth's witches' caldron — and just as dangerous.

Nearby, and filling much of the ground floor space of the printing plant, were shelves — a multitude of groaning shelves — loaded down with type galleys from past printing jobs. These were the seemingly endless stacks of a vast leaden library. Each morning, after my excursion to acquire The Potato of the day, I would start obliterating a designated portion of the treasures piled upon the shelves. A great sin, I thought, for to me these were valuable objects and I must be the savage barbarian and wantonly destroy them.

You see, this plant was where the instruction manuals for many of America's military aircraft were printed. Among its Alexandrian Library of old aircraft manuals were the original galleys for fabled fighter planes such as Lockheed's P-38 and F-80. Sadly, I was to be the one who must destroy these treasures.

Galleys, of course, are the reverse of what you see on the printed page. I was frustrated because I wanted to read this wonderful material before I destroyed it. Dad taught me the trick. To easily read a galley you simply turn it upside down. Now the lines read from left to right, as always. It is much easier to learn to read upside down letters than to read lines from right to left. I soon picked up the trick and, being in those days a lightning fast reader, I was able to digest whole manuals as I was disassembling them before consigning the lines of type to the eternity of the melting pot.

It usually took hours to fill the thick-walled, heavily insulated caldron. Then it was time to light up. A wooden match was stuck in a hole drilled into the end of a metal tube. The match was lit, the pole was inserted among the burners and the gas valve turned. Whoosh, the bank of burners flamed on and the witches brew started to cook.

More hours passed before the last lines of type finally slumped into the growing pool of type metal. As the caldron filled with the dissolution of old knowledge a thickening black scum of dross would form on the surface of the pool of molten metal. This scum was the veritable essence of the destroyed knowledge, for it was the very ink that printed the page.

But not all the ink, and other contaminants, floated on the surface. The massively dense metal pool trapped even the lightest of materials near the bottom. It was nearly time for the Great Sacrifice of The Potato.

The Great Sacrifice required that I don The Ceremonial Garments. As with most elements of ceremony, such garments have, or at least once had, a practical utility. In this case the utility was still both practical and obvious — the garments were to protect me from serious injury. On my feet were thick leather hiking boots. My legs were swathed in Levi's. I wore a heavy sweat shirt and my high school jacket with heavy leather sleeves. Wrapped around my face, like a western bandit's, was a red bandana. On my head sat a sailor's cap with the brim turned down to cover my ears. Over my eyes were safety goggles. My hands were thrust into leather workmen's gloves.

Armored this way, and looking much like a steel mill worker, I was ready to perform the Sacrifice.

Oh, and did I say the tiny room with the burning caldron was hot? Well, it was. The extended range thermometer on the wall showed a room temperature which sometimes almost reached the thermometer's limit of a hundred and eighty degrees Fahrenheit. Rather warm for all that clothing, don't you think? Oddly enough the clothing actually protected against the radiant heat. Still, needless to say, one did not spend much time in the hellish place. One quickly ducked in to do a task, then ducked more quickly back out.

The Potato must now be prepared for its crucial role. Wired to the end of a long, slightly bent, steel pole — The Execution Pole — was an ordinary, rather ancient, tin can (not an aluminum can —that would not work). The open-topped tin can had slits cut in its side, and just enough remained of its bottom to maintain the can's shape. Some additional holes were poked through the side of the can, as well. With great care I inserted The Potato into the can and secured it firmly in place with nails pushed through the holes. This must be done properly for The Potato must not escape during the Great Sacrifice. Escape would mean disaster for me, the sacrificing acolyte.

Final adjustments having carefully been made to my Ceremonial Garments, I stepped into the Devil's closet with its witches' caldron, raised the potato pole up above my head and sloping downward, so that the can holding The Potato was suspended just above the surface of the molten metal, and said The Great Prayer. The Great Prayer usually went: "God, I hope I don't screw this up like last time!"

The immolation of The Potato must be done with precision. Too fast a thrust and a wave of molten lead would splash out of the caldron and drench me with its clinging, searing substance. Too slow and the moisture in The Potato would explode near the surface, flinging a fountain of searing droplets around the room to coat the walls, my garments and any accidently exposed flesh, relentlessly burning deep. Worst of all, if I didn't thrust just right everything might look satisfactory, but substantial foreign material would remain trapped below the surface. This was the greatest danger; the hazard would remain hidden until a time when I would be far more vulnerable.

Thrust the pole into the caldron just right, though, and The Potato, crying in agony its high pitched squeals, would bubble its essence away, stirring the molten lead so as to eject all the trapped dross up to the surface. It took much practice, and many accidents, before I got the hang of it. Even then, The Potato, in its death throes, did not always behave as a Proper Sacrifice should and blazing hot molten lead would explode out from the bubbling caldron, or too much dross would remain trapped below the surface. To this day parts of my arms and face, where my garments had briefly pulled away, show the scars from those torturous times in Hell's Closet.

At last the hissing, bubbling, steaming, death agonies of The Potato ceased, the molten surface slumped back into quiescence and the Execution Pole could be withdrawn and set aside. With growing experience I could now have reasonable assurance that the molten lead was purified. It was time to perform *The Skimming*, skimming off the dross.

The Skimming was done with a wire mesh soup strainer, the kind found in most every kitchen. The principle of The

Skimming was easy, the practice of it was hard — and, at first, terrifying. Try pouring molten lead through a soup strainer. You've never done that? Well, I assure you liquid lead really doesn't want to pass through the mesh. Lead is exceedingly dense and the drag as this fluid is forced through the fine openings of the mesh is tremendous. To skim off the dross it was necessary to fully immerse the circular mesh of the strainer in the pool of lead. But then, the only way to supply enough torque and force to drag the strainer through the resisting liquid was to firmly grasp the strainer at its neck. This meant my fist was only a small fraction of an inch above the wavy surface of the molten lead.

Back and forth I would slowly force the strainer through the strongly resisting liquid - keeping an eagle eye on the small gap between my hand and the deadly surface. Back and forth until all the dross was swept up and the pool of metal was mirror shiny, slivery and smooth. With a sigh of relief I would carefully withdraw the strainer and tap the dross out onto the ever growing pile of waste beside the caldron. Then I would flee the hellish room to drink in a refreshing draft of the much cooler, but still desert hot, air outside.

My job wasn't finished yet. Now came the final exam — the test to see if I had done the job right. Unlike in school, failure in this exam meant immediate, painful and scarring punishment. For now I had to cast the ingots.

The specific gravity of lead is more than eleven times that of water. The liquid pool in the caldron was more than three feet deep. The pressure at its bottom was equivalent to that of forty feet beneath the sea — more than a full atmosphere. Scuba divers will appreciate the significance of this number. Sudden release of so much pressure can have explosive effects.

At the bottom of the caldron was a spigot. This spigot delivered the molten lead alloy to an open, water cooled, mold. If all went well, a turn of the spigot and the silvery liquid would flow into the mold and quickly solidify into an ingot which could be lifted out with a special tong and stacked on the slowly cooling pile of previously cast ingots. In and out of the room I would slide on a low, wheeled dolly. Slide in, turn open the spigot, slide out. Let the ingot mold gradually fill, then slide in to turn the spigot off and slide out while the ingot solidified so I could remove it from the mold. Repeat until the caldron was empty.

However, if the liquid metal was not immaculately clean, if there was any dross remaining in its depth, the sudden release of pressure as the liquid flowed out of the spigot would cause the dross to violently explode and a spray of molten lead droplets would fly through the room like shrapnel. In the beginning many were the times this would happen. But, with these hard and pitiless lessons, I quickly learned this devilish trade, and I survived.

The summer finally ended and I migrated off to the University, never again to experience the Devil's life in printing's Hell on Earth — though as I said, I carry its scars to this day.

TEACHERS

OF COURSE MY MOTHER AND FATHER are the greatest teachers I have ever had, or ever will have. They not only gave me life and language and knowledge, but they also taught me *how* to live.

We are, all of us, surrounded by teachers: our friends, our bosses and colleagues, our lovers, our children, our clergy, and the people we most enjoy reading and listening to.

And, I haven't forgotten, our teachers in the classroom. School, for good or for ill, controls much of our formative years. Thus it was for me.

Certain individuals stand out in my experience of school as teachers of true excellence. Let me take this opportunity to honor them with a few good memories. But before I tell of the good, it is well to lay out a contrasting background against which their light can better shine. So I will begin with the bad.

First grade was bad. We devoted a whole year to learning: a..b..c..d..e..f..g...., and the little hand on the clock goes here and the big hand goes there.

My teacher was of the new, *progressive*, school of education. For her, the only thing that was important was to provide some solace to the slowest kid in the class. The rest of us didn't count, and so the rest of us were restless. I was particularly so. Instead of my first year of schooling being a joy, with new adventures of learning being opened for me, I spent my time wondering what I was doing there, and chattering with my fellow classmates, most of whom had completely mastered this excruciatingly slow trickle of knowledge in the first five minutes.

The teacher was fit to be tied with my behavior. She called my mother in for a conference. Mom listened patiently to the teacher's complaints about how I was disturbing the class and, worse, did not want to obey her or to give her any respect. The teacher concluded I was mentally deficient and should be placed in a school for the retarded. At the end of this diatribe my mother quietly replied: "Has it not occurred to you that Chet might simply be bored?"

The teacher was way overmatched, and she was just barely able to know it. There was something about the way my mother had responded that told the teacher she was treading on dangerous ground. That was the end of the matter, but I did have to continue suffering through the rest of the school year. It wasn't quite as bad as before because now Mom knew what I was going through and could, to some extent, help me through it all.

Second grade was the bright day which followed the dark night. We were supposed to be reading by the time we got to second grade. But, as I have implied, our first grade teacher did not believe we were capable of such advanced learning, so we remained illiterate.

Our second grade teacher gave out a sigh. She had dealt with this before. She rolled up her sleeves and went to work. She did not make a big deal of it, she simply quizzed each student to probe for abilities, and made some seat reassignments. After that she divided the class into side-by-side red, white and blue sections. She told us this was so she could attend to each group while the others were doing their assignments. It was no surprise to her when each color made progress at a different rate. It was no surprise to me that she spent almost all of her time with the other colors.

She began to teach: The alphabet had a purpose. Its purpose was to communicate sounds. String the letters together in different ways and the sound of words magically popped out of the page. Our Readers were time honored: *Dick and Jane* and *See Spot Run!*

Within only a few weeks our color had completed the fourth grade reading curriculum and the slowest color had already finished second grade and was moving into the third.

After this my parents moved and I relocated to a spanking new, and "progressive" school where I languished for the rest of the school year. I continued to read on my own and vacuumed up everything I could get my hands on. I soon far outstripped anything the school was able to provide.

My earliest second grade teacher deserves the highest honors, for she was *a teacher.*

Fourth grade provided the next moment of darkness — a brief eclipse which scarred me for decades. By this time school was no great challenge. Classes, for the most part, repeated subjects I had already absorbed. A two month sojourn in a Brooklyn school, at the beginning of third grade, had provided me with full mastery of all the math I would experience in California schools until I reached Junior High. By fourth grade I was already reading at the college level, so there was little new for me in the classroom. Because we had moved around quite a bit I repeated Social Studies three or four times in succession, but got no English Grammar. To this day I still don't what a participle is, though apparently I merrily dangle them with abandon.

The scarring eclipse occurred in one of our weekly art classes. I had always looked forward to art class. Some years before, I had taken art classes at the De Young Museum in San Francisco. Mom was told by the instructor I had real artistic talent and art was to be my destiny. I wasn't aware of his assessment until many years later. By then it was too late; the critical period when fundamental drawing skills are deeply engraved had passed.

On this particular occasion our regular teacher was absent and a substitute took over. The assignment was to paint a landscape. Use our imaginations, we were told, paint a bright and cheerful scene. Something delayed me at the start of the class. By the time I reached the supplies table all the bright paints were gone. There was no blue, no green no yellow or red or orange. The only colors left were the dull shades — brown, gray and black. I was disappointed, for I had very much wanted to paint this beautiful flowered countryside I could see so vividly in my head.

I stood by the table, trying to think of what I could do with these inadequate materials. "Get to work," the teacher prodded, "this isn't a time for day dreaming." I looked once more out the window. Brown Mount Verdugo rose up and faded into the brownish-gray, smog filled, Southern California sky. Suddenly, and maybe for the first time, I saw the world around me as it really was. The sky was not always blue, the hills are not always green and flowers do not always bloom. Inspired, I grabbed the paints available and went to work. I would paint the real world, not the world of imagination!

Finished, I was very pleased with what I had done. I had truly captured what was visible outside the schoolroom window — even to the crevices and canyons of the mountain and the fade of the mountain into the haze. I had the *spirit* of the scene. Proudly, I raced up to the teacher to show her my masterpiece. She recoiled in horror. "What have you done there?" she asked. "Don't you know the sky is always blue and the hills are always green?"

She grabbed my ear and hauled me over to stand in the corner, facing the wall. Worse, she fashioned a tall pointed dunce cap and plunked it firmly on my head. She announced to the busy class that I had committed a terrible sin.

She was our "art" teacher for a couple of more weeks. Through that terrible time I was not allowed to go near the art materials. I had to stand in the corner with that silly hat on my head.

When our regular teacher returned, she could not understand why I was no longer interested in art instruction. She could not understand, either, why the class laughed at the mere mention of my name. I understood, though, for the laughter was the same as I had heard while I was standing in the corner.

I don't want to leave the impression schooling was all bleak — something out of a Charles Dickens novel. It wasn't. Indeed, the majority of my teachers were quite dedicated and several had real teaching talent. I was quite taken with many of the subjects being taught, particularly unfamiliar ones, such as biology, geography and most especially, history. Still, I had been badly damaged by the *art class* incident, and subsequently I could only rarely put my full trust in teachers. They had to prove worthy.

The ideal relationship between a teacher and a student is one of trust. The student takes a considerable risk when he exposes to the teacher he is struggling with these new ideas and needs the teacher's help to master them. Teachers, after all, have the power of grades, and grades are the main gateway to one's future. Without trust instruction is crippled, and so is the student. Sadly, in my experience, only a few teachers understood this crucial fact, or cared.

One more tale of darkness before I pass fully into the light. But not too dark. In the end, I was well entertained by this experience.

As an undergraduate I was enrolled at the University of California, Berkeley. Although Berkeley had its full share of dark shadows — professors who believed students were merely necessary nuisances — this tale is about an academic missionary on sabbatical from NYU. I'm quite sure his intention was to instill in us California primitives the superior Wisdom of East Coast Culture. Unfortunately for the enlightenment of the savage natives, here, his exalted message fell on unfertile ground. Perhaps it was the way he cast his pearls among us swine that led his labors to be barren. Or perhaps his pearls were merely plastic.

I was a physics major and physics is considered by the University to be a Liberal Art, so it is housed in the College of Letters and Science. This is undoubtedly a holdover from medieval times when physics was called natural philosophy. A physics student therefore has to meet the full requirements of the Liberal Arts curriculum. This meant we had to take a year of English.

First year English courses at Berkeley were mostly poetry readings and I didn't believe such pieces were going to be of much utility. But there was an alternative available: I could substitute courses in Speech.

It happened the Speech Department was kind of a dumping ground for subjects which did not fit well in any other Liberal Arts department. Thus, my first semester of "speech" was in reality a course in modern philosophy. Okay by me.

The professor opened his first lecture with the pronouncement that he had once coauthored a paper with the Great Bertrand Russell. I was not impressed. Neither, apparently, were my classmates. The professor was visibly disappointed at the lack of instant adulation. West Coast primitives! He harrumphed a bit and continued with an outline of the course.

I expected the course to be interesting. But the first couple of lectures were a mix of philosophical dreariness and polemics against religion and the capitalist way. There was only an occasional interaction with his students as the professor droned on, and on. In those few exchanges the professor was mainly looking for affirmation of his superior intellect from the students.

And don't forget, he would frequently remind the class, he had once coauthored a paper with the Great Bertrand Russell.

After a couple of weeks the professor lighted on the topic of evolution. Man, of course, had no part in evolution. *This is utter nonsense,* I thought. I raised my hand. "Professor, are you telling us people had no hand in domesticating and breeding dogs and farm animals, and the different varieties of crop species? Aren't breeding and domestication examples of man controlled selection rather than natural selection?" I had obliterated his entire thesis and his plan for the rest of the course.

He didn't have a clue who I was, but he was not about to have his philosophical juggernaut derailed. He perched his reading glasses back upon his nose and peered down at the seating chart. "Mr. Richards, is it?" I acknowledged that was me. He proceeded with a blistering personal attack covering all my ancestors — starting with Adam and Eve (in whom he didn't believe). The class was shocked into tomblike silence.

Having been to a Catholic High School, I was untouched by his invective. Catholic Schooling had equipped me with near impervious armor. When he got to my dad I did get mildly annoyed. What the professor said about my father sounded familiar, for Dad had been keen to make his lazy son more industrious, and I had had a rather different opinion on the subject. But I was the proper judge of Dad's intentions, not the professor. When this pretentious person got onto the subject of my mother I put an instant halt to his diatribe. Mom was definitely, and forever, off limits.

From then on there was a thick wall of ice between the students and the professor. The students would answer a direct question but no more. We sat in stone silence. No one ever again asked a question of the professor.

I contrived to somehow get even. For the first, and only, time in my student career I went to the university library and checked out my professor's entire reading list. As it turned out there were only two copies of each book on the list — the professor had one set and I had the other. This was no good service to my class mates but, at that point, I didn't care.

Comparing my class notes with the library books I discovered something very interesting: The professor was plagiarizing. His lectures were cribbed, word for word, from the books on the list. With this knowledge I could forecast, precisely, what he was going to say in each lecture. Early on he would call on me to try and trip me up on some obscure issue. Of course he couldn't. What was worse for him, I would anticipate the next point he was going to make in his lecture: "Professor, I expect next you are going to say thus and such." My uncanny prescience must have spooked him. I *had* to be reading his mind — which was not possible in his materialist Marxist view of the universe. He soon ceased to call upon me.

The semester dragged on, but eventually drew to its final days. There had been no midterm exams. Our grade rested entirely on a single term paper. I figured I was going to flunk the course, anyway, so I decided to have some fun in the process. I chose to refute every major point the professor had made during the entire course. It took some doing, but I did find effective counter arguments to each of his major theses.

When I received my grade I was rather astonished to find I had gotten an A+. I hunted up the T.A. to find out what had happened. He told me, rather sourly, the professor had left a week early and he had been stuck grading the papers. The T.A.'s reaction: He was delighted someone had "finally put that creep where he belonged."

And now for the light. I was unsatisfied. I didn't feel I had learned much from Speech 1A (of course I had — but not what the professor intended). When I complained about this to my senior class roommates they suggested a grim alternative for the second semester. "You could always take Wolfson's course." They warned me there was extreme hazard in this alternative. Professor Wolfson rarely gave higher than a C grade, and he was even pretty stingy about giving out C's. "Wolfson's tough, he'll work you to death and he'll wreck your G.P.A., but he's fair and you'll learn a lot from him." I was willing to give it a try. Besides, I needed a stretch. So the next semester I signed up for Wolfson's course.

What a difference! I felt I had been tossed into the stainless steel clutches of a Marine Corps Drill Instructor. (My high school phys ed teacher had been a Marine Corps D.I., so I know what I'm talking about.) The rumor Wolfson was tough didn't *begin* to scratch the surface.

I didn't realize it at the time, but I was getting a dose of classical rhetoric straight out of Cicero. Any ancient, hardnosed, Roman senator would have immediately recognized Professor Wolfson's method.

The method was simple enough on the surface. Each week Wolfson took apart a published essay to show what made it tick. The essays were carefully selected for their flaws. Each week, for homework, we were assigned a similar essay and we were to write an analytical paper in response. He started us with easy ones — essays obviously flawed in their logic. As the weeks progressed the challenges grew more difficult.

I poured over my first week's essay and easily picked out the flaws. I wrote my analysis and turned it in. Wolfson read my paper and red penciled it. My paper was graded F. I was stunned. Wolfson wasn't kidding, either. As I worked my way through his comments I was chastened at how much I had missed and how badly flawed my own logic was. I resolved to do better on the next assignment.

One thing became clear right at the start. Professor Wolfson did the grading work himself. He did not trust teaching assistants to have the analytical skills and dogged persistence needed to bring this lout into the light. The down side was there was no way I was going to pull the wool over Wolfson's eyes. I had to perform.

Each week's classroom analysis showed different kinds of failures in the offerings of various authors. Frequently the author's use of language was unskilled and confusing. Almost always there were problems with the logic — often the conclusions did not follow from the premises. Sometimes the logic was impeccable but the premises were nonsensical. Sometimes the logic itself was self-contradictory. Circular reasoning was a common fault — the author assumed his conclusions. In many cases the premises were unstated and needed to be dug out. We learned how to work backward from the conclusions, through the logic, to establish what premises the author, often unconsciously, had started with. In most of those cases the premises turned out to be utterly implausible.

Each week I turned in my analysis paper. Each week I got back an F, together with an exposition of items I had missed and where my own logic had failed. This was frustrating. I was spending more and more time on this one class until its demands exceeded all my other studies — math, physics, German, biology — put together. While I was clearly learning, I was still failing. My frustration increased.

Then, one day, I received a D -. I was making progress. In a few more weeks I migrated from D + to C. There was some hope. I even occasionally received a treasured *good* when I had uncovered a particularly obscure error. Slowly my skills improved until I was getting a consistent A on my papers. Maybe I was going to pass this course after all.

And maybe I was turning paranoid. It seemed to me that in classroom questioning Wolfson always directed the hardest questions straight at me. This happened with increasing frequency, too. He always scowled at my answers and usually made no comment unless my answer was incorrect. Never once did I get an attaboy — a grunt was sometimes given in lieu of good. But a grunt could also mean the opposite.

We had been warned we would conclude our semester's work with a speech. Much too soon the time for this grew near. Instead of the common essay that was each week's usual assignment, Wolfson, this time, required each student to analyze a different essay. We went up to pick out our essays from the pile. As I approached the stack Wolfson drew me aside. He had selected a particular essay for me. He told me this essay had been written by a close friend and colleague — a fellow founder of the Americans For Democratic Action. Wolfson said he wanted to see what I would make of it.

The author turned out to be a noted expert in labor relations. It was well written, concise and transparently clear. The premises were fully stated and completely acceptable. The logic was well laid out and appeared perfectly correct. The conclusions followed directly from the logic. But the conclusions and policy recommendations troubled me.

Dad had been a labor leader, later a manager, and then a businessman. When a strike was called and it turned intransigent and bitter, Dad, respected by both sides, was asked to arbitrate — which he did with great success. Labor relations was in my blood. I had grown up with it. The conclusions offered by this paper not only didn't make sense to me, they appeared a recipe for disaster. Something *had* to be wrong with the paper, but I couldn't see it.

I reread the paper and still could not find a thing to criticize. On the third reading I discovered a problematic area. I would focus there. On the fourth reading I found a loose end. I tugged on the loose end and the logic disassembled. Upon detailed examination I discovered one logic component was flawed. I made the needed correction and carefully reassembled the logic. Now, tracing the logic flow from premise to conclusion, I discovered the machinery provided exactly the opposite conclusions and policy recommendations from the original. These new results now made sense to me.

But for all my efforts I now had a real problem. The problem wasn't technical, I knew I had gotten that part right. The problem was political. There had to be some reason Professor Wolfson had so carefully pointed out his deep friendship with the author. Just how Machiavellian was Wolfson, anyway? Was he trying to trap me? Sly as he was, I wouldn't put it past him.

My latent paranoia increased when I discovered Wolfson had scheduled me to give the last speech — out of order. I remembered all too well Wolfson had not given any of the other students a special assignment.

I had to make a decision about what to present. Should I simply regurgitate what appeared to be a perfect paper? That appeared to be the safe course. Or, should I report what I had discovered — and risk Wolfson's legendary wrath?

My roommates had claimed Wolfson was fair, and I had seen nothing since that would indicate otherwise — tough, very tough, explosive at times, but fair. Should I trust Wolfson? A difficult decision for a teenager to make, but you have to grow up sometime. The worst that could happen is I would flunk and have to repeat the course. Admiral Farragut said "Damn the torpedoes, full steam ahead!" I chose trust. *What the hell*, I said to myself. *Damn the torpedoes. Let's go for it.*

I had the elements of my speech blocked out on file cards. I had noticed Wolfson's earlier reaction to the students who read out a prepared speech. He clearly didn't like it. He preferred a more extemporaneous approach.

Wolfson was standing at the rear of the classroom, leaning back against the far wall, his arms folded across his chest. On his face was the usual scowl.

I took a deep breath and began. I simply followed what had transpired when I sat down to analyze the paper. I laid out the contents of the paper with its premises, its logic flow, its conclusions and policy recommendations. I told of my reactions and how I had repeatedly reread an apparently perfect paper and how I finally found the loose end. Then I disassembled the logic for the class and made the needed correction. Upon its reassembly I showed the logic now gave precisely the opposite conclusion.

Throughout all this Wolfson's scowl got deeper and deeper. I could hear an occasional grunt from the back of the room. Clearly I was in deep trouble.

Trembling with excess adrenalin, I watched as Professor Wolfson stalked towards me from the back of the room. As he moved up beside me I naturally turned towards him. He grabbed my shoulder and spun me around to face the class.

"This," he said in a penetrating voice, "is *exactly* what I've been trying to teach you all semester! I'm glad that at least *one* of you got it!"

I nearly fainted. My grade for the course was a B.

Looking back on those four years at Berkeley I realize in that one semester course I got as much education as in all the rest put together.

LEARNING PHYSICS

OVER THE YEARS OF MY HIGHER EDUCATION I have had many fine teachers of technical subjects (along with a few truly abysmal ones). One teacher towers above the rest: Dave Pandres, my graduate school instructor in Classical Mechanics.

Dr. Pandres, at the time, was the Director of Theoretical Physics at the Douglas Advanced Research Laboratory. At the time the lab was one of the jewels in America's crown. That was before James McDonnell purchased Douglas Aircraft Company and, in a fit of tyrannical rage, shuttered the lab and fired the staff. His rage was caused by the refusal of the lab's staff to pack up, at his behest, and forthwith move to St. Louis. How *dare* they!

But my association with Dr. Pandres was before that piece of idiocy. Dave Pandres was a stocky, jolly faced individual, with a kindly disposition, a slow, deep south drawl and a razor keen intellect. It wasn't only his technical skills that impressed me, great though they were. I was mesmerized by his extraordinary creativity in the classroom.

I want to emphasize professional physics is *hard*. The brightest students struggle to master the discipline. The time honored method of presenting the subject doesn't help in the least.

New physical ideas are presented in the form of mathematical derivations — a highly abstract and difficult, but essential, technique. A derivation is a form of mathematical manipulation which takes the starting equations of a theory, inserts an assumption, and evolves a prediction of some interesting outcome. A simple example is to put a mathematical model of the Earth's force of gravity into Newton's famous force equation, F=ma, and develop from that the equations describing a satellite's orbit around the Earth.

Physics students are normally challenged to "sink or swim." The material is often thrown up on the blackboard with only a minimal explanation as to its meaning. Most students, at the time they take a physics course, do not fully digest the material — the lectures move far too fast. The process can be brutal.

Our experience with Dr. Pandres was completely different. As a teacher, Dave Pandres was a magician! In two quarters we completely mastered what might normally take three full semesters, or more, to present. Goldstein, the traditional Classical Mechanics textbook, we demolished in less than six weeks. We moved on to explore the transition from Classical Mechanics to Quantum Mechanics. Finally, we delved into the mysteries of General Relativity. Moreover, the students simply aced the exams, and the exam questions were usually *very* hard.

How did Dr. Pandres do it?

He did it by moving very slowly. This sounds paradoxical. It isn't.

Dave Pandres had a novel teaching approach. He believed in making sure each student in the class fully understood each new idea before he was willing to move on to the next.

Physics is usually presented in a standard way. Professors learn this way from their professors who learned it from their professors, and so on. However, there are sometimes multiple ways of approaching the same basic concepts. Dr. Pandres usually introduced a new idea pretty much along standard lines, but with greater elaboration than usual. The real novelty, though, was this: Before he would go on to the next topic he would quiz each of the students, in some depth, to make sure the new ideas had settled in and were fully understood. There were only six students in the class so this was easier than if the class had been much larger. Sometimes the new material clicked in on the first try. Much more often a student would not have grasped its essentials.

It was at this point Dr. Pandres' splendid creativity blossomed forth. On the spot, during his questioning, he would diagnose any conceptual problem the student might be having. He would then develop and present an entirely different approach to the material. The new technical approach would be custom tailored to solve that particular student's problem. Once he was satisfied the student fully understood the point he was trying to make, he repeated the process with the next student.

On occasion Dr. Pandres would create no less than six different mini-lectures, each one custom tailored to remove a road block he had detected in each student. It was a dazzling tour-de-force. I discovered my understanding deepened with each such custom presentation until my grasp of the material became rock solid.

When Dr. Pandres moved on to the next section of the course he was able to construct it on the firm foundation previously laid for each student. As a result, he was often able to fly through difficult material because, with a solid foundation, new topics were much easier to grasp.

Not all the students fully appreciated what they were experiencing. I well remember one student complaining to me the lectures were deadly dull because Dr. Pandres kept repeating the material, over and over. I was dumbfounded at this complaint. My classmate was blind to the privilege he had been given. He had no idea he was witnessing a Grand Master in full, prodigious, flower.

In this story and another I have told of three teachers who rose far above the crowd. I especially honor them as exemplars of what might be achieved in the classroom. But not all who teach have that astonishing magnitude of talent and commitment. Nonetheless, the integrity, dedication and knowledge of the majority of my teachers will always have my full respect. They did well by me.

PROFESSOR PELLAM'S
FABULOUS FISH TALE

Note to the reader: The following is a reconstruction of a story told to me half a century ago by Professor Pellam, now long since deceased. In effect, the story is much like a Hollywood "based on a true story" movie tale. I have recorded accurately as much as I can recall, with guesswork as to some of the fine details.

Part of Professor Pellam's role in the wartime antisubmarine effort is described in the official US Navy history of its Operations Research efforts: "The Operations Evaluation Group," by K. R. Tidman. Unfortunately, this book only briefly mentions the episode described here. That mention is enough to establish, in broad outline, what I am reporting below. The detailed documentation of the event is undoubtedly buried somewhere deep in Indiana Jones' vast warehouse. Fortunately, I have also been able to verify the award mentioned at the end of the story through other sources. I take full responsibility for any errors that may have crept into the narration.

The written word cannot capture this great man's vibrant personality. Only those who knew him have those special memories. It was indeed a privilege to have worked in Johnny Pellam's laboratory and to have been mentored by him.

IT WAS HALF CENTURY AGO. By a series of odd coincidences I found myself in the Charter Graduate Student class of the newly opened University of California, Irvine. I was one of a small handful in that initial Physics cadre.

Sometime after the first year I caught the attention of Professor Johnny Pellam. Perhaps it was because I couldn't stop myself from hanging around the exquisitely lovely Lilly Fong, Pellam's secretary. Rumor Control reported Johnny Pellam was always accompanied by the most gorgeous secretary in World of Science. Lilly certainly fit the description. Rumor also had it eminent physicists (and others) would travel half way around the planet just to bask in the company of Johnny's beauteous secretary.

Maybe that was true, but the professionally distinguished Dr. John R. Pellam — former Director of Low Temperature Physics for both the National Bureau of Standards and the California Institute of Technology, author of numerous pioneering scientific papers, Fellow of the American Physical Society, Presidential Science Advisor — was sufficiently magnetic on his own account.

In any case, perhaps Dr. Pellam picked me out for entirely different reasons from hanging around the delectable Lilly Fong. Whatever the circumstances I soon received an invitation to work in his newly constructed laboratory.

Johnny Pellam had a strong physique, a craggy face and a great shock of silver hair. His voice was deep and gravelly, his demeanor gruff but grandfatherly. When the occasion called for it, his language could become quite salty — perhaps the consequence of his time at sea. He matched my ideal of a wise, elderly teacher. I am much older, now, than he was then but my sense of the man, his strength, and his eminence remains the same.

For all his gruff exterior and formidable reputation, Johnny Pellam was a delightful fellow — totally accessible and wonderfully willing to trade experiences and opinions. Garrulous, too. He could spin a yarn with the best.

One day, while waiting for a vacuum pump-down, we were sitting and chatting. I mentioned back in the 50's my folks took me on an excursion to Catalina Island. We had flown over on a big old four engine flying boat. It was a lot of fun, especially when we landed. The plane didn't just skim the surface and settle in. What it did when it hit the water was to sink the windows below the surface of the sea. For many long seconds I was in a high speed submarine with a large picture window revealing a seemingly endless panorama of crystal clear water. I was entranced with the splendid kelp sea gardens and the huge schools of fish we so quickly passed as we slowly decelerated.

"Flying boats and submarines," he mused. "That reminds me of something that happened to me many years ago."

"Tell me about it," I said. So he did, settling himself in for a long saga. The story ran something like this.

It was during the war. In the spring of '43 I was a graduate student, dividing my time between Harvard and MIT. At Harvard I was engaged in sonar work. This took most of my time. But there was another project I had been roped into. This was operational analysis of antisubmarine warfare. The Navy had already sent me to Newfoundland to become acquainted with what the British were doing to protect their convoys.

One gloomy day I was alone in the sonar lab, making some measurements the Navy thought were important. These two beefy, grim faced guys pushed through the door, pulled out official looking ID's, and announced they were from some Government agency I had never heard of. They told me to stop what I was doing and come with them. I asked what was going on, where did they want me to go? They didn't respond, except with a 'Just come with us.' Just like government types, I thought, they like to be mysterious.

With big solid guys like that I didn't argue. I started to put my notes and apparatus away. They said to just leave things like they were and come with us. OK, I'll play along. –

In the hallway I was tightly sandwiched between those guys. They hustled me out of the building and shoved me into the back seat of a big black car. One of them slid in beside me and pinned me against a door whose handle would not turn. I asked again where were we going. They said nothing, and continued to say nothing as the car drove around Cambridge until they came to where I was staying. I had not told them where I lived but they knew anyway. The driver stayed in the car, its engine running, while the other guy walked me up to my room. 'Pack one suitcase,' he said. I started packing the usual variety of clothing. I was told to forget all that stuff. 'Just lots of thick socks and extra underwear. And don't forget to put in a warm sweater and one change of your warmest clothes.' He said to take a few things to read – this thing was going to take a long time.

I picked up a couple of textbooks I had been struggling with. He told me to drop those. Just plenty of light reading was all I could bring along. Then he hustled me back to the car.

We drove fast, very fast, to the railroad station. The cops we passed just ignored us.

I was worried. Who was going to pay the rent, what about my bills. I had classes and seminars to give, and the Navy very much wanted my latest measurements. 'It's all taken care of' was the curt reply. I wasn't happy with that answer.

The car was left at the curb, right in front of the station – just like that. One of them picked up my heavy suitcase, as if it were light as a feather, and the three of us ran to meet a train that was about to pull out. The train was jammed with people – mostly soldiers on their way somewhere. But my guys already had tickets to a first class compartment, so we were alone. The train went south, towards New York City.

On the train I asked those guys for about the fourteenth time where we were headed. I was told when I got there I would find out. Meantime, I was to tell nobody what was happening. That was easy to do since I had no idea what was going on, and they weren't going to leave me alone by myself. The guy went further. He told me I was never to talk about this. In fact it would be best if I didn't talk to anyone, ever. 'Just keep your mouth shut.' If anyone asked, just tell them I was really very sick. A happy thought!

In New York we transferred to the Long Island train. At one of the stops we got off. A car was waiting. The car's driver handed my driver the car keys and we were on the road again. After a while we reached the sea, and drove to a dock where I was put aboard a giant Pan American Clipper flying boat waiting in the water. The government men gave me their final caution: 'Talk to no one.' Okay, but where was I going, who would I meet, where would I stay, what was I to do? 'Don't worry,' I was told again, 'it's all taken care of. Just relax and enjoy the trip – and don't talk to anyone.' That sure helped.

Not many years before the Pan Am Clipper was the height of air travel luxury. But during the war, luxury was a luxury and the plane had been stripped down to bare essentials. Priority cargo and special passengers were on board, but little else. Needless to say, the flight was long, very long, and very noisy. I was uncomfortable and got no rest.

As we droned out over the ocean it soon became pretty obvious, from the sun angle and such, that we were headed across the Atlantic. The only break we had was a short stop in the Azores to refuel and get fresh food. After that we headed north to England.

I was totally bushed by the time we reached land. I was really worried, too. After many hours in the air, and some conversation with fellow passengers, I had discovered where I was headed, but I still had no idea what to do when I got there. Now I was there.

I was standing on the dock, shivering with the cold, when this small guy walked up to me. He looked like he had just stepped out of some old British cops and robbers movie, with a neat suit and mustache and accent, and all. 'Mr. Pellam, please come with me.' he said. I asked who he was and how he knew me. He pulled out my photo and a very fancy British Government ID. He also told me he knew the boss of the project who had sent me to Newfoundland. Then he handed me my credentials for this excursion. It seemed like a good idea to go with him, so I did.

For the first time in days I had a nice hot bath, a fresh change of clothes (just my size, too) and a really good hot meal. I still didn't know what was going on, but I was feeling much better. Maybe this was going to work out after all.

I got a good night's rest – nice and long after that mostly sleepless flight across the pond. Then, with a knock on the door, things started to happen. My guide treated me to a hearty breakfast, making sure to keep me well isolated from everyone. I'm sure glad he did, too, because we got lots of nasty stares from those half-ration starved Brits around us. After breakfast I was hustled into a car and we started a drive along the coast.

That certainly was England and it certainly was wartime. Military gear and soldiers were everywhere. Barrage balloons were all over the place. Lots of planes were in the air, too. The traffic jams were awful and endless. But eventually we got there. It was a Navy Base of some kind. The guards really checked out our credentials, and then we drove through the gate and down to the docks. There I saw a submarine making ready to go to sea. I wondered what I was doing here. Perhaps I was going to interview the skipper about his patrol experiences.

No, that couldn't be it. The sub was clearly getting ready to leave. I still hadn't been told anything. Was I supposed to be on board? What was going on? I can tell you, at this point the butterflies inside me were really fluttering.

It was just as bad as I feared. We got out of the car and my new friend opened up its boot and hauled out a sea bag. 'All your belongings are in here,' he told me. 'Everything is fresh washed and ready to go. Also, extra clothing you will need is packed away.' He reached into the car and pulled out a heavy wool pea coat and handed it to me. 'You'll need this,' he said. 'And, here are two packets. Give these to the Captain when you go aboard. Good luck!' He smiled, grabbed my elbow, and hustled me halfway up the gang plank. My friend was a little guy, but he sure was strong, I'll give him that. A big seaman grabbed my arm and my sea bag, and pulled me the rest of the way up. I had little choice in the matter. Someone had really gotten me in a fix.

I crawled down through a hatch in the deck and down a narrow ladder into the bowels of the submarine. The interior was very cramped. From the movies I had seen I had thought that the insides of a sub would be roomier. And the place stank! People were piled on top of each other with poor plumbing and with ever present smells of old food, sweat, oil, grease, and just plain B.O. No wonder the Germans called them pig boats. But after a bit I didn't even notice the funk.

I was led to an empty bunk and my sea bag was slung onto it by the sailor who was with me. At the time I didn't realize that my bunk was considered a special privilege because I had it all to myself. Most of the people on board shared a bunk with at least one other sailor – things were that tight.

After he showed me how to stow my gear, and explained the toilet – the head – and various critical procedures, my guide took me to the Captain's cabin. The cabin was about the size of a closet, but at least it had a small desk and a door that could be closed for private conversations. The Captain was courteous but very cool. He obviously did not want me aboard. Like me he had no idea what was going on. He had simply been ordered to standby to take me aboard and then await further orders.

I handed the Captain the two packets I had been given. One of them was to be opened immediately, the other at an appropriate time after we were out to sea. The Captain broke the fancy wax seal of the first packet, read the orders to himself, and then told me to stay as much as I could in my bunk – especially to keep well out of the way. Then he headed to his command station to give the order to get underway. He also sent back one of the junior officers to give me instructions on safety procedures, meal schedules, protocols and such.

For a long time afterwards I had no idea what was going on or what I was doing there. I mostly stayed in my bunk, as ordered, and read. However, I did eat in the wardroom with the officers and I did spend lots of time outside up on the conning tower – the deck below was too dangerous. This was normal because subs mainly traveled on the surface. They would dive only to attack or to escape from attack.

After a bit I found the other officers and the men to be friendly, and even curious. I became something of a celebrity when people found out that I had lived out west in prairie country, and that I even

*knew, first hand, about cowboys and such. So my first days aboard
were really OK.*

*In the beginning we sailed far out, westwards, into the Atlantic.
Someone told me this was to avoid German air patrols. Along the
way we were constantly accompanied by our own aircraft. They were
there to protect us from German attack. Also, some clever person had
figured out how to keep our boys from accidently attacking us, so we
felt safe and could relax a bit.*

*I tried figuring out what this mission was. My best guess was we
were out to discover something about German wolfpacks in the North
Atlantic. This theory sounded plausible because of the research I had
been doing on antisubmarine warfare back in the States. Instead,
and much to my surprise, we turned South.*

*After several days plowing through the heavy Atlantic swells, we
turned back East. It had been very cold on deck during the early part
of our voyage and I was quite glad I had been given that pea coat and
told to bring a warm sweater and extra socks. But now, in the more
southern and spring time seas, things were warming up.*

*All through this early part of the voyage the Captain and I had
been avoiding each other, except at meals. But now the Captain called
me to his cabin and told me to close the door. He pulled out the second
packet. He told me his orders were, when we reached this location,
to open the second packet with me there. The packet was a thick one,
but it had a cover letter which was addressed to the Captain. The
Captain took out the letter and read the short instruction typed there.*

*I'll never forget the look of surprise on the Captain's face as he
read that letter. I was to take immediate command of the sub! If the
Captain was surprised, I can tell you I was simply stunned. In all my
thinking about this trip, taking command of a warship, much less a
submarine, was the last thing I expected. I can tell you, it took a bit
for both of us to get our feet back under us.*

I think the Captain might have been testing me when he finally asked for my orders. At least so it seemed to me at the time. Maybe he expected I'd be some wild cowboy and start bossing everyone around. I simply told him it didn't matter what the Admiralty said, as far as I was concerned he was still the Captain. For sure I had no idea how to run a submarine and I said so. Whatever this mission was, I probably was going to goof it up, a bit. I asked the Captain to keep me from doing anything dangerous or stupid. The Captain relaxed a bit. But again he asked for my orders. I told him we had better dig into the packet and find out what we were supposed to do. I was still dreading this was going to be some kind of secret penetration into the Nazi inner sanctum. I took a quick glance at the papers. To my surprise I realized: 'Hey, I can do this. Piece of cake!'

Since there were quite a few papers in the packet we decided to go to the wardroom where we could spread out. Before leaving the Captain's cabin he got on the intercom and asked the steward to meet us in the wardroom. Since I was now in command I should have the Captain's cabin. I pointed out to him his cabin had instruments and communications that were vital to his guiding the boat. No thanks, I insisted. We made other arrangements that made me a bit more comfortable.

This whole thing had to do with Operations Research, a science the British had invented a few years before. In addition to my sonar research, the Newfoundland excursion had been part of the newly established US operations research initiative. Probably those factors, together with my knowledge of hydrodynamics, had caught the attention of whoever had dreamed up this stunt.

In those days Nazi subs were running wild in the Mediterranean. The Brass were going nuts trying to figure out how the subs got through our tight anti-sub screen across the narrow Straits of Gibraltar. Then, some smart OR guy noticed a pattern. Radar on patrol planes showed German subs were briefly surfacing just outside the straits and disappearing before our planes could get to them. These events were correlated with later attacks on Allied shipping. Obviously the Germans were somehow slipping through the net. It was my job to figure out what the Germans were up to and how they got in and out of the straits.

The Captain and I laid out a bunch of maps, got out some scratch paper and a couple of slide rules, rolled up our sleeves, and got to work. We had a few clues to work with. We had a list of the sightings, and their locations, outside the straits. We also had a list of subsequent attacks, and when and where they occurred inside the Med. We also had the most up-to-date hydrographic information the Admiralty could supply us. This all explained why the second packet was so thick. We spent a lot of time plotting all the data on the maps and talking about what it could mean. After a lot of this we needed a fresh perspective. A bit of rest would help clear our minds. We decided to call it a day.

Sometime during that first long break I had the inspiration: If we could map out the current flows through the strait, we would have most of our answer. Of course the surface currents were well known, but what was going on under the surface was pretty much a mystery. I decided this was going to be our primary objective. If we knew the full three dimensional flow of water we probably would be able to figure out what the Germans were up to.

The Mediterranean Sea, being entirely landlocked with only a narrow entrance, is a giant evaporation pond. The hot land breezes suck up water from most of the Sea's area and drop it far inland where some of it could run off into other oceans. This accounts for the extra saltiness of the Med and for the fierce current running from the Atlantic into the Mediterranean. Obviously the German subs were riding that current into the Med. But how were they doing it, why were they surfacing, and how were they getting back out?

The Captain and I discussed my idea and together we figured out how to do the job. We would use our submarine as a neutral buoyancy tracer. That much was clear from the beginning. This meant wherever the ocean current went the submarine would go too. If the current flowed downwards, the submarine would go down. If the current flowed up, the submarine would go up. Thus, by tracing the actual motion of the submarine we realized we could map out the three dimensional movement of a particular flow line of the ocean current. As you know, water is incompressible and in motion it follows flow lines. If you start in a certain place, you will go with that particular flow line and end up where the continuity equation says you should.

All this was pretty elementary. Although the Captain had not studied hydrodynamics he immediately caught on to those basics. There were three major problems that needed to be solved.

First, how do we do this job safely. In order to completely map the flows through the straits we were going to have to go pretty close to some shoals. My knowledge of the continuity equation, and of eddies would greatly help with this problem. We really didn't need a very close approach to the danger areas because we could extend our knowledge of the flows in the safe areas to those in the dangerous ones. Furthermore, we would start right down the middle of the straits and later work our way to the sides. That way we would be gaining valuable experience as we progressed.

The second problem was how were we going to know exactly where we were at any given time. It's nice to say we were going to create a three dimensional current map, but we were almost flying blind. We could measure our distance from the bottom with sonar and we could measure our depth by pressure readings, but that was about it. It was evident we were going to need substantial assistance from surface ships. The Admiralty had also realized we were going to need to be escorted by a destroyer simply to protect us from being inadvertently depth charged by a friendly warship. Our escorting destroyer could provide one anchor of a measurement system, using shore based radio location techniques and sonar, but I felt we also needed two other sonar equipped surface ships to precisely determine our sub's three dimensional position at all times.

The third problem was security. A submarine operating in concert with a surface warship in repetitive patrols was bound to raise curiosity and, on leave, sailors were bound to talk. And Nazi spies abounded in that part of the world. After all, Spain was, for all practical purposes, Germany's ally. Moreover, we didn't want German subs anywhere near while we were making our measurements. They might guess what we were really up to.

We solved our various problems with a subterfuge. When we reached Gibraltar, and after I had made contact with the Allied forces in Morocco, I called up a captain's conference. Only the captains and I knew exactly what we were about. We cooked up a charade – we were a new kind of hunter-killer group with our submarine acting as an underwater scout equipped with special detectors. This cock-and-bull story was leaked out and it scared off the German subs long enough for us to do our job. Naturally we didn't find any German subs. So, after a few weeks the task force was disbanded as being ineffective and a waste of resources. This too was part of the charade, because by then we had developed a pretty good idea how to trap and kill the Nazi subs.

After some hard work we realized the German subs were surfacing so they could accurately determine their location. With this information, and presumably spy observations of British anti-sub activities, they could pick the right flow line into the Mediterranean.

Drifting silently with the current, some distance away from the anti-sub patrols, and with all machinery shut down, they were essentially invisible to the Allied defenders. It was evident the Germans had really done their hydrographic homework before the War. Most probably they had been using submarines in concert with specially equipped merchant shipping to create the needed three dimensional current maps.

The big surprise to me was how the subs might get back out into the Atlantic. It turned out there was a substantial amount of water flowing back from the Mediterranean to the Atlantic. The Med's water was saltier than the Atlantic's, so the Med's water sank beneath the inflow and travelled out along the bottom of the straits. We thoroughly mapped these outflowing bottom currents, as well. We also guessed the Nazi subs could surface on the Mediterranean side of the straits to get their bearings before slipping down into the outward bound current.

By the end of the project we pretty much knew where the German subs would be taking their observations, which flow lines they were likely to follow, and where they would be at any given time during their transits.

Now that we knew the ocean currents through the straits, the ocean became our friend. The captain and I started working with the US and British air crews, and surface fleets, to develop tactics to trap and attack enemy subs. Of course we used our sub as a practice target. Within a few months after starting our hard work our job was done and we headed home.

By now the captain and I, having worked so closely together, were quite good friends. The crew, of course, had long since figured out what we were really up to. It's almost impossible to keep secrets aboard a submarine. But though those submariners must have had some sympathy for their enemy counterparts, they had too many family and friends among the surface sailors for them to leak out what we had accomplished. Besides, England itself was at stake.

I was given a hearty farewell during our final approach to England, and again as I left the boat. Sure enough, there was my small companion waiting for me on shore.

The trip back to the States was almost an exact reversal of my trip out. Except, this time, I was going home.

As the plane reached its Long Island mooring I saw the same two government agents waiting for me on the dock. They brought me back to Cambridge and parted with the usual admonition not to tell anyone about my mission, not that I was about to. My cover story – I had been sick and in the hospital – was supposed to be effective because I had lost quite a bit of weight while I was at sea. My suntan came from convalescing in the hospital's solarium. Of course, none of this fooled anyone. My guardians and I said our goodbyes. This was the last I would ever see them, or so I thought.

It was hard getting back into the laboratory routine. After my great adventure what had once been fascinating research now felt rather dull. Months passed, when suddenly the two agents reappeared in the lab. Once again they told me to drop everything and come with them. Once again they drove me to my lodging. This time I was instructed to pack my best suit. I was going down to Washington and I would need it.

The train trip to Washington was quite pleasant. By now the agents and I had become well acquainted so we could talk about almost anything but my old mission. When we reached Washington they put me up in a first class hotel. My suit was sent out to be cleaned and pressed for the next day's meeting. In the morning I was barbered and manicured and immaculately dressed.

We got in the car and started out. I had it in my mind that I was going to the War Department to brief some Admirals about my *mission. But we did not go that way. Instead, we drove to the White House and pulled up to its portico. I was ushered inside the building. We walked passed the public area and into the working offices of the White House. Finally, I was directed into the inner sanctum, the Oval Office.*

President Roosevelt was sitting behind his big desk. 'Ah, Mr. Pellam', he said, a big smile on his face. 'I'm so glad to finally meet you. I've heard a lot about the work you've been doing.' He wheeled himself out from behind the desk and towards me. I had heard rumors about the wheelchair, everyone had, but I didn't believe them. In newsreels the President had always stood tall and strong.

The President motioned me to take a seat on the sofa. He called for refreshments and asked me a bit about my background. After some small chit chat Mr. Roosevelt conjured up a small box and a certificate of some kind. He opened the box and handed it to me. In it was a medal. A Presidential medal. The certificate was a Presidential Citation. 'You should have this,' he said. 'You've really earned it. The Prime Minister tells me the Royal Navy is nailing every Nazi sub that tries to slip by Gibraltar. Our ships in the Mediterranean are very much safer. All thanks to you. Well done,' he said. 'Well done!'

He leaned forward and patted my arm, his face alight with a twinkle in his eye and that famous jolly grin. In a low voice, as if in a conspiracy, he continued: 'Now we don't want word of this to get out, do we? Let this be our little secret, eh?'

As he finished his story Johnny Pellam, too, had a grin on his face and a twinkle in his eye. Maybe this all had been a tall tale. But then again, maybe not.

The vacuum chamber had completed its pump-down, so we got up and went back to work.

BLESSINGS

THE TRUE TREASURES OF THIS WORLD are not material. They are not gold or jewels or palaces. They are intangible. You may not even know those are your true treasures until you lose one of them, a loving parent, for example, or a dear friend. Sometimes you only realize what you have been given in a moment of epiphany.

When I was young I went through a rite of passage young men of that time suffered through. I received a formal letter from the government stating I had an appointment for my pre-induction physical. I was not going to be drafted because I was working in the defense industry and was, for the time being at least, deferred. But this was 1964 and a war was on. All young men had to be processed through the system, regardless.

The place of examination was an old building in downtown Los Angeles. It reminded me of a rundown gymnasium. We, the members of a vast crowd of young men, stripped down to our underwear, stored our clothes in lockers, and joined a long line. This was the first stage in a long established process of dehumanization which the ancient Roman Army invented.

The line snaked its way, back and forth, passing various review stations. Questions were asked and answers were stamped on the paperwork we carried. Then came the embarrassing place where we dropped our underwear and a rubber gloved examination was made of "private parts," no doubt meant to introduce us to what it meant to be a private in the Army.

But soon this unsettling experience was over. We put our clothes back on and several of us were herded into a large room and "invited" to take a seat at one of the many school desks there.

This last part of the day was devoted to an IQ exam. Two hours were allotted for the exam. For me, and for some of the others, the exam was easy. We started filtering out after twenty minutes or so. The conducting sergeant told us to be back before the exam was to finish. I wandered out of the building and found a small café where I could get a bite to eat.

I returned to the exam room a bit early and before the other wanderers. The room was empty except for the sergeant and two who were still taking the exam. Struggling to take the exam is a better description. One of those young men was black the other was white. As the clock wound down the emotions of both were visible. It was obvious they were failing this exam they so very much wanted to pass. The Army was their ticket to a better life — or so they obviously believed. But they were not going to make it.

Shock flashed through me as I realized what I was witnessing. My heart went out to those two, but there was nothing I could do. The scene changed my life. For the first time I fully understood how blessed I am. To this day I cannot look on the struggles of others without my attitude being tempered by what I saw that day in that lonely room.

Mom and Dad
Circa 1980

GENES

I CHOSE EXCELLENT PARENTS. My father's family were Wild West pioneers. My mother's parents were Sicilian immigrants, and pioneers too, of a different kind. The odd chance meeting that produced me is a typical American story. Classic melting pot.

Families such as these — pioneers who have to figure things out — create their own traditions and ideas. They pass this pioneering viewpoint down through the generations. As the inheritor of this way of looking at the world, I count myself blessed.

My mother, Catherine (Kay) Richards, born January, 1918
Portrait by Dad, 1950

MOM

SHE WAS A SMALL WOMAN, though she loomed large in my life. A small woman, petit, that is, slender, dark haired and beautiful. To be sure, every mother is beautiful to a small child. But old photos declare my mother was quite lovely. It didn't matter much to her. She was an everyday lady in her own estimation, and in the way she presented herself to others. If she stood out at all, and she did, it was because she was bursting with intelligence, sweetness and good humor.

Mom was born in Brooklyn in 1918, the third of five sisters. Her father, Giovanni, had emigrated from Sicily shortly after 1900. He and his older brother had been selected by their family to go to America to establish a foothold and work to import the rest of the clan. After some years of hard work the two of them prospered and my grandfather sailed back to Sicily to marry my grandmother, Lucia, and bring her to this country. Lucia was only seventeen when the first of her daughters, Angie, was born. In swift succession, Josephine, my mother Catherine, and Dunette followed. The youngster, Fran, was born several years later. It was a classic immigrant family of that era.

My grandfather earned his living from his fish market in Harlem. He and his market were well liked, and well-guarded by the locals, so my grandfather prospered. Giovanni, now John, was an enthusiastic adopted American. He insisted his daughters speak only English around their apartment. They did, when he was present. Mom's fluency in Sicilian tells me when Grandfather was away working they chattered with Grandmother in her language. And so Mom grew up in a two language household — Grandmother never became a fluent English speaker.

Mom was an excellent student and was able, for a couple of years, to attend nursing school at Hunter College in New York. There, after residency at the fearsome Bellevue Hospital, she became a registered nurse. Mom's stories about the place said its frightening reputation is not exaggerated. She came out of the experience tempered and tough. That steel served her well in the coming years.

Mom liked to read. The best place for it, with its nearly infinite resources, was the New York Public Library. It happened a certain someone also liked to read. This was a young soldier, a sergeant in the Army Air Corps who was posted to the air station on Long Island. On his leave days, instead of heading for the nearest bar with his comrades, this young soldier headed for the New York Public Library.

One day it chanced that these two youngsters were standing together on the corner across the street from the library. While waiting for the signal to change they got into a conversation. Mom was fascinated with the handsome and highly intelligent young soldier. The fascination was reciprocal. This quick witted beauty certainly drew one's attention. It is unlikely any reading was done that day. Romance was in the air, and so, after a suitable time, was marriage. Mom and Dad became one. They stayed one for sixty-six years.

In the beginning, with a wedding and a family in his immediate future, Dad started looking around for a different assignment from the dangerous aerial photography he'd been doing. His dream job became available, and he jumped at it. After the wedding Dad was foreman of the Army's giant printing plant at Fort Benning, Georgia. There in Columbus, nine months after their honeymoon in New Orleans, I was born. It was eight days after Pearl Harbor and the nation was now at war. After the wedding Dad was foreman of the Army's giant printing plant at Fort Benning, Georgia. There in Columbus, nine months after their honeymoon in New Orleans, I was born. It was eight days after Pearl Harbor and the nation was now at war.

Mom joined the Department of Public Health. Her job was the most demanding and dangerous they had to offer. She was a circuit nurse taking care of the sick in Georgia's backwoods.

Dirt poor farms covered much of the rural areas of southwestern Georgia. The Depression hit hard for all, white and black alike. The diseases were those of poverty and swamps. The big four were malaria, pellagra, intestinal hook worms and yellow fever. These weren't the only diseases, of course, but they were the worst. Pellagra was a vitamin deficiency. Worms a parasite. The poor were their principal victims. Malaria and yellow fever were mosquito borne. They affected everyone, including those passing through. It took courage to minister to these impoverished people. That was my mother.

When I was a teenager Mom told me I had nearly died when I was only a few months old. I had a lethal case of bronchial pneumonia. I didn't respond to sulfa drugs, the only antibiotic available at the time. I did respond to a miracle, however. The miracle was penicillin. But penicillin didn't exist in early 1942, so how could this possible?

Actually, it turns out small quantities of the drug did exist, and Mom found a way to get it to me in time to save my life. How little was available? It is reported that by the end of 1942 fewer than one hundred doses had been produced. One estimate puts the number at thirty. Since I took sick early in the year there could not have been more than a small handful of doses yet produced.

What is more, the very existence of penicillin was a closely guarded military secret. The curative molecule from the penicillium mold was widely known to be antibacterial, but it was a long road from scientific discovery to a widely available pharmaceutical drug, a road yet to be traveled. How Mom discovered the existence of this military secret, and how she obtained the necessary dose she never said. However she did it, she must have fought for that dose with great intelligence and diplomacy, especially since time was of the essence. That was my mother.

I might mention the earliest application of penicillin in the historical literature was to save the life of a woman hospitalized with a fatal staph infection. This was in March of 1942. No other medical interventions that year are in the published literature. Nevertheless, I would have been given my dose about the same time.

When I was only a couple of years old Mom became seriously ill. I said backwoods Georgia was a dangerous place. It was, and Mom suffered the consequences. My parents would not tell me the details. Dad took me on the train to Brooklyn to stay with my grandparents until my mother recovered. Several months later he picked me up and we rode back to Georgia. When I greeted my mother she was astonished and amused — I was babbling away in Sicilian. I remember my grandmother spoke to me with a funny kind of English. In the beginning she was hard to understand. Her accent was thick, her words were mostly new to me and her speech was all twisted up and backwards. That was all right. If she wanted to speak that way, I would too. We got along just fine.

Mom worked during the day. Dad was in the Army and usually slept in the barracks, except on occasional weekends. Someone had to take care of me when Mom wasn't around. So teenaged Laura Mae was engaged. I knew Laura Mae was different, but that was okay. I had my mommy and I had my mammy. It should not be a surprise I sometimes was a bit confused as to who was who for a while. Indeed, I loved Laura Mae almost as much as I loved my mother. For me she was part of our family. Laura Mae's own family was large, with many kids — brothers, sisters, cousins — not much older than myself. The children in Laura Mae's home were my playmates until the war was over, and we moved. We both, Mom and I, treasured our memories of Laura Mae.

Dad was released from the Army shortly after VJ Day. He and Mom decided it was time to go back home. We packed up and moved to Dad's hometown of Seattle. We didn't stay long. Mom was depressed by the endless drizzle in exceptionally rainy western Washington. So, *California Here We Come* became our song as we drove south. We landed in San Francisco.

Mom found public health employment in the rough Hunters Point district while Dad was developing new skills as a color lithographer at the region's largest printing establishment. Postwar Hunters Point was a taxing assignment. This was the Navy's shipyard area. During the war the massive crowds of roughnecks needed to repair combat damaged ships had magnified the area's already bad reputation. Postwar was worse.

The wartime workers were moving on only to be replaced with an influx of Afro-Americans. Racial tensions were intensified by predatory real estate practices which penalized both blacks *and* whites. Tough as Mom was, it is little wonder she would occasionally come home frazzled.

What bothered Mom was not the work, but the climate. For all its physical beauty, San Francisco can be a miserable place to live. Much of the year, especially in the summer, the climate consists of bone chilling fogs made more penetrating by icy winds. In its own way San Francisco's weather was as punishing to Mom's morale as Seattle's. Mom and Dad started looking for a happier place.

Me, Dad, and my sister Marie, 1959

Desert warm Southern California beckoned. And so in 1949 we headed south, and landed in Glendale. For the next seven years Mom worked at the local office of the Los Angeles County

Department of Public Health. There, as before, she was making house calls, but the duties were far less demanding than what she had already survived. The only thing sometimes frying Mom was office politics. This organization had them in abundance.

By this time I had grown up enough to begin to understand the world from the point of view of an adult. My introduction to this strange office milieu began at the dinner table. Mom and Dad always treated me as an intelligent member of the family, especially when we were having our evening meal. My questions were answered in a straight forward way. My opinion was always respected. So, I was part of conversations about what went on at work. Office Politics was my introduction to a kind of bizarre fantasy land. I still am repulsed by this selfishly destructive behavior.

In 1957 Mom took a leave of absence to give birth to my sister, Joan Marie. The next several years were devoted to raising this delightful child. While Marie was growing up — fast — Mom decided to return to school to achieve her dream of a well-rounded college education, and a Bachelor's Degree. This brought her fully up to date in modern nursing.

Returning to work was her next goal. She contacted LA County Health for reinstatement. She was in for a shock. Her leave was voided. The county would only hire her as an entry level nurse. No credit was to be given for the years she had already worked for the county, no credit was given for the many years she had earlier nursed under the most demanding conditions. To add further insult, she was to be posted to the farthest extent of Los Angeles County, out in the desert a full hour and a half's drive from home. Office Politics! Those shriveled souls were not about to allow a seasoned old pro to intrude on their precious empire. Go away! Don't bother us.

Mom took retirement. From that time on her focus shifted more and more to taking care of Dad, now retired from the printing industry but still active as a successful inventor. After her retirement Mom and Dad found they had a new freedom. Not having any great reason to stay in California, they decided to move to the east coast. The local smog was causing Dad severe lung problems, and Mom had family there. Eventually they settled in Virginia near where Marie, now active in the U.S. Foreign Service, had established her home.

Mom's gone now. She passed in her ninety-fifth year. Still, she lives on in me. She lives on in how I live, how I view the world, in my sense of what is right and what is wrong. She lives in my most basic moral foundations.

I think of my life with Mom as something like the course of a long beautiful day. An endless time when I felt she was always there, somewhere near me. I became aware of her at dawn. That was the time for being nurtured. As the day brightened she was always there, encouraging my development, binding my wounds both physical and emotional, showing me how to live, showing me how to shrug off inevitable reverses. As I came into my own she cheered my achievements. Inside me she was always there, like the warmth of sunshine, wherever in the world I might be and whatever I might be doing. She is alive within me still.

It is difficult to convey Mom's personality. It is difficult to evoke the grace, humor, intelligence and fearless tenaciousness of this extraordinary person. A couple of incidents only hint at the sheer pleasure of having this great lady as my mother.

I was visiting home for the weekend. My young sister was caught in the emotional throes of becoming a woman. We four were sitting at the kitchen table having supper. For some reason Marie threw a tantrum — over nothing consequential. She surprised me with her vehemence — explosions like this were quite unlike the Marie I knew. Mom studied this outburst for a while. In a quiet voice, she said: "Nine point five," and went on eating. Dad picked up this sally and increased the score to nine point seven.

Marie was having none of it. Up she jumped from the table, tears beginning to stream down her face. She ran down the hall to her bedroom and slammed the door so hard the walls of the kitchen shook like we were in the midst of a California earthquake. The three of us looked at each other, said nothing, and resumed our meal. We knew what was coming.

After a little while my sister came back down the hall and rejoined us, all sunny and giggling. She had been had. She knew she had been had, and by a true master. The game was permanently up. It was to be the last of her emotional outbursts.

A few years before the tantrum, Marie and our parents were vacationing in the midst of a grove of Sequoias in the Sierra Mountains. One evening there was a rustling on the front porch of the cabin in which they were staying. Some kind of animal was pawing at the door. Did it want to come in, or was it simply curious? After a while Mom was fed up. Time to do something about the nuisance. She grabbed a broom, opened the door and confronted . . . a bear! Raising the broom Mom shooed the bear off the porch and into the woods. "Get out of here!" she commanded. "Leave us alone. You don't belong here." Dad looked at her with wry amusement as she reentered the cabin. "Kay," he said with a smile, "the bear lives here. We don't."

That was my Mom.

Dad, age 9 or 10, and his older brother Trummy, about 20
Circa 1923-24

DAD

Dad's father, Truman L. Richards, was unusual for the time, for he was a university graduate, having been one of the few students matriculated at the still young campus of the University of Washington. Always interested in literature, early in the last century he set up a print shop in Seattle and married my grandmother, who became his partner in business as well as in life. The small family printing enterprise, later known as Greenlake Press, prospered, and my grandparents became the publishers of several community newspapers.

Dad and his father were evidently quite close. Dad used to tell stories of his father's excursions with him into the Great North Woods near Seattle. The land of constant rain, western Washington is, but it did not matter. Into the woods they went, regardless. From his father's experience, and, through his father, from lessons handed down by his pioneering grandfather, Dad learned woodsman's skills: how to build a fire in the wet, how to camp warm and dry despite the rain, how to properly sharpen a knife, how to carry an axe — blade out — so as to avoid injury in case of a fall, how to safely use a rifle, how to hunt.

The first shock of many followed. Shocks that profoundly changed my father's life. Dad was fourteen when it happened. It was an automobile accident — a collision. Dad's father smashed through the windshield, leaving him with a fractured skull. He lingered for some time, and finally succumbed from his injuries.

Printer's ink was in my father's blood from his earliest childhood until his passing at the age of ninety-three. Working in the print shop when he was young built his muscles. Newspaper galleys of lead type metal, ready for the press, could weigh fifty pounds, or more. It was normal for the boy who was to become my dad to lug around two of these at a time. Not that Dad was tall, or heavy set. Dad was medium height and lean. Yes, that's the word — *lean*. He weighed only about a hundred and twenty pounds until he reached middle age, by which time he finally maxed out at a hundred and forty. But, slim though he always was, he was, for his size, the strongest man I ever knew. I remember it was no trouble for him to hoist a couple of fifty pound sacks of ready mix concrete and haul them over to some backyard construction. He could do this all day long without tiring.

His great strength served him well while he worked summers as a ranch hand near Ellensburg, Washington. Working the ranch did not always mean herding cattle. More likely it meant lifting heavy bales of hay.

When he came of age, Dad entered the University of Washington to study engineering. But it was still the Great Depression, and long hours of work conflicted with long hours of study. The mix was not a good one.

Two years was all Dad could manage of university studies before finally succumbing to reality. So he hopped a freight and headed east. Bad business, riding the rails. Bad and dangerous. Inevitably, Dad fell in with a rough crowd. Hobos were not always, indeed seldom were, the romantic figures of later mythology. Dad was lucky, though. Somewhere along the way a railroad detective caught him and yanked him out of the box car. The detective saved his life. He explained Dad's companions figured to murder him and split up his belongings. It had happened before. I remember Dad telling me this story, and telling me in his calm, matter of fact way.

The kind-hearted detective kept Dad with him and saw him safely to Chicago, where he got Dad a job in an ice cream factory, hauling blocks of ice. Once again Dad's great strength served him well.

War broke out when Germany invaded Poland. Dad figured we would someday be in it, and those who got in first would be best off. So, he joined the Army. Actually, he joined the Army Air Corps. Those good folks sent him to Long Island and trained him as an aerial photographer, not too much of a stretch given the skills he had already acquired.

Air Corps aerial photography still had an archaic flavor. Already the British and Germans were equipping their fastest fighters with automated cameras. We did things differently over here. Dad flew in an antique bomber — one with an open cockpit up front. Snugged into a leather harness, he leaned far out the door and snapped off photos with a hand-held camera. The photos, I remember, were superb. New York City was a sharply etched grid with a multitude of tall buildings reaching up as if to try to snag the old plane out of the air.

On his leaves Dad would oftentimes travel into Manhattan. Unlike most soldiers there, his destination frequently was the New York Public Library. One day, while waiting on the corner across from the library, he could not help but notice the pretty young lady, headed for the library as he was, the charmer who was my mother to be.

It didn't take long before Romance was in the air, and the friendship started to get serious. Mom took Dad home to meet her Sicilian-born parents. The Old Country had certain customs which must be adhered to, one of them being The Formal Meal. Dad did not know how this meal worked, but he was, nevertheless, on his best behavior. The consequence was interesting.

Picture this: Dad at the time weighed less than 120 pounds. Lean is a word I have used, but skinny is probably a better description. There Dad was, sitting straight up, army stiff, in his chair at the dining table. A dish was brought in and Dad was encouraged to sample it. I can attest to the fact that my grandmother's English, such as it was, was not exactly easy to understand. Undoubtedly Dad was doing his best, but he was definitely in over his head. Instead of sampling from the dish, Dad thought this was part of the main meal, so he took it all.

This was a bit of a surprise to the rest of those present, but everyone was being extra polite and the formalities proceeded as usual. More of the same was brought in so everyone could also eat. Still more samples arrived and again Dad overindulged. This continued through several courses of these delights until soup and salad and, at last, the main meal was served. By this time, of course, Dad was more than stuffed. Nonetheless, he somehow managed to get it all down. Then came desert. A rich desert. Followed by coffee and cookies. Again, Dad somehow achieved the impossible. We laughed about that sensational supper for decades.

Dad loved the Air Corps. And the Corps was good to Dad. Getting in before the great military expansion was good. Becoming a technical specialist was good, too. Within a year after he joined up he had already been promoted to the rank of Staff Sergeant. As it happened, something soon occurred to change his mind about flying.

Out on a training mission one day, Dad's plane was lumbering along on its way to the target. Things were a bit too relaxed during this routine flight. Dad had lashed his parachute to a cabin fixture and he was sitting, probably not comfortably, and drowsing. The pilot and copilot were also probably half asleep. Certainly they were not looking around as they should have been. Suddenly, out of nowhere, a giant Pan American Transatlantic Clipper sped right past the nose of the old bomber.

The prop wash from the huge, four engine transport knocked the much smaller bomber totally out of control. Dad's plane promptly fell out of the sky. The bomber didn't spin out, it just tumbled towards the ground.

So there Dad was, in the center of the cabin, suspended in midair, the plane rotating slowly around him, everything out of reach. Dad couldn't even swim over to grab his parachute. Fortunately, the pilots managed to recover the plane or I would not be writing this.

The incident woke Dad up, as well. Deeply in love and committed to marriage, he started looking for another job. He landed one down in Georgia. He was going back to printing. So he and Mom were soon married and living down South. I was born the regulation nine months later, only a week after Pearl Harbor.

With the war now on, Dad was appointed foreman of one of the Army's largest printing plants — the one at Fort Benning, Georgia. Dad's job was to print the battle maps for upcoming campaigns. The Army had no more sensitive job than Dad's. Dad was not entirely happy with his position, though.

He wanted to go to the war. He applied for officer's training, repeatedly. His captain turned him down, repeatedly. Finally the captain explained second lieutenants in combat had a life expectancy of only a couple of weeks. Given Dad had a wife and son, and was doing war critical work, he was of much more value where he was. Dad acquiesced to this wisdom. But still he wondered what he had missed.

Shortly after the war, when we were living in San Francisco, there was a parade. It might have been the first anniversary of VJ Day, or it may have been the mustering out of the final lot of war soldiers. Dad, for the last time, put on his old Army uniform — a uniform with more stripes on it than before. We got in the car and drove downtown. The crowd was dense, excited and proud. Dad hoisted me on his shoulders so I could see the phalanxes of soldiers marching by. "Remember this," he told me. "You may not see this again." I have not, since.

After the war Dad was finally able to get his prized Union ticket — a hard thing to come by. He worked for many years at the bench as a color lithographer — camera man, dot etcher and stripper. Having mastered these highly exacting skills, he was well enough thought of by his colleagues to be elected as an official of his union, the Amalgamated Lithographers of America.

Eventually Dad accumulated enough savings and experience to join with two of his friends and start a shop of his own. Strictly speaking this was not a print shop. Rather, Dad's trade shop specialized in preparing the color separations (in the form of photographic films) needed for creating the printing plates used in four color printing. Dad's business prospered because it was known throughout the industry for delivering the highest quality product.

I never heard Dad brag about anything. He did seem to be proud once, when he said that Frank Sinatra, in his contract with Capital Records, specified no one but he was to do Sinatra's printing preparation.

As I wrote in The Potato, I worked in Dad's shop during the summer months and weekends. I was maybe eleven years old when I started. In the beginning I had only two tasks. One was to mix the chemicals — developers and fixers — needed for processing the photographic films. These chemicals were dry powders which had to be dissolved in distilled water. (Yes, they were toxic; Ferro cyanide was one of the components.) Mixing was critically important, for any flaw in the process would ruin the films. My second duty was equally important. I had to keep the shop immaculately clean. No dust was permitted, for a speck of dust on the films would also cause their ruin. This was a particularly hard thing to do because the shop fronted on a busy street with automobile traffic constantly stirring up dust and debris. Mopping floors and careful dusting usually took most of the day. It was also my duty to clean the toilets and keep the bathroom in an attractive state. My reward was to be paid the princely sum of a dollar an hour (good money at the time).

A couple of years after the shop opened Dad proudly announced, over dinner, he had purchased a press, a small proof press. This would allow him to do short four color runs and highlight any corrections needed before the color separations were to be delivered to the customer.

The next day I eagerly accompanied Dad to the shop to see this new marvel. There it sat, bedraggled, encrusted with decades old residues of multicolored inks. These days so-called fine artists would probably swoon over such a rainbow swathed found object. But Dad was a real artist and the press was merely a tool.

Dad admitted the press needed some work to get running. "Don't tell Mom," he cautioned, for he did not want her to think he had made a fool investment. "Some work" actually meant taking the press completely apart, down to the last nut and bolt, and cleaning all the parts until they were as immaculate as if newly manufactured, and where appropriate, oiling or greasing them. Cleaning involved soaking the smaller parts in buckets of kerosene and scrubbing the encrusted inks off. The larger parts and the framework had to be cleaned separately, a much tougher job. For weeks Dad and I sat on the floor, disassembling, cleaning and reassembling. Miraculously, nothing of this complex machine got lost and the reassembly came out fine (try taking an old fashioned mechanical clock apart and putting it back together so it runs perfectly — a much easier task).

The day came, at last, for the "smoke test." The machine was plugged into the recently wired up heavy duty electrical outlet. Dad pushed the big green 'Run' button. It worked! Slowly the machine accelerated to full, clattering, speed. Dad showed no reaction. He stood still for a couple of minutes, looking and listening. Slowly, he walked around the mechanical marvel, his ear cocked, listening — always listening. "Not good," he said. He shut the machine down and we began taking off the covers.

Hours later, the press having been partly disassembled, tinkered with, and reassembled, we were ready for another go. Again the machine clattered to life. "Better," Dad said, but it was still not good enough. "Tomorrow we'll work on this some more." And so it went, day after day. Each time, Dad would hear something new in the tumbling mechanisms inside the whirling machine. Each time we would disassemble it and Dad would make a correction. Each time, the expression on Dad's face would become slightly more relaxed.

The day came when Dad finally smiled — a great happy grin lit up his face. The machine sang a sweet song only my father understood. The press was finally ready to go to work, good as brand new.

Then came the strike.

Printer's unions had always been a hotbed of radical agitation, especially in Los Angeles, and the Lithographers Union was no exception. Its history was laced with long and bitter strikes; just a generation before, people had died. This new strike presented Dad with a dilemma. Though he worked at the bench quite amicably alongside his employees, nevertheless they were his employees, and Dad was now Management, no longer a member of the Union.

The conversion to management and the subsequent strike did not modify Dad's inclinations. They remained strongly sympathetic to the skilled craftsmen who produced the product. Nevertheless, he had learned a great deal about the pressures and responsibilities of meeting a payroll.

The strike hit the industry hard. As with his employees, it put my father in a difficult position. All of us were small fry with few resources to sustain us through a long walkout. Dad made the best of it, though. He set up a table, with a rented awning to shade his workers. This was in the parking lot behind the shop. There, he kept plenty of refreshments for his striking employees. In turn, his men "picketed" only in the back, rather than on the street where they were supposed to be. While the employees sat outside and chatted the hours away, Dad and his partners worked hard inside to meet their contractual commitments. Through the summer I worked there, keeping the shop immaculate.

The strike stretched on through the summer and into the fall, past the opening of school. No resolution was in sight. Finally, the Union and Management could agree on one thing: They wanted my father to mediate.

Mom and I did not see much of Dad after that. He would come home, exhausted, late at night, only to be up before dawn to go back to the bargaining table. Dad put his heart and soul into finding some formula both sides would accept. Eventually he hit on something that turned out to be magic. Suddenly, each faction discovered they could get more than what they had originally wanted.

The strike was settled. Dad's magic formula remained magic and the basis for settling all subsequent disputes. Dad proved himself to be a wizard. More than half a century has since passed and the formerly turbulent industry has had relative peace. Perhaps achieving that settlement was Dad's proudest moment.

Dad's business folded after one of Dad's partners died and the shares had to be liquidated.

By the time I was well along in high school, Dad had become Plant Manager of a major printing company in another part of Los Angeles.

Later Dad went into the business of printing money — literally. He took on the management of a large and highly secretive printing plant. In this heavily guarded establishment much of the world's money was printed.

Before finally retiring from the printing business, Dad established a demonstration trade shop which introduced computer controlled laser color separation scanners to Southern California.

All along, Dad had been tinkering with inventions for the printing industry. After his formal retirement as a printer he started a new career as a professional inventor and engineer. He did quite well in this endeavor, too, licensing several inventions which quickly became standard tools in the printing industry.

Word got around about his expertise and the newly born integrated circuit industry called him in as a consultant to teach their engineers how to produce, and precisely align, the photo masks needed to manufacture those early integrated circuits.

Well into his eighties Dad was still learning, still striving, still inventing. His last endeavor was to develop microprocessor-controlled machinery. Eventually, though, the advent of personal computers, and automated color separation software to go with them, made the skills of the traditional lithographic tradesmen obsolete, along with most of Dad's inventions. Dad retired a second time, this time for good.

My father, all his life, was a kind man. He could be quite stern with me, but only when I got completely out of line. And always he treated me respectfully, though sometimes he had to fight to keep his temper in check.

Dad's respect was most clearly shown at the dinner table. As we'd sit and discuss the events of the day, he'd never evade any of my questions. He always treated my opinion as if they were coming from someone who was his equal, disregarding our age difference. This I remember from my earliest years.

After dinner Dad and I would do the dishes, thereby taking some of the burden from my hardworking mother.

Helping clean the house was another chore he gladly performed, though often exhausted himself. He helped with the cleaning right up to the last days when he, physically, could no longer carry on — and still he complained about no longer being able to help.

As soon as he saw I was up to it, he introduced me to progressively more dangerous, but interesting, tasks. At an early age I learned how to safely use a full size table saw and other power tools. Together we built various pieces of electronic equipment — Dad teaching me how to form a perfect solder joint. Together we built substantial structures out of concrete and brick. The education I received at home was far more important, in its way, than anything I brought home from school.

Of course, like all of us, he evolved over time. Early on he was gregarious and loved a good argument. He laughed a lot in those early years. Later on he became quiet and introspective. He took the ribbing we gave him about his increasing taciturn demeanor with grace and good humor. "Silent Sam," we'd call him. But his intelligence, wit and interest in the world remained keen.

Who could ask for a better pathfinder to show me the way to live.

GREAT-GRANDFATHER'S HERNIA

OSCAR P. SAYLES HAD A HERNIA. My great-grandfather had a hernia. This is a matter of some consequence.

I learned about my great-grandfather from my great-uncle, Chet Sayles. When he was very old Uncle Chet reminisced into a microphone about his years on the western frontier. His parents' saga began the long tale. It is likely that I had heard the story ages before, but it had slipped out of memory.

Shortly after the Second World War we moved to San Francisco. On occasion Uncle Chet kept me company in his ginger bread Victorian town house, while my parents went out for a night on the town.

I remember one night. Fed milk and cookies, I curled up in a deep stuffed chair. It was time for the stories. I was fascinated by the telling, though I had little understanding of what Uncle Chet was relating. But what five year old boy was not entranced with cowboys and Indians and outlaws?

Soon, drowsy from the cookies, I drifted into dreams. Briefly I was aware of my father gently lifting me from the darkened bed. Time for home. That is all I knew until sunshine. Happy memories. Now it's Uncle Chet's turn...

Pilgrims on the Plains, sketched by Theo R. Davis

ory of
Mother's telling about it, it was in '63.

The first year of the Civil War Father wanted to go into the service, but he had a double hernia, and always had to wear a belt (and he never did have an operation), so he was excused. So apparently he got on a horse and rode out because he wanted to come West.

Well, they didn't organize these wagon trains east of the Mississippi River, so he came out and landed in the east border of Nebraska, on the Missouri River. At that place they were organizing this wagon train. I can't remember the name or even if there was a town there, but anyway it was a congregating place, and started west.

They only traveled about fifteen miles a day, and most of the train was pulled by oxen.

But they had a big train, and therefore very little Indian trouble on the way across. However, they did have one Indian mishap, which I'll tell you about.

I don't know where it was, but it seems that one of their people, a man that belonged to the wagon train, had killed – shot – an Indian squaw. The wagons were going along and the Indians came up pretty close to them and this idiot of a person shot the squaw and killed her. Well, pretty soon then the Indians surrounded that train, all around it. They just came from everyplace, behind every bush it seemed like, according to Mother. They wanted that man. And apparently they knew who it was, because they could see.

So the wagon train leader decided that giving him over was the only thing to do to save a lot of lives. So they turned him over to the Indians and the Indians skinned him alive, right in front of the *wagon train. They just took a knife, cut his skin and pulled it off in strips, you know.*

That was 'bout the only thing that happened of any consequence. Father said they never had much trouble with the road until they came to the Snake River in Idaho. Now, I think the Snake River in this place borders Idaho and Washington, I'm not sure.

Father apparently was what they call an outrider. The train would roll along in a big long string, and they would put these riders out, about one half to one mile away depending on the terrain. If it was level they'd be a mile away looking for Indians or trouble. And if it was hilly country they'd be at the right place so that they could tell if they were going to have any trouble.

So, when they got to the Snake River, he was one of their outriders, and in order to get across the river – it was in flood stage, which was apparently the end of summer when the snows were melting in the Canadian hills – these riders would go upstream and attach a rope there, a long rope. Then they'd swim across on their horses with the long rope and they'd used it to pull over other ropes until they had one that was big enough that they could get the wagons over.

Now the wagons, they would float them across on logs. The logs were there apparently from people ahead of them. They would attached the logs to the wheels and pull the wagon across. The horses would slip, and it took a long time. Now the river was so high that they lost a couple of outriders there: Their horses tripped over something and the riders went down the river and drowned.

About my great-grandmother

On the journey west my great-grandfather became very close to the Mills family. One of their (ultimately six) daughters was eleven year old Sarah Eliza. She was to become my great-grandmother. But Sarah had to grow up to the age of seventeen before the two were married in 1871.

I have the high school graduation photo of my grandmother, Alta Sayles — Uncle Chet's older sister. She was a very pretty young lady. The Washington branch of my family produced some women of spectacular beauty. Genes being what they are, I suspect that my great-grandmother, Sarah, was quite lovely when she was young — someone to attract the devotion of my great-grandfather. Uncle Chet's memory of his mother would have been that of a much older woman — a woman weathered by pioneering.

Now my mother, she was a short, chunky little woman. Pennsylvania Dutch. I remember her talking about it so much, and I think at that time they wore the Dutch clothing, like the bonnets and that sort of thing.

Her folks, their name was Mills, and her father was a captain in a Northern Army regiment, or whatever it was, from Pennsylvania, and I think he was in the war about two years when he was wounded and discharged. Now I don't know anything about the wound, or his discharge or anything, but when that happened he wanted to move west too. So they left Pennsylvania and came out and happened to come to the same spot where Father was (and of course they didn't know each other before then).

Well another thing, when that big wagon train got to the Continental Divide it was just above Rawlins, Wyoming, at Rock Springs, Wyoming. Well, when I went through there years later I stopped and talked to an old timer there and asked him about where the wagon train went. 'Well,' he says, 'it went right through here.' 'Well,' I said, 'Did it go to California or Washington?' 'Well,' he said, 'the dividing place was about fifteen miles up here on the Continental Divide.' So that's where this wagon train split up, and about half of them went north into Oregon, and the other half went south, down to Salt Lake and California.

Years afterwards, when I went over to eastern Oregon, hunting, I asked about the Oregon Trail. Father told me about that. He says when you get out on this road, about so and so, you look carefully and you'll see two tracks where the Oregon Trail went through here and down to The Dalles, Now, It ended at The Dalles, one of the most beautiful spots on the Columbia River. Then from The Dalles (this is in '63, I believe) this group split up.

Trail's End

The part of the Oregon Trail which headed for the Willamette Valley ended at The Dalles simply because it could not go any farther. Prior to this location the Willamette fork of the Oregon trail had followed the south bank of the Columbia river. At The Dalles a lava flow, part of the northern skirt of volcanic Mt. Hood met the river. Here it formed high, and impassible, cliffs.

During the early years of the migration the settlers had no choice but to make rafts from the local timber and float their disassembled wagons on the treacherous waters of the Columbia. Hopefully they would fetch up safe before reaching the dangerous rapids of The Cascades.

In 1846 the notoriously bad and expensive Barlow toll road was opened which provided an alternative. This road looped around the southern end of Mt. Hood. It was very long, and it negotiated steep and difficult ravines, but many considered it safer than trusting the water route. The river run remained in use, however, and that's the route that my great grandfather and the Mills family took.

Father took the northern route because he had always been a woodsman. He had been raised in the New England states (though born in Illinois), *and he was an expert with a saw and an axe, and that sort of thing. He wanted to get into wooded country, so that's the way he went.*

By that time my father had gotten acquainted with the Mills family and they were rather close – and they all went together down to Willamette Valley.

They spent, oh I guess, about a year there, because when you've come three thousand miles to start a home, you kinda want to look around and see where you want to live. So Dad prospected that whole country, and finally decided that he didn't want to stay there. The Mills family, probably the whole group of them, decided this also. So it was decided.

So they gathered together a wagon, and of course Dad took his tools – the main thing was a big two handle saw – along with other saws, his axes, and his sharpening tools.

They started across the Columbia River. You went up from Willamette to Portland and then you met the Columbia. The Columbia is a big river. The only way you could cross it was a ferry at a little town called Kalama which is about, uh, oh, I think it was about twenty miles, maybe thirty miles north down the river (the river runs north, the Columbia river runs north from Portland and turns west and goes to the ocean). Well, they crossed by this ferry, and then started out to get through the country.

The Northern Trail

The Oregon Trail split into multiple routes as it approached Oregon territory. The main route went to the Willamette valley. This route is what most people think of when they think of the Oregon Trail. The branch to the north of the Willamette trail passed across central Washington territory and through the Cowlitz River gap in the Cascade Mountains. When it was due south of the settlement of Olympia the trail turned a right angle and headed north to the new Olympia settlement, and then on to Seattle. The distance from this corner to Olympia was about 35 miles — two days on the well-traveled Cowlitz Trail.

From Kalama to the right angle turn of the Cowlitz Trail was forty miles of densely wooded — and impassible by wagons — wilderness. It is this forty mile stretch which Uncle Chet is referring to. With a clear wagon road a wagon train could traverse this stretch in an easy three days. Without such a road it took much longer.

There was no road from there (Kalama), there was just trails. I don't know how long it took them to get from there to Olympia — that's where they were going — but it was a long time. Mother said that they'd go a little ways and there'd be a tree fallen across the trail. They'd look around, try to find a way to get through, but couldn't do it. So Dad'd get the big saw out, cut the thing in two, put his team on, get the thing out of the way, then drive through. It probably took them months to go to Olympia.

In Olympia, it was just a little settlement and Dad still didn't know where he was going to settle (course he could homestead most anyplace), so he prospected that part of the Puget Sound area.

He went to Seattle, and while he was there, he got acquainted with Mr. Yessler, who was the founder of Seattle. Mr. Yessler had a sawmill there — the Yessler Mill.

Well, Father talked to Yessler, and Yessler tried to get Father to get together a logging outfit, so that he could go up the hill and log for

Yessler. Yessler owned the land and that was the area on the first hill in Seattle, above Pioneer Square.

Mr. Yessler said, 'If you can, get a team and go up there and clear out ten acres,' (it was beautiful standing timber), he says, 'I'll give you half the land.' And that meant, if Dad could have arranged to get in there, he'd have five acres of land right in the center of Seattle (four city blocks). *Anyway, Dad couldn't do it, so he went back and decided to take a homestead just outside of Olympia.*

Now Dad, he figured that Olympia, being the end of Puget Sound, was going to be the big city, which was a mistake. So he took a homestead, I think about ten miles south of Olympia, at a place called Bush Prairie. Bush Prairie. And it was nothing in the world but timber. As the old Arkansas traveler said, 'As thick as hair on the back of a dog.'

He stayed there about twelve years. He built a barn (I'll tell you about that a little later). He cleared off and drained forty acres of forest, swamp and pasture lands, and raised hay on it. And pretty near every year he'd mow his hay – and he had to do it with that axe – and then the rains would come and spoil his hay. He was raising cattle, so he'd have to buy hay to feed them, or sometimes he'd just turn them loose – all that sort of the thing. Anyway, finally he got so disgusted with Puget Sound weather that he finally gave up and he decided to go to Ellensburg.

Now I believe it was probably the first year that the Northern Pacific Railroad was open. The railroad went through Ellensburg and on to Seattle. That's why Seattle grew big and Olympia did not. They went to Ellensburg and bought a little sixteen acre ranch over there, because of the weather.

One day Mother said, 'Chet, couldn't you take me over to the old homestead sometime? I'd like to see it.' She must have been around 70 or 75. And I says, 'Well we sure will.'

We drove out what is known as the 101 highway to a certain place and then we, instead of making a turn, we went straight ahead and out into the Bush Prairie. Mother hadn't been there for, oh, years and years, and it had all changed. Finally she said, 'Now take it easy.' So we were going along slow, and she says, 'Stop here.' And she says, 'Now, I'm sure that's the road that goes into the homestead.' Well, we had to stop and open the gate. Apparently the people that owned it were using it for pasture land. So we opened the gate and drove in, and we could only go a little ways because the road hadn't been kept up and there was fallen trees on the road and everything. So we parked the car and walked in. We had gone some distance and there was a big tree. Mother said, 'Stop here.' So we did.

And she said, 'Right over there, under that tree, is where my twins were born. Father and I, Oscar and I, were out here. We lived in a little lean-to, there, and I was going to have a baby. The pains came on, and Father was afraid to leave, and I was afraid to let him go, so we just had to fight it through ourselves. But when it was all over, we had twins and they were both born dead.'

'Right over there, there was a little maple tree, it stood eight or ten feet high or something. And,' she says, 'look at it now.' And I stepped across: It was 60 feet from one side to the other. My twin brothers – they were brothers – lay under that tree.

So anyway, we walked down the road a ways, and finally came to the house. And it was just an ordinary old log cabin. But Father had built a picket fence around it, where he had his garden and all that sort of thing. Just before we got to the house there was this big meadow, about 40 acres. Father had cleared, just with a saw and an axe and a team of mules (he had mules that time) and planted it into sometimes oats but mostly wild hay.

Mother, was just, oh, she was just in heaven. She told all about that, how Father would work daylight to dark, made no difference, and had built that place, built the house himself.

Right alongside the house was what they call a lean-to, and she said, 'Now, Chester, here's where you were born.' It was kinda fallen down, but it was just a little addition onto the shack. It was about, oh, I'd say, five feet wide and ten feet long, something like that. That's where I was born.

And she had the nerve to say that I was a beautiful baby! Can you imagine that? 'Course I've had lots of people say it since, later. So I went down to the barn and I said, 'Mother, would you come down here?' I said, 'Do you mean to tell me that my father built that barn all by himself?' She said, 'Yes, he did.' Now Father was a pretty good sized man, he weighed about 175-180 pounds, and was just under six feet tall. But he had timbers up there ten, twelve feet in the air, cross-pieces, that he had to put up with a block-and-tackle and his team. He put a big pole up, anchored it down, and put the team on. Mother'd go out and lead the horses, or the mules, and pull this timber up. Dad would get up there and set it where he wanted it. He built this barn all by himself. If you ask a person that was remarkable.

And don't forget, clearing this land. Every stump had to be dug out with a shovel – you have to be pretty good with a shovel, too. You'd dig around at the roots, get a pry, chop 'em up, get a pry and pry 'em out. And sometimes you'd let 'em lay there a while until they got dry, and then you built a fire out of them. Dad had fires all over the place, you know, burning these stumps out.

Father was the greatest man that I've ever known, I believe. But he had one fault, and that is, he had been raised and trained to abide by the Golden Rule, and if he was going to sell something, he wouldn't charge any more than he would want to pay for it.

I tell you, it's just remarkable what that man did. If I saw the work that he did in his life stacked up in front of me, I would quit right now, I'll tell you.

Uncle Chet's narrative now passes from the story of the migration to his own experiences growing up near Ellensburg. And what adventures those proved to be — scary encounters with still savage Indians; the great fire that flattened Ellensburg, and the Sayles ranch as well; successful appendicitis surgery on their kitchen table; frontier justice for murder and for the last of the Wild Bunch — these tales and many more.

And then there is the road. Oscar Sayles and the Mills family cut the road north from Kalama, following the Cowlitz River, to Cowlitz Corner in 1864.

The new road was an instant success. It is easy to see why. Prior to my great-grandfather's endeavor, the way from Willamette to Olympia and Seattle was long and hard. At Portland there was an expensive ferry crossing of the Columbia. Then you headed east along the north shore of the Columbia until you had passed the Cascade Mountains and a wilderness on your left that is roadless to this day. The path then led north to Yakima and the northern Oregon Trail. Then you proceeded west on the northern most branch of the Oregon Trail through the Cowlitz Gap in the Cascades to the Cowlitz Corner. This all was about four hundred miles and one month's time.

Now, with a wagon you went north from Portland two days to Kalama, then three more days on the new Sayles road to the Cowlitz corner. Or, you could travel three days by stage coach all the way from Portland to Olympia. Big difference!

My great-grandfather could have made a fortune with tolls on his new road, as the other road builders in the region were doing. But Oscar Sayles would have none of it. As we know, Uncle Chet said, he *"had one fault."* He had been *"raised and trained to abide by the Golden Rule."* He would *not* exact a toll from fellow settlers.

With no toll being collected, no name was attached to this vital road. Memory of who built the road quickly faded. Not that it mattered to passing travelers. It would be of interest only to local historians and to our family.

In 1870 the newly chartered Northern Pacific Rail Road sent surveyors down the Sayles road to define the rail route from Tacoma to Olympia to Kalama –– and thence by steamboat to Portland. The rail line was completed in 1874.

Traffic insured the Sayles road was well maintained and broadened. Half a century later, with continuous use by the new-fangled automobiles, the road was paved, then widened, and new names were progressively attached to it. With linkage to other roads, the Sayles Road section became part of a major highway. The road was further improved. Its name changed again.

Today we call it I-5 — Interstate 5 — part of the great Pacific Coast Highway stretching from Mexico to Canada.

I have a special regard for my great-grandfather's hernia. Without it he would never have met his beloved Sarah. Without it my grandmother, Alta, would not have been born. Without it Uncle Chet would not have had stories to tell. Without it I would not exist!

Wedding Photo, Author and Bride Sarah Noel
Mission San Juan Capistrano
September 17, 1987

CODA

FATE BROUGHT US TOGETHER. Fate brought us together *again*. We had been together at birth but had gone our separate ways. We followed very different paths until our lives joined to complete a circle. You see, Sarah and I were born, only months apart, in the same country town clinic on the same birthing bed with the same doctor and the same nurse. Our births were witnessed by the same county clerk. Our nearly identical birth certificates give the proof. But we never met. We never met until destiny brought us together in a distant time and place.

War brought us together that first time — World War II. When we first were together it was in the weeks after Pearl Harbor. At the time our fathers were stationed near each other. This was when my dad was at Fort Benning; Sarah's father was stationed at the Air Force Base nearby. The country town in the vicinity was Columbus — small then, at the very beginning of the war, much larger now. Only in later years did we discover our strange connection. It seems that we were meant for each other.

For some reason my memories of that time and place in history remain clear and sharp. Sarah's, by contrast, were cloudy. So I carried for us the burden of memory. Sarah liked hearing those memories — the observations of a very small child — of the years of war and its dramatic end. The story instantly became her favorite. My memories became hers.

Christmas, 1942
Dad, Mom, and Me, age one

THE ORIGINAL WAR BABY

I AM THE ORIGINAL WAR BABY! I was born a week after Pearl Harbor.

Not good enough. There must have been a new birth every fifteen seconds during that long, long week. Try again.

I still maintain I am the Original War Baby. I base my claim, in part, on the fact that the war was the reason for my existence.

My father bailed out of depression weary Seattle, his old home, and hoboed his way cross country; riding boxcars and sometimes coaches with good men and evil who were regulars on the rails. He arrived and found work in Chicago, hauling blocks of ice.

The nation still slumbered in fitful dreams as the lightning clouds gathered to the east and west. Then Adolph cracked champagne across the bow of War. Middle Europe cheered. "America First," we mumbled and rolled over to try for a few more winks.

When Dad read the war clouds and signed up. he was smart. A draft was inevitable. He was right — the Army was glad to have him and gave him his choice of jobs, as he expected. He chose aerial photography, a romantic trade which matched his skills. Now aerial photography in those days meant Long Island, a foreign land to my father, and where he went.

My mother was born and raised in New York. In her experience the city was the whole world, or at least most of it. One should not forget parts of Long Island, especially her home town, Brooklyn. One should especially not forget the Old Country, Sicily, her immigrant parents would remind her. With the usual improbabilities, much assisted by Mr. Adolph across the pond, Mom and Dad met and became friends.

The Big Man in the White House could see what was coming, and had started gearing up the country for the inevitable. Goaded by him, the nation finally woke up, rubbed the sand from its eyes and rolled up its sleeves. The Army wanted everything. The Army wanted planes, it wanted tanks, it wanted men. The Army wanted maps. Maps, my father mused, maps meant printing. Maps meant giant multicolor presses, chugging away like locomotives, day and night. Hot Dog! My father started pulling strings. He wanted into maps.

You have to understand my father's family was a printer's family. Everyone, father and mother and brothers and sister, and stray relatives, were engaged in the family printing business. They had to be. They had a small struggling newspaper on their hands, the kind thrown on doorsteps as an advertising flyer. In the Depression there was no surplus, and everyone helped out. If you live in a print shop you either learn to hate it, or printer's ink gets into your blood. My father was in love with printing.

He wanted most of all to get his hands on the big color presses. It had been his dream for years, but there was a thing called the union. In depression America the unions were not about to let smart youngsters get their hands on the precious printing machines. No, sir. That would mean competition, and maybe old timers out of work.

My father got his wish and was posted to Fort Benning, Georgia. He was going to print maps at one of the biggest printing plants in the nation. That sped things along and he proposed. Mom and Dad were married within a few days of their arrival at the Fort. A bit of fiddling around, called a honeymoon, and I was on the way, timed with precision to be dropped in the aftermath of the bombing at Pearl.

So you see, I have a pretty good claim. But still, with fifty thousand rivals there is bound to be someone else who can establish similar Bona Fides. Thus, I lay out my ace: I remember the war. I remember it well. It was my whole life for a long time.

It helps I was precocious. It helps, also, that my father was a photographer, which gives me the critical evidence my memories are strong and sure. I remember the circumstances of a remarkable photo. I remember crawling across the floor through a landscape of giant's furniture. I remember the giants, my parents, talking of things I somehow comprehended. I wanted to tell them I knew what they were saying, but I could not find any words of my own. I was entering the great world of language and understanding.

My father lifted me up and sat me atop a bookcase which had been cleared for the occasion. He gave me a prop, a leather case with keys dangling out. I was all set for my portrait. He turned on the "floods." I smiled, all delight at the attention and ceremony. I have the photo still. It is dated. I was eleven months old.

The war. The war was furious activity, mysterious, with strange schedules. The war was long lines, sometimes neat, sometimes ragged, often raucous. The war was people, young, strong, vibrant; living each day with energy and wonderful laughing gaiety. The war was khaki, and brown and green, but mostly khaki.

My father had two homes. When he could he would stay with us in our half of the little duplex apartment. But often he slept with his mistress. We visited him and his other lady, the Army, when it was possible, which was not often enough. We would drive onto the post, negotiating our way through the inevitable columns of marching and join him at the plant or sometimes the barracks. There were occasions when we would simply sit on the lawn under the shade of the spreading trees and delight in each other's company.

Much of the time a certain looseness made life tolerable. But the Army made its demands, especially when a big push was on and maps and instructions were needed in vast quantities to cover expected new conquests.

I remember one such occasion. We drove onto the post, Mom and I, in our big old Chevrolet. The world was as usual, with men marching everywhere, their lean figures painted with the light colored khaki uniforms in the warm southern sun. We stopped and a column tromped smartly across the road ahead. We drove on slowly, catching up with a longer line snaking on about its business. The front, in the distance, was gyrating with precision, a vast, many legged organism. Things grew ragged towards the end of the line. Something there was not quite right.

Mom scanned the line and suddenly caught sight of a familiar face, more as many friends came into view. "Look," she said. "There's Daddy!" I looked, but could see only the long tan caterpillar. "Look! There he is, at the end of the line, out of step, as usual." I detected a faint note of wry amusement. Her hero evidently did not exactly emulate all the military virtues.

The men marched on, indistinguishable to my young eyes. We followed and watched as the marching caterpillar reached its destination, wheeled about, and froze for a breath or two before shattering into little milling clusters of men. Mom parked the car and we greeted Dad, who had seen us and come over. He led us through a little door set in the end of a huge structure. There, in a cluttered room, carrying the wonderful aromas of fresh ink, we got reacquainted.

I was fascinated. There were so many things to play with. Pictures of planes and tanks and ships. Instruments with curious calibrations and bright polish. And those wonderful maps. I didn't know what a map was, of course, but I was impressed and thoroughly charmed by their size and complexity and color.

Occasionally the door to the interior would open as someone would come out to solicit Dad's opinion about something. Conversation would temporarily be replaced by the overwhelming clatter of the mechanisms beyond the now open door to the sanctuary. I positioned myself so I could glimpse those hidden marvels. A greater thrill came later when I was at last led, all wide-eyed with wonder, into the vast cathedral of machines. I was convinced then, and for a long time after — here was the heart of everything. And my father must be a very important man to be supervising this key to the whole world.

My mother was, as all mothers should be, warm and tender and loving. She raised her young child with a gentle and sparkling humor. My mom was tough, too. But her tough side was generally reserved for the necessities of her profession. She was a Registered Nurse, steeled in the hell of Belleview. Her services were desperately needed in the ramshackle, rural south. She spent her days in the disease-ridden hinterlands, tending to the poor, both blacks and whites. Sometimes she spoke of people who had sent their beloved sons to the war. People who somehow managed to get on with life, with pride, honor and dignity.

Mom wasn't home much during the day. But I didn't mind. I was twice blessed. I had my Mommy. And I had my Mammy. My mammy was Laura Mae, a young woman full of joy and laughter.

Laura Mae. Photo by Dad

Laura Mae was famous. Her picture was on every box of Aunt Jemima's flapjack mix. My parents tried to convince me the lady on the box was someone else, but in my infant wisdom I knew better.

While the war was gaiety and laughter, the war was also shortages and improvisation. One day I wandered off from my play area on the lawn in front of the house. I didn't go far, just down the street and into the courtyard of an apartment building. There I found a boy. He was sitting on the broad concrete step in front of his door. Spread out beside him was a newspaper littered with fragments of this and that. He was working on something. It was a kind of square lattice made of wood. I watched for a long while as he fumbled with his materials, annoyed with them, wishing he had better, but making do. Carefully he whittled a stick of wood into shape and tacked it in place, holding it tightly until the glue set, working another piece until it was as he wanted it. He laid paper across the span created, glued it down, and trimmed the edges meticulously with a knife.

Fascinated, I plied him with questions, trying to fill the void of knowledge I suddenly felt within me. His concentration broken by my childish insistence, he grew annoyed and chased me away. Hurt by the rejection, and by my unsatiated curiosity, I wandered home, leaving my brief acquaintance to struggle on with the construction of a model airplane, built of Popsicle sticks and newsprint.

The war was tanks. But I didn't know about this; they were kept out of sight. There was, however, one old friend. It was huge, a lozenge shaped steel box with treads wandering up and out of sight across its far away roof. Its sides bulged into sponsons from which thick tubes poked out at odd angles. It was like some antediluvian creature which had once bellowed its way through the world. Now, in its retirement, it slept the years away, resting silently on its grassy bed amidst the buildings of the fort. A retirement safe from the long ago times when it adventured across the blasted landscape of a distant nation. Perhaps it took notice of the small boy who crawled among its many feet and looked up at it in wonder.

The war was planes, shiny silver fighters, fresh born, lined up in their multitudes with military precision. These were in another part of the country, glimpsed form the window of a speeding automobile. The planes were familiar as they roared overhead in mock combat maneuvers.

I remember a party. People jammed noisily into the living room of a small house somewhere miles away from ours. The men were all soldiers, still wearing their uniforms from the long day of work. They had their wives and gals with them. Beverages flowed as freely as the loud, earnest conversation.

Mischievously, I hid for a while behind the floor-hugging drapes which covered the main windows of the room. After a time I was missed and a search began. But they couldn't find me. At last some small motion on my part betrayed my hiding place. Someone grabbed my arm and pulled me back into the light of the room. I was giggling. Though now discovered, I was pleased I had fooled them. By way of compensation for the loss of my secret hideout I was handed a deck of airplane flash cards. Intrigued by the shapes — racy black silhouettes with details sketched in fine white lines — I dreamed for a long time of flight and fast machines. These objects of wonder helped me fight my increasing drowsiness. I awoke briefly later, while being gently carried from the car to my bed at home.

The war was ships, celluloid ships, gray shadows cast on a giant screen. Everyone put out documentaries, and newsreels showing the folks in the States how things were going. But the Navy had a gift for talking to the public. The Navy did theirs in color.

We would see the long, low, lean shapes sliding swiftly and silently through the endless waves. Alert faces scanned the horizon, waiting, waiting. Far off, so far you could only see specks against the sky; the neat formations would follow. Puffs of black would begin to fill the scene, shattering the precision of the incoming clusters of aircraft. The scene would shift and suddenly the image of a wildly dancing airplane would fill the screen, bright red spots emblazoned on its wings. Another shift and a similar aircraft would be racing low over the water, pursued by the tall, spindly splashes of cannon shells biting the sea. Suddenly, an explosion, raising a cheer from the audience.

Another time and it might be night. Suddenly the screen would fill with a flash, like lightning, as the big guns fired. For an instant strange fret works and knobby projections would be silhouetted, winking out to leave crazy afterimages. The screen would fill with the traceries from pyrotechnic firehoses arcing out, red and gold and orange destruction, across the reflecting water. Far off in the distance something would begin to burn. The flames would rapidly mount until, in an instant, all would let go in a frenzied cataclysm of fireworks, exploding, dazzling, with all the colors of the rainbow.

I felt the pride my elders had in those ships. Great ships, the embodiments of strength and majesty. I saw those ships once. It was in a later time, only months after the war. We were living in Seattle. On a rainy day we drove out along the north shore of the Olympic peninsula, headed for the Pacific. The narrow straits were filled, the whole distance, with the gray shapes from the sea. This was not a dead fleet. Not quite yet. The sound of klaxons and sirens bounced from the green clad hills as fast shore boats ran to and fro, splitting the glassy waters with their long, wide wakes. We stopped occasionally as some notable sight caught our attention — a grouping of aircraft carriers or the massive outline of a battleship.

Below me, assembled for my review, was the great Pacific Fleet. This, the most magnificent of all history's naval armadas, was together in a single place only once, only here and only for a brief while.

Ships of the Pacific Fleet, 1945

The fleet was already becoming a ghostly legend, an armed force to stand beside the phalanx of Alexander, the legions of Caesar, the galleons of Elizabeth. The vessels would soon scatter, some to mothballs, some to the wrecker's yard, some back to sea to guard against the predators of a still troubled world.

The Fleet is forgotten now, by all but a few: antiquarians, lovers of wild old stories and the fast diminishing ranks of men who were there.

There was much more to life than the war. People sacrificed heavily for the war, but joined in celebration of victories, and otherwise the days passed with an air of normality. These were dark times, but occasionally a special magic broke through to light up our lives.

We lived in those days in the heart of the Old South. Its charm lingered to cast a spell upon these years of conflict. The Fort, and its small, sleepy civilian counterpart, the town of Columbus, fronted on a large river which divided Georgia from its neighbor, Alabama. Sometimes evenings enchanted us with soft balmy breezes carrying perfumes from the spring-flowered countryside, and stars glittering sharp in the blackness above. On such an evening we went down to the river's edge, to the levee, to the bright lights and crowds. There we saw an apparition, conjured as if by some sorcerer, from the remote past.

It floated gracefully on the water, tied to the land with massive cables. The vessel gleamed white, its brilliant lights collaborating with wooden fancy work to trim the vessel in filigreed shadows. At one end a strange pinwheel contraption of slats and struts lay motionless, attached to the hull with massive beams and crooked connecting rods.

The old steamer brimmed with life. Somewhere up above a brassy band played syncopated tunes. Gaily colored dresses swirled amidst the sober khaki as the young couples delighted in their too brief time together.

The festivities swelled until, at some signal, a parting occurred. The shore crowd flowed back from the dock's edge as stragglers from the boat fled in haste over the long plank connecting the boat to the land. Once passengers bound for this stop had departed, puffs of smoke hissed upward to freedom from the tall, flower-topped stacks high above the deck. The pinwheel contraption began to turn, slowly, splashing as if testing the water. The thick cables were cast free and suddenly all accelerated as the fabulous old boat once again tasted liberty.

The river was broad and long. We stood beside its dark, lapping waters watching the luminous white castle glide away, shrinking with distance as it disappeared back into the mists of time. A slight shift in the breeze and we caught again, for a brief moment, the delicious sound of wonderful music.

On another such night we drove out into the darkened fields beyond the town. Down a straight and narrow road we traveled until the lights of the city merged into a sparkling necklace hung on the horizon. We came upon a scene of activity and pulled off the road, parking our automobile among the long rows of tin can cars, red dusted from country roads. We didn't have far to walk until we were caught up in the lights and color and frenzy of the attraction.

I was entranced. I kept tugging my amused parents from one novelty to the next. I had never dreamed of anything like this. It was thrilling. The whirling machinery, decked out in Christmas tinted bulbs, the bands and organs pumping music into the night air, the green and blue and red and yellow striped tents, the milling throng all joined forces to overwhelm my imagination.

My parents escorted me through the entrance of a large tent. Inside various stalls lined the fabric walls, each occupied by a purveyor of exotic skills. My mother chose one and sat me down in an old stiff backed chair. I faced a partition hung with curiosities. To my left a little lady, neat and prim, fussed busily with something. Fully charged with energy absorbed from the bustle outside, and bursting with curiosity about the lady's activity, I kept squirming around to get a better look. My mother rode herd, reminding me constantly to keep looking straight ahead. But still I caught glimpses of quicksilver fingers snipping, nibbling with tiny scissors at something black.

It must have been only a few minutes, though it felt much longer, before the refined old lady delivered up her small miracle. The black piece of paper had been transformed into a perfect silhouette of a small boy, complete to its tiny eyelashes. This was a rare treasure. It is lost now, somewhere in the sweep of the intervening years. But that fragile shape, lovingly framed and held for so long, remains a bright memory, a talisman of my first country carnival.

There were other entertainments, more regular, more familiar. Our favorite was the movie house. It was downtown, in the middle of the block. We would park in back and walk around the corner onto the main street, there to be greeted with the long line of service men waiting for entry. It was the same khaki caterpillar, or perhaps the black sheep member of the species. For this long line was not neat and precise and machine like. The creature who inhabited this corner of the world was spirited and boisterous.

We'd walk past the restless animal, straight up to the box office window. My father evidently had privileges, the consequence of his wife and child, or perhaps the multitude of stripes sown onto his sleeves. The theater was spacious inside with a large balcony projecting out towards the screen. We usually sat in the center of the main floor along with the townsfolk and the men whose uniforms were fancier. The balcony would fill with the offspring of the caterpillar, the lights would lower and, as the curtains swept aside, the screen would come blazing to life with the opening newsreel.

There was not, in that time and place, a great respect for the dignity of the motion picture. Not many sat quietly, absorbing the events portrayed before us. Boos and catcalls boomed down from the ceiling's plaster when the villain strutted across the screen. The hero was egged on with encouraging cheers. Thunderous approval filled the air when the bad guys met their inevitable doom.

Sometimes, when a story of intrigue was playing, the theater would grow silent for a brief while. There would be a beautiful lady in distress. In a smoky cafe below the level of the street the lady would have a chance rendezvous with a mysterious stranger. Some evil, hidden, never fully exposed, always seemed to be lurking about. The stranger managed to be remarkably adept at acquiring important papers. After violent tussling in darkened alleys and half lit corridors with the minions of evil, the stranger and the beautiful woman would flee to freedom and happiness. But stories which silenced the audience were aberrations. After they were over the theater would return to its normal unruliness.

There was one night when something different happened. The crowd exhibited an extra lightness of spirit, as if

306

a great, dreaded weight had suddenly been lifted. Everyone was smiling and happy and noisier than they had ever been. I don't remember the first movie of the double feature playing. It's what came after that sticks. It's always been there in the back of my mind.

After intermission it was time for news of the day and the war. The theater grew silent, hushed with anticipation. The new film was in black and white. There was, at the beginning, some ceremony with dignitaries lined up and signing papers. The scene shifted to dockside. High sided troop ships lined the wharf. Each had a long gangplank slanting down next to the ship, leading to the landing below. Long lines of soldiers, arrayed in battle gear, descended the ships' ramps and formed up ashore.

We joined a jeep for a tour. The drive took us past curiously constructed houses and quaintly dressed people. We broke out into the countryside. Peculiar flooded fields on either side of the highway reflected the sky. The roadside was lined, the whole way, with throngs of people, pulling piled high carts and carrying bundles.

We drove up into some hills and along a winding road. Suddenly the view opened up again to flat, broad countryside, but it was a country of strangeness. A grid was laid across the silent land, reminiscent of broad, neat streets. Hugging the ground within the squares of the grid was a raggedness which at first carried no meaning. The camera panned the scene, and shifted into the center of the strangeness. There were glimpses of things dimly recognizable — faint shadows of normality: a fragment of a concrete wall jutting up like some half completed construction; metal webbed girders, twisted about and partly melted; shadows of people burnt into a wrecked wall; people aimlessly poking about the alien landscape.

Not a breath could be heard now, in the theater.

Another shift of scene and we were suddenly amidst crowds of people. Doctors and nurses in white masks tended a multitude of horrid injuries. The camera moved closer. Surgical instruments and gauze in skilled hands were being laid across a charred unrecognizable object. The object moved slightly and I glimpsed, with fascinated horror, a remnant of humanity beneath the hideousness.

The reel ended. The house lights waxed on for intermission. The audience, mostly men who had been training for a feared invasion, rose and slowly, courteously, silently, drifted out. No one returned. There was no second show.

I am the Original War Baby. I remember an age which is no more. I remember the moment when it vanished. Who else of my generation carries such visions?

I am the bridge between times.

Steamboat City of Savannah. Source unknown, circa 1900

Sarah

EULOGY: A GREAT LADY

GREATNESS IS SELDOM ASSOCIATED WITH GREAT WEALTH, or great office, or great title. Greatness is something you *feel* when you are in its presence. My beloved Sarah was truly a Great Lady.

She didn't start that way. Her remarkable spirit grew as she matured, helped I think, by adversity. Before she was three years old, her father, a fighter pilot, was shot down in the Philippines. She was an orphan before she knew what the word meant. Her mother remarried, but this was not a happy event for Sarah. I will not go into details. Some things are best left buried with the dead. To get the sense of it, remember the story of Cinderella. That was my Sarah.

As she grew, Sarah also grew rebellious. To spite her mother she married unwisely — with disastrous results. This marriage was ultimately annulled so she was free to regain her life. There were only two happy outcomes from this misadventure — her son Paul, and the well planted seed of Wisdom.

Young Sarah became a ravishing beauty — radiant, witty and charming. And captivating. For a while, as in Cinderella's story, she was romanced by a young prince, a prince from some province of India. He proposed, and she would have become a Maharani with great wealth and estate. But she turned him down.

She turned him down because her dream was to become an archaeologist. She studied the subject's ancient worlds, and anthropology, geology and mechanical engineering. Alas, archaeology proved ruinous to her health. While in the field, Sarah discovered her body was too frail, the sun too strong, and her skin too fair.

Sarah changed course, acquiring a Master's in English Literature and a Master's in Music. For a while she was a high school teacher. Later she became a crackerjack psychotherapist, with many lives turned around for the better.

One summer she took time off and went up to a mountaintop. The U.S. Forest Service hired her and she became a Forest Ranger. This would not expose her to the blazing sun as severely. Pregnant, she was stationed in a lookout tower, high atop a mountain, deep in the Idaho wilderness. Once a week she made the long trek down the mountain to the base station to pick up supplies. As she walked along, Sarah was not alone. A momma bear with a small cub happened to be living near the tower. Sarah and the bears became friends. Momma bear and her cub would accompany Sarah to the base and back, keeping pace as she walked, a few feet to one side.

I was charmed to discover my strawberry blond Sarah was an American Indian, among her other pedigrees. Her unusual affinity for animals and sparkling personality had attracted the attention of Ella, the shaman of the Nez Perce Indian tribe. Ella took Sarah on as her apprentice. She taught Sarah Nez Perce tribal lore and spiritual beliefs. She taught her about plants and about animals. In the end, the Nez Perce adopted Sarah as a full member of the tribe, and as a shaman.

Sarah constantly amazed me with her understanding of animals. One afternoon, in the woods on the ridge above Bryce Canyon, we came across a herd of skittish wild deer — mothers protecting young fawns. I tried to approach the herd to get some photos, but to no avail. The deer backed off. I was repacking my camera gear when I noticed Sarah had walked right into the middle of the herd. Not one of them showed the slightest sign of distress. Instead, they closed in around her, made her a member, and together Sarah and the deer wandered off into the woods. A long time later, as I was becoming anxious, she reappeared, matter-of-factly, as if nothing extraordinary had happened.

In subsequent years Sarah repeatedly showed the same talent for taming wild animals. I asked her the secret. "It's easy," she replied. "Just believe you are one of them. That's all. They *know* what you feel."

Usually one has to make a living doing ordinary things, and if time is left over, one chooses what one longs to do. For Sarah this was music. She was a fine singer with perfect pitch and the rare gift (Mozart's gift) of permanently capturing a melody with a single hearing. On occasion she would entertain me with perfectly replicated jingles and songs from the early days of television.

For a long while Sarah made ends meet as the Bishop's Cantor in the deeply Catholic town of Spokane. This made her a local celebrity.

Stage performances delighted Sarah. She sang with the Spokane opera and also with the Seattle opera. Mostly she had bit parts — walk on, do some stage stuff, sing a little ditty, and walk off. Simple enough business, but with Sarah the result was extraordinary. You would have had to see her on stage to fully appreciate her comedic gifts. During one memorable dress rehearsal all the folks were laughing so hard at her antics the conductor involuntarily dropped his face onto his music stand to hide his tears. On this occasion the Prima Donna — a famous singer imported as a special attraction — stormed off the stage. People later reported there was much screaming and smashing of things. Sarah had stolen the show.

On another occasion Sarah was part of a small nun's chorus which was humming some tune prior to the curtain being raised. This one was not Sarah's doing. By some fluke, all the nuns' habits got caught in the folds of the curtain. As the curtain ascended to heaven, so did the nuns' habits. For a moment the souls of the ladies must have ascended with these garments, for they simply stood there in stunned disbelief — until pandemonium broke loose.

I can only relate these incidents as hearsay, for I did not meet Sarah until sometime later. But I did, once, see a bit of her stage magic. She had the part of General Cartwright in a production of *Guys and Dolls* — at least she played him until Valley Fever closed her stage career. Now, if you've seen the movie, or the Broadway production, you know the Cartwright character is straight-laced and stern. At rehearsal Sarah played it differently. I'm not sure what she did. She certainly exercised the authority of the General, as required. But for some reason we were all in stitches. The director hid his face in his hands, he was laughing so hard. All of us were rolling on the floor. Except for her fellow actors. They stood stock still, mouths hanging open. "My God! I've got to play against *this!*"

Sarah was so good she received an exceptional invitation — to join New York's Metropolitan Opera without audition. She turned it down because it would have meant abandoning her young son for Career.

Maybe because of the public adulation she received in Spokane, Sarah felt boxed in. She also had been permanently injured through poisoning by an inmate while she was working as a psychotherapist at a half-way house. This injury created permanent physical pain. She decided to move herself and her son Paul to Southern California to escape an increasingly stifling environment, and to find better medical care.

I met her at a party shortly after she arrived. On the occasion of our acquaintance she was sitting with a mutual friend. He invited me to take their sofa's remaining seat. Sarah tested me, the stranger, with her Dumb Blond, Bubble Head routine. It didn't fool me as it had many of the others present. The three of us were giggling so hard at her routine some poor guy wandered over and asked, in all seriousness, what we were smoking. Perfect! Bullseye! We doubled over with laughter. The guy wandered off, utterly bewildered. Sarah and I, of course, were smoking Romance.

My wonderful lady and I were together for twenty years. During that time a series of permanent injuries took their toll on a progressively frail body. The pain became constant and increasingly intense. Almost two years ago, Sarah contacted bacterial pneumonia, which became septic. We nearly lost her, but a medical miracle worker worked his miracle, and she survived, radiant as ever.

But it was not to be like old times. As a result of the sepsis, she suffered from progressively more severe brain seizures. These seizures provoked falls which created still more injuries and increased pain. In the end Sarah's heart could not withstand the strain and simply stopped.

In time of legend some blacksmith discovered how to turn an unpromising lump of ore into an extraordinary sword. Firing the material to incandescence, hammering it into submission, folding it to build up intricate interior structures. Shaping it into refined curves. Tempering it in such a way the humble lump became tough, resilient and keen enough to slice through all the protections people use to armor themselves. And finally, polishing the material to bring out its hidden luster, creating a thing of wondrous beauty.

In the last epoch of her life I was privileged to sit beside, and assist, the Smith as he finished shaping my dearest Sarah into a truly splendid lady.

For many years, every evening when I arrived home from a good day, or a bad, I would be greeted with a cheery "Hi Chet! Welcome home. I love you Chet." And we'd sit and chat. I would relate my small triumphs, or misadventures. And we would giggle over the silliness of office politics. That is gone, now. It is only a sweet memory.

PHOTO CREDITS

Sarah in the Field page xii. Photo by Chester L. Richards.

Bouquet of White Roses, page 5. Photo by Alena Yanovich from Pexels. https://www.pexels.com/photo/close-up-shot-of-white-roses-7834307/. Reprinted with permission. Modifications: Converted from color to black and white

Popped an oar, page 6. Photo by Chester L. Richards.

Grand Central Airport, page 32. Cover of Grand Central News, Grand Central Aircraft Company magazine, March, 1953. Company closed in 1959. Photographer unknown.

Sam Street, page 44. Photo by Chester L. Richards.

Lava Falls, page 61. Photo by J. Brew from near Seattle, USA, CC BY-SA 2.0 <https://creativecommons.org/licenses/by-sa/2.0>, via Wikimedia Commons. Modifications: converted to black and white from a color image. Reprinted with permission.

Land of Troubles, page 62. Photo by Chester L. Richards.

Monkey at Awash Camp, page 70. Photo by Chester L. Richards.

Omo River hippos charge into the water to stand guard over baby as we approach on our rafts, page 82. Photo by Chester L. Richards.

Hippos Waiting for Dinnertime, page 87. BS Thurner Hof, CC BY-SA 3.0 <https://creativecommons. org/licenses/by-sa/3.0>, via Wikimedia Commons. Modifications: converted to black and white from a color image. Reprinted with permission.

Boatman with undersized Omo River catfish, about three and a half feet long, page 88. Photo by Chester L. Richards.

Rocket launch from Vandenberg Air Force Base, (now Vandenberg Space Force Base), headed for Kwajalein Atoll, page 96. https://nara.getarchive.net/media/a-minuteman-iii-launch-580ccb. State: California (CA). Country: United States Of America (USA). Scene Camera Operator: F. Franz. Release Status: Released to Public. Combined Military Service Digital Photographic Files

LAMP (Large Advanced Mirror Program), page 146. Photographer unknown. Believed to be original manufacture, Itek, photograph

Sather Gate, UC Berkeley, page 172. Architect: John Galen Howard. Added to National Register of Historic Places Locations: March 25, 1982. Photo by Highsmith, Carol M., 1946. Created/published 2012. Carol M. Highsmith Archive, Library of Congress. Rights Advisory: https://www.loc.gov/item/2013633500/

Charles Music, group photo after a recital, given to all members of the band, page 184. Photographer unknown.

Mergenthaler Linotype Machines and Operators, page 206. Photo Public Domain, Australian Copyright Council (ACC): https://commons.wikimedia.org/wiki/File:Linotype_machines,_Anthony_Hordern_and_Sons_department_store,_c._1935.jpg

Mom and Dad, page 252. Family archival photo.

My mother, Catherine (Kay) Richards, born January, 1918. Photograph 1950, page 254. Portrait by Dad (Chester Lewis Richards).

Me, Dad, and my sister Marie, p 260. Family archival photo.

Dad, age 9 or 10, and his older brother Trummy, about 20. Circa 1923-24, page 264. Family archival photo.

Pilgrims on the Plains, page 278. Sketched by Theo R. Davis, 1869. Reproduction Number: LC-USZ62-133213 (b&w film copy neg.). Rights Advisory: No known restrictions on publication. Call Number: Illus. in AP2.H32 1869 (Case Y) [P&P]. Repository: Library of Congress Prints and Photographs Division Washington, D.C. 20540 USA

Wedding Photo, Author and Bride Sarah Noel, Mission San Juan Capistrano, September 17, 1987, page 290. Family archival photo.

Christmas, 1942. Dad, Mom, and Me, age one, page 292. Photo by Dad (Chester Lewis Richards).

Laura Mae, page 298. Richards family archives. Photo by Dad (Chester Lewis Richards).

Ships of the Pacific Fleet, page 302. https://upload. wikimedia.org/wikipedia/commons/7/75/ US_Pacific_Fleet_ships_steam_toward_the_Panama_ Canal_in_October_1945.jpg. U.S. Navy, Public domain, via Wikimedia Commons.

Steamboat City of Savannah circa 1900, page 309. Source unknown.

Sarah, page 310. Photo by Chester L. Richards.

Made in USA - Kendallville, IN
57957_9781880882306
08.02.2022 1306